DATE DUE

DEMCO 38-296

THINKING BODIES

✛

Irvine Studies in the Humanities

Robert Folkenflik, General Editor

CONTRIBUTORS

✦

Peter Brunette

Peter Canning

Frieda Ekotto

Mira Kamdar

Jeffrey S. Librett

Juliet Flower MacCannell

Jean-Luc Nancy

Dorothea Olkowski

Avital Ronell

Benigno Sánchez-Eppler

Greg Sarris

Peter Schwenger

Gary Shapiro

Gayatri Chakravorty Spivak

Anne Tomiche

Laura Zakarin

Slavoj Žižek

THINKING BODIES

✛

Edited by

Juliet Flower MacCannell
and Laura Zakarin

Stanford University Press, Stanford, California

1994

R

Stanford University Press
Stanford, California
© 1994 by the Board of Trustees
of the Leland Stanford Junior University
Printed in the United States of America

An earlier version of "Hiroshima in the Morning"
by Peter Schwenger appeared in Chapter 3 of
his *Letter Bomb:*
Nuclear Holocaust and the Exploding Word,
© The Johns Hopkins University Press, 1992;
reprinted with permission of
The Johns Hopkins University Press.

CIP data appears at the end of the book

Stanford University Press publications
are distributed exclusively by
Stanford University Press within
the United States, Canada, and Mexico;
they are distributed exclusively by
Cambridge University Press throughout
the rest of the world.

A Note on This Series

This is the seventh in a series of volumes on topics in the humanities and the second in the new series published by Stanford University Press. This volume originated in the April 26–28, 1990, meeting of the International Association for Philosophy and Literature held at the University of California at Irvine on the subject "Bodies: Image, Writing, Technology." For help with a broad range of problems, I am indebted to the Editorial Board of Irvine Studies in the Humanities: Ellen Burt, Lucia Guerra-Cunningham, Anne Friedberg, William J. Lillyman, J. Hillis Miller, Spencer Olin, John Carlos Rowe, and Jon Wiener. Joann McLean and Nancy Tablyn provided secretarial help for Irvine Studies.

Robert Folkenflik, General Editor

Acknowledgments

We gratefully acknowledge the following people, and also the offices they represent, who made this volume possible: the Vice Chancellor and Associate Vice Chancellor of the Office of Graduate Studies and Research, the Dean of the School of Humanities at the University of California, Irvine; the Organized Research Initiative in Women and the Image funded by the President's Office of the University of California; Professor Robert Folkenflik, general editor of the Irvine Series, and the Board of Irvine Studies in the Humanities; and Helen Tartar, editor at Stanford Press. All of these offered us not only approval but encouragement. Our thanks also to Nancy Atkinson, our copyeditor, and John Ziemer, who has seen this volume through production.

We are ultimately most grateful to the authors who have lent their minds and talents to this crucially important concern.

We gratefully acknowledge permission from the Cumberland Packing Corporation for use of their logo and material for "Sugar in the Raw."

Finally, infinite thanks go to the Marin Headlands Center for the Arts, for providing Juliet MacCannell space, time, and atmosphere to accomplish the final editing.

J.F.M.
L.Z.

Contents

Contributors

PETER BRUNETTE is Professor of English at George Mason University. He is author of four books on film and visual art: *Roberto Rossellini*; *Screen Play: Derrida and Film Theory* (with David Wills); *Shoot the Piano Player*; and *Deconstruction and the Visual Arts: Arts, Media, Architecture*. He is working on books on Michelangelo Antonioni, and on the visual representation of bodies.

PETER CANNING is Assistant Professor of Comparative Literature at the University of Minnesota. Author of articles on Deleuze, fabulation, Nietzsche, and the Holocaust, he is completing a book on libidinal time and event.

FRIEDA EKOTTO is currently completing a study entitled *The Relationship of Law and Literature: Jean Genet's Melancholic Writing and Legal Discourse*. She is at the University of Minnesota.

MIRA KAMDAR is Senior Fellow at the World Policy Institute at the New School for Social Research, working on international and domestic policy issues with regard to race and gender; and on cultural issues, especially the conflicts between women's rights and community rights.

JEFFREY S. LIBRETT is Assistant Professor of German at Loyola University of Chicago. He has published essays on Kant, Schiller, Nietzsche, Heidegger, and de Man and translated, among other critical works, *Of the Sublime: Presence in Question*, by Jean-François Courtine et al. He is currently at work on a book concerning Jews and Germans in the eighteenth century.

JULIET FLOWER MACCANNELL is Professor of English and Comparative Literature at the University of California, Irvine, and is author and editor of several books on Lacan, semiotic theory, feminism and psychoanalysis, and postmodern culture and politics. Her current work is on the interplay between democratic social theory and modern philosophy and literature exhibited in the relation of women to love and war.

JEAN-LUC NANCY is Professor of Philosophy at the Université de Strasbourg, and author of many renowned books on community, Spinoza, Descartes, Lacan et al. The essay in this book also appears in English in his *The Birth to Presence* and in French in his collection *Corpus*.

DOROTHEA OLKOWSKI is Associate Professor of Philosophy and Director of Women's Studies at the University of Colorado, Colorado Springs. She is co-editor of *Deleuze and the Theater of Philosophy* (with Constantin V. Boundas).

AVITAL RONELL is Professor of Comparative Literature and Theory at the University of California, Berkeley. Her books include *The Telephone Book, Dictations: On Haunted Writing*, and *Crack Wars*. She is currently working on *The Test Drive: Nietzsche's Gay Science*.

BENIGNO SÁNCHEZ-EPPLER is Assistant Professor of Latin American Studies and Comparative Literature and Manheimer Term Assistant Professor of University Studies at Brandeis University. He is author of *Habits of Resurrection*.

GREG SARRIS is Associate Professor of English and Native American Studies at the University of California, Los Angeles. He is currently working on a teleplay.

PETER SCHWENGER is Professor of English at Mount St. Vincent University in Halifax. His books include *Phallic Critiques: Masculinity and Twentieth Century Literature*, and *Letter Bomb: Nuclear Holocaust and the Exploding Word*.

GARY SHAPIRO is Professor of Philosophy and Tucker Boatwright Professor in the Humanities at the University of Richmond in Virginia. His books include *Nietzschean Narratives* and *Alcyone: Nietzsche on Gifts, Noise and Women*.

GAYATRI CHAKRAVORTY SPIVAK is Avalon Foundation Professor of the Humanities at Columbia University. She is translator of Derrida's *Of Grammatology* and author of *In Other Worlds: Essays in Cultural Politics*; and *Outside in the Teaching Machine*. Her research interests continue to be deconstruction, Marx, Freud, feminism, and globality.

ANNE TOMICHE is Assistant Professor of French and Comparative Literature at State University of New York at Buffalo. She has published articles in *Poétique, Revue de Littérature Comparée, L'Esprit Créateur*, and is working on writing and cruelty in Artaud, Stein, Duras, and Burroughs.

LAURA ZAKARIN is currently writing a long study of Freud, George Eliot, and Claude Lanzmann on history, the "woman's question," and the "Jewish question," while completing her studies at the University of California, Irvine.

SLAVOJ ŽIŽEK is Senior Researcher at the Institute for Sociology, Ljubljana. He is author of *Tout ce que vous avez toujours voulu savoir sur Lacan sans jamais oser le demander à Hitchcock, The Sublime Object of Ideology, Le plus sublime des hystériques, Hegel passe, Looking Awry, They Know Not What They Do: Enjoyment as a Political Factor,* and numerous other books on philosophy, popular culture, and politics. His work astutely links Lacanian psychoanalytic theory to idealist and materialist philosophies.

THINKING BODIES

✛

Introduction

Juliet Flower MacCannell

*I*n one of Poe's odder tales, a sickly, housebound narrator, Egaeus, is obsessed with his healthy, pretty young cousin, Berenicë—or more precisely, with her teeth: "Ses dents étaient des idées," he explains. Eventually, his absorption in these idea-teeth leads him to ask for her hand in marriage. Egaeus's fascination seems to stem from his having been born in a library: he is prone, he tells us, to deep and compulsive reveries. Unlike those of his romantic contemporaries, however, his reveries do not spiral around numinous and ever more sublime unpresentable Ideas. They center, instead, on phenomena, concrete physical minutiae, like, for example, Berenicë's teeth. So foreign are *concepts* to his sensibility that Egaeus purposely meditates on the printed words in books (recall that the library is his natal milieu) until they become mere meaningless marks, purely concrete physical phenomena, devoid of all further signification.

Once Berenicë becomes engaged to Egaeus, she unaccountably and visibly begins to alter. Normally robust and vigorous, the fiancée starts to decline physically, suffering spells marked by the most complete lapse of signs of life. In one such fit, her comatose state so resembles death that she is taken for dead and placed in the family vault. After her "death," Egaeus, unconscious of what he is doing, one night descends to the crypt and extracts the entire set of her *dents/idées* (which are all that remain unchanged of her *ident*ité) from what is, in fact, the still-living body of his Berenicë. In the last lines of the tale, these teeth have finally lost contact with their minimalist, enigmatic *idées*: Egaeus sees them only as white cubic structures that can be measured, described, counted, and placed in a box. He thus completes the trajectory of his reveries upon the material body of his "beloved."[1] Berenicë's natural, phenomenal body has become incorporated in its own way into Egaeus's world, a world of only apparent concreteness, composed entirely of the formal representation of the categories of time, space, and number. Natural content, the body, is lost to the categorical representations of the imagination.

An obvious parody, Poe's framing of Egaeus's apparent hypermaterialism within an *idealist-romantic* literary and philosophical idiom (of compulsive love and intense, detached reverie) is not without some relevance when bodies of thought, thinking bodies, or the relationship of philosophy to the body are at issue. By arranging the material, physical body in time and space, Egaeus's dental surgery parallels the idealist costuming of his reveries that turned the materialist into the phenomenologist, and permitted philosophy to disregard the body in pain and pleasure. In a sense, the Poe story parallels a series of odd turns taken in the post-Cartesian history of our efforts to think the body and to embody thought. When Lacan rewrote Freud's phrasing of the unconscious as "I am there where I do not think; I think there where I am not," he returned to and radicalized the import of the Cartesian utterance that pronounced the definitive gaping between the body of the real and the hallucinatory-symbolic field that defines human being.

The articles in this volume have at least this purpose in common with the project of the earliest *idéologues* (e.g., l'Abbé de Condillac), reacting against yet strangely with Descartes: to synthesize or establish contact between body and mind (formally, as Reason and as Unreason), that is, to put it into a relation with a logic that dreamed of going its own way.

The materialists of the eighteenth century took as their point of departure the 1754 *Traité des sensations*[2] by Condillac, for whom no thought, no impression of the world, could be born *disembodied*, because only the body could *feel*: "penser et sentir sont la même chose." Now we know that Kant's revolution made Condillac's "pathological thinking" philosophically untenable: the Idea, the universal concept, had to be made independent of the sensations and sensitivities, of suffering and pleasure.[3]

For Kant (in the *Critique of Judgment*), bodying forth the ideas of pure reason through sensible representation is impossible.[4] Only the Understanding (concept categories) is available for such embodiment, and then only through the concourse of the Imagination, which mediates sense perception and understanding, making its concepts available to consciousness through phenomenal schemata.[5] Crucial links with the "thinking body" thus broken (the phenomenal, "natural" body could be understood, but thought itself could not in itself be so), the morality of sentiment and the Horatian ethic of pleasurable and rational instruction likewise collapsed.

A certain split therefore became permanent: between the two major ideological streams concerned with *synthesis* that have narrated philosophy's body—one rooted in Condillac's attempted synthesis of Lockean empiricism and Cartesian rationalism, the other rooted in Kantian will. Choice between them became necessary, and coexistence impossible.

Condillac tried to bring Descartes's *pensée* directly to Locke's body to overcome the opposition that had led to a detested metaphysics—the opposition of *feeling* and *reason, mind* and *body, penser et sentir,* that so astonished Pascal. The good Abbé (whom Rousseau thought the highest genius and man of good faith among the philosophes) plotted his synthetic trajectory on the *tabula rasa* pushed to extremes: on the rigid, unified, but neither dead nor unintelligent body of a marble statue,[6] brought to life— and consciousness—through a single sense perception: smell. This single sense perception, repeated, combined, remembered, reflected upon (in short, judged), contains the seeds of everything into which the "higher mind" develops. Mind begins with body. Yet the reverse is equally true; body can develop no sense of sense in the absence of a so-called "sense perception." This "sense perception" already has the form of the signifier; it is a marking out, a marking off, a limiting device.[7]

The other kind of synthesis, Kantian and historically received as having saved philosophy from Condillac's materialism,[8] locates the transcendental (especially the *transcendence of feeling*) as critical to thought. As a kind of crisis of experience, which it splits, the transcendental is not—as in Condillac and others—a *judging mind* so much as it is a sustained *will* with which the subject can be united only by an act of identification with it. Kantian goodwill will and must match the will to the Good, to an impersonal yet sustainable will to enjoyment[9] apart from considerations of a "pathological" sort. Only identification with that will could "bridge" the gap or splitting of the subject implied by the transcendental.

Kant's philosophy did double work, in the sense that it theorized what was surprisingly an accurate description of how people and not just the structures of the mental faculty comported themselves: we are most desperate to maintain the distance between the phenomenal natural body and the noumenal world of Reason. The absence of any experience of things-in-themselves, supplemented at its source by an original synthesis, becomes the principle of nonidentity from which "more" is made of "less," something is made of nothing, excess is made of lack. But if the synthetic a priori judgment, which must contain more in its predicate than the matter contained in its subject, protects us from the excess of pleasure we might endure, it strangely does not protect us from a certain pain, experienced in the very void of pleasure, inhibiting pleasure in its heart, but experienced as the painful correlative to the ethical act (*Schmerz*). In any case, after Kant, what the body-of-the-subject suffers, its pains as well as its pleasures, would no longer, as it still did with Condillac, carry an *epistemological* function;[10] it could only deny itself the knowledge of its split through an act of willed ignorance.

Of course, there is an analytic story to be told as well. An alternative sort of parody to the one in Poe's tale had already appeared earlier, at the height of the Enlightenment, in the writing of the "materialists" (or neo-Spinozists). These include Diderot, who, like Poe, used literary *contes* to express skepticism about the philosophical separation, canonical since Descartes, between bodies and ideas. If in Kant it is the Idea (Reason) that is "unpresentable," in the philosophes' jokes it is the other of Reason, the Body, that is (for political, sexual, and other agendas) kept offstage and made obscene to thought. The marked analytic propensity of the materialists to demystify the unacknowledged sensuality and sexuality at work in moral ideals is primarily evident in their "literary" rather than their "philosophical" texts.[11] The sensuous root of ideals is repeatedly evoked among those with materialist leanings who claimed to follow Locke if not Spinoza, especially Shaftesbury, Helvétius, and Diderot himself.[12]

The firm technical linkage made by Condillac between *sensation* and *idea*, between *feeling* and *reason* or *rational thought*, is underscored by Diderot in particular as a positive if somewhat dangerously humorous enterprise.[13] Diderot went further, indeed, than a mere critique of morals and ideals: he meant to examine even scientific thought in this light. Here a renewing synthesis rather than a demystifying analysis touches philosophy and science (as in the *Rêve de d'Alembert*), but Diderot implicitly advocates a productive or creative reconnecting of mental processes with physical ones. That this enterprise is abandoned, or rather, radically redirected with the advent of Kant may not, however, mean that the tradition is entirely lost to philosophical thinking, and persists, not exclusively through literature, but through ideology critique and psychoanalysis.

The Ideologues Versus Kant: The Formal Side of Synthesis

We have long since lost touch with the radical tenor of the "ideologues" and their particular tradition. Stendhal claims in *De l'amour*, fragment 91, that we lost it because of a few "slips of the pen" made by Helvétius, who was inept at defining his terms, like "self-interest" and "generosity."[14] We must confess, however, that the subsequent alternative direction taken by romantic and idealist philosophy also leads to impasses where thinking bodies are concerned. Kant was able to bring together *sense* perception and *ideas*, largely within the Imaginary (hypotyposis, schemata, etc.). But the level at which the materialists took firm aim, the level of *ideas-in-themselves*, is what Kant moved to keep sacred, safe from any representation other than oblique, allegorical, or weakly Symbolical (conventional, contractual). There is, in essence, a premonition of the Symbol (à la Peirce or Lacan) in Kant, even a Symbolic that operates effectively as lack. But it will take the relay through Freud and psychoanalysis for the body to be put into that peculiarly heterogeneous yet nevertheless critical relation to thought adumbrated in the notion of the symbol.

As heirs to Kant, we cannot ignore the separation of the pathological, the pathetic, and pathos in general from the realm of Reason that he made the cornerstone of his ethical and universal imperatives. When he dislodged affect from ethics (almost) and placed mood, feeling and sensibility—as "aesthetic" in the etymological sense—in the realm of art, he effectively kept the pathological, bodily origins of pure reason safe from being thought in the opposing direction.

To return to a certain Condillacian moment, however, would be to wend one's way from the early inspiration in Spinoza through a continuously subsidiary, minor branch of "philosophy" (materialism, ideology critique) or at most to a philosophy diverted toward politics, economics, psychology: Helvétius, Diderot, d'Holbach, La Mettrie, and ultimately even Marx, not to mention the Nietzsche who devoured the *idéologues*. It is also to find oneself before a wondrous, neglected body of thought, named such by Destutt de Tracy, *Idéologie proprement dite*.[15]

The *idée* that constitutes the base of *idéo-logie* is the hybrid product of body as it effects mind and mind as it defines body. As developed by Destutt de Tracy from his criticism of the limits of Condillac, it was constituted by the marking off, in the field of consciousness, of a sense experience. This experience is one that quite simply fails to flow through without leaving any trace; it is a blockage that nonetheless roots consciousness *as such*. The source of the blockage (and therefore, the birth of the *idea* as a concept) is, however, a *judgment* made about the experience by a body that endures it as either a pain or a pleasure. But again, this judgment is made in a way that refers specifically to the body: what appears to lead away from the enjoyable culmination of an experience (*souffrance*) is deemed "painful"; what seems to be tending to successful consummation (*jouissance*) is judged "pleasurable." These "judgments" are, as Rousseau put it in his *Dialogues*, what constitute a "sentiment distinct," permitting the whole range of mental faculties to come into play—memory, imagination,[16] perception, and so forth—as the different markings made regarding sense experience by this judgment.

Now the *correctness* of such marking judgments is always at issue. Regarded closely, the *idée* that operates between body and mind is that absolutely clear yet absolutely obscure point around which every human and not so human cultural structure crystallizes. Being, ultimately, a relation to *jouissance*, it is a relation that the greater part of human culture is designed to avoid recognizing, to demand sacrificing. Small wonder that philosophy and speculative thought found other syntheses, other routes less perplexed.

Change is in the wind. As the essays in this volume attest, there is clearly a renewal of philosophical interest in how bodies think, how thought is embodied. Lacan, Deleuze, Irigaray, Nancy, Lacoue-Labarthe, all confirm in their own way that a philosophical accounting of the *reason* (which is also the *madness*) of the body in pain, the body in enjoyment, is being called forth again. But if it appears that we have only recently (say, after Freud) discovered the knowledge of/in the body, the working of thought in the body marked by/as its suffering and its enjoyment, the history of philosophy—and of literature—indicates otherwise. Recovering this history may take us back to materialism, if not to Epicurus, but it is a detour made necessary by the loss of the Kantian body of rational feeling. That the body is the work of thought and vice versa is not a new idea, but it needs, perhaps, some reviving. The idea that the body is the slate on which the letters that seal its destiny are marked as its "thinking" surface is newer, or at least a modern twist. It is what makes literature (at the very least, but also all kinds of signifiers dropped from the "logical" chains of metaphysically organized and ordered "understanding") a vigorous and much-needed partner of philosophy. And if it also harks back to Condillac, it reminds us of his ancestors—Montaigne, Pascal, Descartes.

Cutting the Body

I see a common stake, in the essays in this book, in what Lacan called "immixion" or "inmixing." Inmixing is that apparent desubjectivization that permits a licentious yet punitive Superego—the "non-barred Other" of *jouissance*—to be set up as a "Symbolic" machinery that "liberates" organ pleasure from what we used to call "the body." By way of clarification, I should explain that, in the later Freud ("The Dissolution of the Oedipus Complex") and the early Lacan (*Seminars I–III*), the setup of the Superego (who is *not* the oedipal "Father") derives from the ascendance of secondary, not primary, narcissism. Indeed, Lacan said that all of Freud's formulations of the "Father" were destined to culminate in this Superegoic form. Ironically, it is the masturbating boy-child's failure to renounce his *organ pleasure* that structures this Superego: for in permitting one organ and its *jouissance* to assert absolute claims, the child effectively and definitively remains a "fragmented" body, a body in pieces, *morcelé*. While such a disruption of "symbolic identity" might be greeted positively by postmodernites, the residue—the Superego or Other as *objet a*—is possibly a hazardous waste—a toxically Ideal Ego, a hyperbolically beautiful, unified body whose very existence belittles our body, divided into so many clamorous organ-parts.

There are, thus, two different versions of the "cut" body, and though these eventually converge in the regime of the Brother, we might profitably return a moment to precisely *what* was supposed to have been "cut" by the signifier. Lacan's "cut" creates the subject *by separating it*—judiciously—from its rival self (fraternal twin or maternal body). The paranoid structuring of the bonded ego is by no means limited to early infancy; indeed a recent observer has termed ours an "age of paranoia";[17] Lacan called it psychotic:

The human ego is the other and . . . in the beginning the subject is closer to the form of the other than to the emergence of his own tendency. He is originally an inchoate collection of desires—there you have the true sense of the expression *fragmented body*—, and the initial synthesis of the *ego* is essentially an *alter ego*, it is alienated. The desiring human subject is constructed around a centre which is the other in so far as he gives the subject his unity, and the first encounter with the object is with the object as object of the other's desire. . . . This dialectic always carries the possibility that I may be called upon to annul the other, for one simple reason. The beginning of this dialectic being my alienation in the other, there is a moment at which I can be put into the position of being annulled myself because the other doesn't agree. The dialectic of the unconscious always implies struggle, the impossibility of coexistence with the other, as one of its possibilities.[18]

Lacan characterized our time as the "era of the ego," meaning that the primordial, cardinal relation of our time is a *narcissistic*, intra-egoic relation. One pole of this split ego is located in a fragmented body "before the mirror" (subjected to partial drives and inchoate organ pleasures) and its *alter Ego*—a synthetic, ideal, and whole unfractured Other, "beyond the mirror." The illusion of a divine/dividing Other, the mirror's edge as a "truly" separating signifier, the "third party" required by all social pacts, has given way, displaced by the fantasy of fulfillment—of multiple organ-pleasures, of the *jouissance de l'Autre*.

The Id-eal ego (variously termed the maternal, narcissistic, or artistic Superego—sometimes it is called feminine, but I disagree) has apparently claimed (if not reclaimed) precedence over the paternal metaphor. Classically, the signifier, the symbolic pact, the social contract of speech is what divides us from each other as mutual aggressors ("in so far as this involves a third party. Speech is always a pact, an agreement, people get on with one another, they agree—this is yours, this is mine, this is this, that is that," writes Lacan; p. 39). Division and separation are supposed to create a fortunately unsatisfiable *desire* (the ego neither assimilates—eats—the other nor is eaten by it; nor does it foreclose the other, excluding, rejecting, and relegating it into the Real, where It enjoys and the ego does not "know" it). Nevertheless, as Lacan was first to point out, this "symbolic" agreement retains a certain stamp: that of "the aggressive character of primitive competition [which] leaves its mark on every type of discourse about the small other, about the Other as third party, about the object" (p. 39). In each of these the potential for a paranoid, "primordially competitive" relation remains. The fragmented ego, belittled by comparison with the fullness of the Other, is literally tormented, the ironic butt of the commands to an enjoyment that can never be complete for it *qua* fragmented body. In the regime of the Superego, the signifier-as-separation has become its opposite, an imaginary phallus that holds a place, fills in a gap, solidifies against (or so it imagines) a real and pervasive substance—that of *jouissance*. Indeed, it is as *objet a* alone that the "material signifier" gives the *body* (as Žižek puts it, following Lacan's *Encore*).

Its field is fantasy. All the essays in this book take their positions around these two pulsations of the same structure: on the one hand, the primordial division or cut; on the other hand, its suture and panic driving by the *objet a*. In truth, wherever questions of "otherness" appear in the text of the essays here—especially those of Slavoj Žižek, Benigno Sánchez-Eppler, Avital Ronell, Peter Canning, and Peter Schwenger—the juxtaposition of the essays has a bizarre result. These essays interestingly converge in unexpected ways on thematics of perversion, figured through an insistence on "coupling." This figure asserts itself just when the body is divided into its organs: the technical (orchestra, telephone, rocketry, sugar-refining equipment, nuclear apparatus) appears not just as a double of but as wedded to the body. The perversity of coupling under the narcissistic regime fascinates several of the contributors here. Were they not placed together here, this seemingly minor theme might not have revealed its intimate link with narcissism: if the couple *ego/It* is truly primordial, then the incompleteness of separation in/of/from this coupling reveals itself by a transference in the plural, fantasmatic couplings arrayed here: man with letter, man with machine, man with language. I use the word "man" advisedly here.

About This Volume

The essays in this volume, selected from many presented at the 1990 meetings of the International Association for Philosophy and Literature held at the University of California, Irvine, offer an exemplary set of differing yet neighboring approaches to this philosophical reawakening to the imbrication of letters in the body of thought, thought in the body. Their authors cross the fields of philosophy and literature, with psychoanalysis as a virtual spirit animating their discussions. Nearly all have been touched by deconstruction, which had in its turn thematized and criticized the teaching of Lacan—but Lacan, who always read philosophy, from Plato to Kojève and Heidegger, *through* Freud, was only repeating Freud's own assimilation of Spinoza, Kant, and Plato.[19] It is necessary to confront, first of all, as Jean-Luc Nancy puts it, philosophy's demand to think the body. Or at least the demand of philosophies that have, over time, enabled thought of the separability of mind and body (Descartes), its domination by letters (Pascal), or the parallel unfathomability of body and mind (Spinoza).

"There has never been any body in philosophy"—so Jean-Luc Nancy tells us in "Corpus"—though its "sense" never stops rushing into the body to make it the organon of the sign. But it is a sign that operates as the signifier, inflicting its cuts and divisions on a body valorized only for its wholeness. Thus philosophy's perplexed relation to the body, he writes, is as old as the oldest metaphysical oppositions (inside/outside; the being itself of the sign, the sign of itself) that issued from Plato's cave. But it is also as recent as the *partage* of the Holocaust, as recent as a wholeness that has exceeded all simpler notions of the "body of the whole." The "becoming palpable" of humanity can no longer appear as a simple universal *concept*, a mere *principle* of generality, but has to be reconceived as a body without organs of a political state formed exclusively by the division and sharing out of the communal body. In the face of the world's eight billion human beings, Nancy poses the question: "Since we know that it is all for nothing, for no other purpose than to exist, and to be those bodies, what will we be able to do to celebrate their number?" This seems to me an appallingly crucial question today, urgent—as experts from the First World begin to explain how certain populations, populaces, peoples, are going to have to be "curtailed" to save the earth, the natural world as understood. (We are told daily in the newspapers that "overpeopling" the world, mainly in India and Africa, for example, is "degrading" the natural infrastructure, the soil, trees, water, etc., of the land, which must be saved from and not for the people.)

Philosophy's reluctant acceptance of the body and its willing rejection of it are as ancient and as modern as Psyche herself, the subject and object at once of a non-knowledge without ignorance. Bodies resist, have weight, extension; without making these attributes an object of knowledge, Nancy tells us, bodies nonetheless experience themselves, are experienced, if only as impenetrabilities, not bodies as incarnations of spirit but bodies as *given*, there. This is the source of philosophy's objection to the body: the presupposition that, as Nancy puts it, the "body" is "the determination of something like an instance of immediate knowledge"—a "contradiction in terms." Yet this is very likely a wrong presupposition, a pretext for philosophy's "mediating" the presumed contradiction of knowledge/non-knowledge with categories like "sense perception," "aesthetics," "representation."

For bodies may be no more than resistances—resistances to knowledge as well as to ignorance; to being touched; to being meaning; to being there. Bodies, says Nancy, are "weighty masses," they can be touched, can be moved, can touch themselves without *being* themselves (being, thereby, bodies without ontological status). Yet they risk themselves by touching at the limit: "Thought is here taken back to its matter; thought is itself this renewing which does not come back, but comes to existence" and manifests itself as a "gram of thought." Nancy's essay, then, seems to me to go somewhat beyond the particular framing of the "ontic" imposed by the ontological difference set forth by Heidegger and even Husserl, that is, the phenomenological/ontological "world" in which the everyday is a constant concern but is just as constantly and stringently revalued. Instead, Nancy is returning to an important body of thought, one that had almost been dropped, a materialism that already challenges Heidegger's view of the body as "extraneous to his project" (see Nancy's note 12). Had philosophy dropped it out of fear of empiricism? Or fear that the empirical self (the physical, moral, gendered body) is simply subject to failing in ways that the transcendental, categorical, empty (linguistic) subject cannot be? And such failing is—as Freud and Lacan have shown us—indicative—vividly so— of a conjunction of mind and body that is not dependent on and guided by a negative transcendence.

Gayatri Chakravorty Spivak's "Response to Jean-Luc Nancy" returns to the Kantian-critical mode, asking the question of the conditions of possibility of Nancy's effort. She characterizes this effort as still a part of a program of "affirmative deconstruction"—a program that she understands "to embrace the familiar, the average, the daily, the chancy, as enabling limits, . . . [and] the acquisition of knowledge in order to suspend it." Spivak's response requires attention. Her complaint is that by making the philosophical argument against the body as object of the knowledge of/by philosophy, he has had to make it a subject without knowledge, a "psyche" whose figure has been repeatedly used to designate who can or cannot ever be "other subjects of knowledge." In her particular blend of Kant, Derrida, and Marx, then, Spivak draws a limit, and draws it in a different place from Nancy: the "ungrounded body" (the natural body relating to itself) is, for her as for Kant, the object of knowledge that is to be distinguished from the "body without organs"—the purely synthetic subject of freedom. Whereas Nancy refers to the model of the embodied, incarnated spirit of God in order to reach the body as given without presuppositions, without its being a representation of spirit, Spivak dismisses certain portions of Western thought on the body as inevitably trapped within this paradigm, which is rooted for her in monotheism. She argues that, although the monotheism[20] of the West has imperialistically divided her from her people and her people from the "authentic" Hindu polytheism of the Indian past, this alternative tradition, much like woman's bleeding and alternative body, should be reinstated at the root of any renewed effort to think bodies.

Gary Shapiro presents a crisp and economical perspective on more than Nancy's book *Corpus*. If Western philosophy has been determined from the beginning by a struggle with the bodily, the need "to distinguish the soul from its other" (a move that too often reduces that "other" to being the object of an incorporation, a mere "moment" in the achievement of its own self-consciousness), Shapiro's claim is that Nancy seeks to break with that line.

Slavoj Žižek's article, an edifying exposition of Lacan's formulation of the *objet a*, explores the fantasy structure—popular and philosophical— surrounding "bliss." Everyone must leave *Shangri-la*—or *Rancho Notorious*—or the land of *King Solomon's Mines*. In the passage to withdrawal, the land of bliss is marked as purely artificial. Where desire is "saturated," it is evidently "unbearable." Žižek notes that this is the "Kantian" problem of "unrepresentability," in perverse or reverse form, running along a Möbius strip where the border between "reality" and the "fantasy" that supports it dissolves. A "reversal into bliss" (or dissolution of this border) is what really threatens. Žižek here re-marks Freud's designation (in "The Two Principles of Mental Functioning") and Lacan's ("The Partial Drive and Its Circuit") of the threat of *jouissance* as being itself the source of our sense of "reality": for Lacanians, "'reality' constitutes itself against the background of such bliss, that is, such an exclusion of some traumatic real." The fundamental antagonism of "bliss" (*jouissance*) and conscious "reality" is offered "symbolic appeasement," the zoning and configuring of the "body" by (enabling) symbolic cuts.

Benigno Sánchez-Eppler's essay is a dramatic recounting of the real effects that "symbolic [read: 'fantasy'] prohibitions" have on the body—of the slave. Here the "symbolic" segregates more than it separates (for Lacan, fantasies of fraternization are always rooted in real segregation)— dark from light sugar, just as dark from white people. The Other in whose service the prohibiting is done is hardly the classic oedipal father of lack, but instead the one who profits from the split bodies of the sugar refinery workers. They are hooked to a machine who is revealed as the "non-barred," or *jouissant* (in this case, profit-extracting) Other.

Avital Ronell's graceful essay locates the necessary symbolic splittings in "the war" between music and language, visuality and aurality, building a case that their split is misread as a perverse access to their traumatic coupling, which she likens to "the transcendental." The coupling moves toward "totality without contamination"—Wagner's dream—by placing "its essential bets on the exclusion of otherness," while pretending to "link two parts of a greater whole." Surprisingly, she finds nostalgia for the "uncut" body—which by now I hope we see in all its fearsomeness—in such advanced critics as Catharine Clément and Jean-François Lyotard's critiques of opera.

Peter Schwenger moves the "machine" of inmixing—and its rejection—into our near past—and into our rejection of this near past. He reads, and revives, "Hiroshima" as an "irruption of the unconscious." In this prelude to an analysis of Pynchon's *Gravity's Rainbow*, Schwenger details with chilling but necessary accuracy the dismantling of the ego, the literal as well as psychic fragmentation of the body image, that the bomb's blast inflicted upon its surviving victims. The blast, described by Schwenger as like "an instant dream," left people in a "state" without "self, without center," without, that is, the "city" (another name for "civilization") that had symbolically promised them all these things. This selfless state is the ultimate expression of what Schwenger calls the absolute condition of war, where the Ego Ideal of a "national self" is transformed into an (Ideal) ego "exempt . . . from being embodied" (he cites Elaine Scarry). Schwenger's piece contributes to the collective meditation on the Lacanian theses on body, image, and ego we have been pursuing here.

Anne Tomiche's reading of Marguerite Duras's *L'amante anglaise* as a kind of perversion of the polymorphous perversity of the *corps morcelé* (Duras reformulated feminine *jouissance*)[21] makes sense of Duras's work as an active parallel to the psychoanalytic insights into the fractioning of the body.

Jeffrey S. Librett's reading of Schlegel's impossible handling of masculine/feminine, spirit/letter, and the perverse couple in *Lucinde* is situated more firmly in the later Lacanian discourse that involved direct address to the situation of the gendered body under the regime of the Superego.

Dorothea Olkowski's essay suggests that we appeal to Deleuze to resist the confusion Superego/Father/Male that dominates theoretical misunderstanding of the technological body as a body of *jouissance* (fullness) rather than desire (as lack). She sees this appeal as particularly urgent for modeling feminism along uncharted lines.

Peter Canning's piece likewise resorts to Deleuze (a "born-again Nietzschean") to make the best of a desperate situation, but he instinctively turns toward Kleinian-affective rhetoric to intimate a more positive turn in the regime of the ego (which is, in the terms I have drawn here, in fact the Superego). Canning attempts to rethink, via Deleuze, the fragmented body less as a "Dionysian" manifestation than as an adumbration of a New Age, the age of nomadic bodies. Though he does not state this, the utopian-nomadic body structurally hangs on whether Deleuze's *body without organs* will suffice to avert the paranoid situation of the fragmented body—subject to organ pleasures, and therefore under constant implied death-threat—"We'll cut it off!"—as strict correlative to the command to pleasure—"Enjoy!" (At the very least Deleuze is premature for our time. The permissive, even licentious Superego even now draws its support from infantilizing the body of its subject, commanding it to multiple, partial enjoyments on the basis of its full organs within a fragmented body, but rendering this commandment completely impossible, incommensurable as such fractional joys are by comparison with its own, full, complete enjoyment as unbarred Other.)

Peter Brunette offers an analysis inspired more by the "Birmingham" school and Barthes than Deleuze on the matter of the electronic or videated body. He works at the level of the significance of form that TV news provides for a body electronically presented, frontal, total-seeming, yet nonetheless incomplete (the news anchors are all head and no body), in a programmatic way that belies the apparent "freedom" of the purely virtual body, composed entirely of mobile electrons. What Brunette argues is that the technical possibilities of virtual reality are subverted by the old dream of mastery over the body, a thought that implicates the work (information, newscasting) being done under its aegis as well.

Turning from the individual to the social "body," three essays—those by Greg Sarris, Frieda Ekotto, and Mira Kamdar—mark the real consequences of the rationalizing of the Western body for non-Western people, and reprise in concrete ways the thematics of Spivak's essay. In the essays by Sarris and Ekotto new resources are drawn from the "catastrophe" of the encounter between formerly "unlettered" peoples and "writing." Sarris and Ekotto both demonstrate that the cultural devastation of this encounter has been met with a resilience that is not that of the mere "survivors" but that of a heightened apprehension (in both senses of the word) of the agency of the letter. Ekotto explores how the power to define the "transcendental forms" are both epistemological and practical weapons within an overall context of conflict. Sarris examines how even those with the best intentions toward "others" and who are most critical of the ways in which non-Western peoples have been represented seem strangely incapable of rendering those peoples "present," of giving them voice, space, time.

But Sarris's essay does more than repeat a truism that is both bland and actually comforting to the conquerors of his people (by reassuring them of the solidity of their victory). His work goes to the heart of the variability of the definition of a self that has its dependence on "writing." What he shows is that "writing" cannot yet close the door on speech, its contractual aspects, its determinations of behavior. Where we see the conflation of the two "cuts" in the Superegoic figure, Sarris finds his split heritage is sutured by his *symbolic* acceptance of infantilization not at the hands of a conquistador or colonial power but at the hands of a woman, an aunt, who literally embodies afresh the principle of the "third party" of which Lacan speaks. Sarris describes his original quest—to "make sense" of his Indian informant, Mabel McKay, by finding her "center," which should in turn yield knowledge for both his "peoples": the white Ph.D. anthropologist and the contemporary disinherited Indian. That this is the wrong way to go about things where the relation to the Other is concerned is a lesson he is taught by his Aunt Violet, who will act, in the specific situation of "the interview," as the "third party." She will do so in a particularly homey way, a way that masks the Symbolic function she is upholding: by asking Sarris to peel potatoes, and judging him not by his product but by his by-product:

the excessively thick, heedless peelings of the potatoes he has shaped (he thought) into the same beautiful, clean, white ovals as she had made.

Mira Kamdar's essay underscores the darker political side of the "liberatory rhetoric" surrounding the body, which rhetoric I have structurally linked to the psychoanalytic "Superego" and which she places in the Enlightenment writer's ambivalence about the imminent loss of "mastery" of his body parts. Her essay on Diderot, the "great materialist," places his postmodern sensitivity toward corporal multiplicities squarely alongside his reluctance to yield mastery ("distance") over the body.

Laura Zakarin's eloquent double exploration of the "student body" shows it aging in hopes of dawning adulthood, which recedes incessantly. The student body is supposed to be temporary, "transitory." Will "adulthood" arrive only with the acquisition of the "job"? She looks to "one of theology's most painful parables" and makes an academic pun *à la lettre* (job/Job). She has read not only the *Book* but the beleaguered body of Job.

Corpus

Jean-Luc Nancy

corpus is not a discourse: however, what we need here is a corpus.

We need a *corpus*, a *cata*log, the recitation of an empirical logos that, without transcendental reason, would be a gleaned list, random in its order or in its degree of completion, a corpus of the body's *entries*: dictionary entries, entries into language, body registers, registers of bodies. We need a passive recording, as by a seismograph with its impalpable and precise styluses, a seismograph of bodies, of senses, and again of the entries of these bodies: access, orifices, pores of all types of skin, and "the portals of your body" (Apollinaire). We need to recite, to blazon, body after body, place after place, entry by entry.[1]

All this would be possible only if we had access to bodies, only if they were not impenetrable, as physics defines them. Bodies impenetrable to language, and languages impenetrable to bodies, bodies themselves, like this word "body," which already withholds itself and incorporates its own entry.

Two bodies cannot occupy the same space simultaneously. Not you and me at the same time in the space where I speak, in the place where you listen.

A discourse must indicate its source, its point of utterance, its condition of possibility, and its shifter [*embrayeur*]. But I will never be able to speak from where you listen, nor will you be able to listen from where I speak—nor will I ever be able to listen from where I speak. Bodies are impenetrable: only their impenetrability is penetrable. Words brought back to the mouth, or to the ink and the page: there is nothing here to discourse about, nothing to communicate. A community of bodies.

We need a *corpus*: a simple nomenclature of bodies, of the places of the body, of its entry ways, a recitation enunciated from nowhere, and not even enunciated, but announced, recorded, and repeated, as if one said: foot, belly, mouth, nail, wound, beating, sperm, breast, tattoo, eating, nerve, touching, knee, fatigue. . . .

Of course, failure is given at the outset, and intentionally so.

And a double failure is given: a failure to produce a discourse on the body, also the failure not to produce discourse on it. A double bind, a psychosis. I have finished talking about the body, and I have not yet begun. I will never stop talking about it, and this body from which I speak will never be able to speak, neither about itself nor about me. It will never experience speech's *jouissance*, and speech will never enjoy it.

This program is known from the start: it is the only program of a discourse, of a dialogue, of a colloquium devoted to the "body." When one puts the body on the program, on whatever program, one has already set it aside. Who can tell, here and now, which body addresses which other body? But should we talk about address? And in which sense? Does one require *adresse*, skillfulness, *tact*—that is to say, the right touch—in order to consider bodies as the addressees they must inevitably be? How does one touch? An entire rhetoric resides in this question. But what would happen if we understood the question non-metaphorically? *Comment toucher?* And as the question or program of a rhetoric, of an art of speech, is it only metaphorical? What does a word touch, if not a body? But there you have it: How can one get hold of the body? I am already speechless.

Of course, the point is not to suggest that the body is ineffable. The idea of the ineffable always serves the cause of a higher, more secret, more silent, and more sublime word: a treasury of sense to which only those united with God have access. But "God is dead" means: God no longer has a body. The dead, rotten body is this thing that no longer has any name in any language, as we learn from Tertullian and Bossuet; and the unnamed God has vanished together with this unnameable thing. It might very well be that with this body, all bodies have been lost, that any notion, any truth, any representation of bodies has been lost. But there remain the bodies themselves, and a discourse divided by them. One should not stop speaking about what cannot be said, one should not stop touching its speech and its tongue, pressing it against them. From this body to body contact with language one must expect a birth, the exposition of a body, which a tongue outside of itself will exscribe, will name by touching and by falling silent.

In truth, the body of God was the body of man himself: the body God had made for himself *ex limon terrae*, with a "putty" symbolizing the whole of his creation. "In oculis est ignis; in lingua, qua vocem format, aer; in manibus, quarum proprie tactus est, terra; in membris genitalibus, acqua." (In the eyes there is fire; in the tongue, which shapes speech, air; in the hands, to which touching belongs, earth; and water in the genitalia.)[2] As an image of God, the body of man was a resemblance to and a manifestation of the creative power *in persona*, the radiance of its beauty, the temple and the song of its glory.

With the death of God, we have lost this glorious body, this sublime body: this real symbol of his sovereign majesty, this microcosm of his immense work, and finally this visibility of the invisible, this *mimesis* of the inimitable.[3]

However, in order to think such a *mimesis*—and to elaborate the whole dogmatics of Incarnation—, one had to dispense with the *body*, with the very idea of body. The body was born in Plato's cave, or rather it was conceived and shaped in the form of the cave: as a prison or tomb of the soul,[4] and the body first was thought *from the inside*, as buried darkness into which light only penetrates in the form of reflections, and reality only in the form of shadows. This body is seen from the inside, as in the common but anguishing fantasy of seeing the mother's body from the inside, as in the fantasy of inhabiting one's own belly, without father or mother, before any father and mother, before all sex and all reproduction, and of getting hold of oneself there, as a nocturnal eye open to a world of chains and simulacra. This body is first an interiority dedicated to images, and to the knowledge of images; it is the "inside" of representation, and at the same time the representation of that "inside."

From the body-cave to the glorious body, signs have become inverted, just as they have been turned around and displaced over and over again, in hylemorphism, in the sinner-body, in the body-machine, or in the "body proper" of phenomenology. But the philosophico-theological *corpus* of bodies is still supported by the spine of *mimesis*, of representation, and of the sign. At times the body is the "inside" in which the image is formed and projected (sensation, perception, memory, conscience): in this case, the "inside" appears to itself as a foreign body, as an object to be examined from the outside, as a dissected eye, or as the hallucinated body of the pineal gland. At other times, the body is the signifying "outside" ("zero degree" of orientation and of the aim, origin, and receiver of relations, the unconscious): in this case, the "outside" appears to itself as a thick interiority, a filled cave, a property prior to any appropriation. As such, the body is the articulation, or better yet, the *organ* or *organon* of the sign: it is, for our entire tradition, that *in which* sense is given and *out of which* sense emerges. But as such, regardless of the perspective used—dualism of body and soul, monism of the flesh, symbolic deciphering of bodies—, the body remains the organon, the instrument or the incarnation, the mechanism or the work of a *sense* that never stops rushing into it, presenting itself to itself, making itself known as such and wanting to tell itself there. The body, *sense*—in this double sense of the word that fascinated Hegel.[5]

In this way, and in this posture, the body never ceases to contradict itself. It is the place of contradiction *par excellence*. Either it is by the body and through it that signification occurs, and then signification falls within its boundaries and is worth only what a shadow is worth in the cave, or it is from the body and on it that signification takes shape and is deposited, and signification never stops reaching toward this proper locus where it should endlessly curl up into itself. There is finally no difference between this opaque darkness and the darkness of the shadows. The body remains the dark reserve of sense, and the dark sign of this reserve. But in this way, the body is absolutely trapped by the sign and by sense. If it is the sign, it is the sense; (How then does one reckon the economy of a soul?); if it is sense, then it is the indecipherable sense of its own sign (And doesn't one still have a soul or a spirit?). The late Merleau-Ponty enjoyed citing Valéry's phrase "the body *of* the spirit."[6]

Literature as much as, if not more than, philosophy exposes this problematic. In a sense, one is tempted to say that if there has never been any body in philosophy—other than the signifier and the signified—in literature, on the contrary, there is nothing but bodies. In yet another sense, one could say that literature and philosophy have never stopped wanting to relate to and/or oppose each other as body to soul or spirit. But actually, literature (I mean here the philosophical determination of literature from which the word "literature" itself can never really be disengaged, though it comes down to the same thing if I say "Literature" according to our "literary" [or "theoretical" or "critical"] understanding of the matter)—literature therefore offers us one of three things: either fiction, which is by definition bodiless, with its author, whose body is absent (in fact, we are imprisoned in his cave, where he gives us the spectacle of bodies); or bodies covered with signs, bodies that are only treasuries of signs (the bodies of Balzac, Zola, or Proust—sometimes, if not often, those signs are in the first

place carnal signs); or else writing itself abandoned or erect like a signifying body—such as for Roland Barthes "the beating (enjoying) body" of
the writer,[7] the body signifying to the point of non-significance.

In this way, we do not leave the horizon of the sign, of sense, and of
mimesis. Literature mimes the body, or makes the body mime a signification (social, psychological, historical, heroic, etc.), or mimes itself as
body. In this way, in all these ways at once, sense always comes back to the
book as such, that is, to literature itself, but the book is never there: it has
never abolished itself in its pure presence, it has not absorbed the sign into
sense, nor sense into the sign. The body of the book, which should be the
body of bodies, is there without being there. Literature, and with it, once
again, the relationship between literature and philosophy, is a long sequel
to the mystery of the Incarnation, a long explication of it, a long implication within it.[8]

In its turn, politics represents the same thing, the same endless explication of the mystery. Either one has to designate the community, the city
as a body, or else the social, civil body, given as such, must engender its
own sense of community and of city. As a body of forces, as a body of love,
as a sovereign body, it is both sense and the sign of its own sense—but as
soon as it's the one, it loses the other.

Sign of itself and *being-itself of the sign*: such is the double formula of
the body in all its states, in all its possibilities. All our semiotics and all our
mimologies are contained within these extremities, in the *materia signata*
that the body according to St. Thomas Aquinas is.[9] (One should also say,
in the most emphatic senses of the word, the *symbol* of itself and the *being-
itself* of the symbol. Or else, one should say that in the body and as body,
the sign demands the reality of the symbol: that is, the material reunion
and co-presence of sense with the senses, the *body of sense* and the *sense
of the body*.)

If the signifier "body" denotes nothing other than this circular resorp-
tion, would this mean that it renders its signification equal to the totality
of sense, and turns it, in the process, into a vanishing signification? Of
course, and it is precisely for this reason that "the body" has not ceased
being stretched, exasperated, ripped to shreds between the unnamable and
the unnamable. Paradoxically, the flesh of Merleau-Ponty—this "texture
which comes back to itself and matches itself,"[10] where the world and my
body are woven together as sense itself, of which Merleau-Ponty writes:
"what we call the flesh, this internally shaped mass, has no name in any
philosophy"[11]—offers a response to the decomposed corpse of Tertullian.

Body is the total signifier, for everything has a body, or everything is a body (this distinction loses its importance here), and *body* is the last signifier, the limit of the signifier, if what it says or would like to say—what it would have liked to say—is nothing other than the interlacing, the mixing of bodies with bodies, mixing everywhere, and everywhere manifesting this other absence of name, named "God," everywhere producing and reproducing and everywhere absorbing the sense of sense and of all the senses, infinitely mixing the impenetrable with the impenetrable.

It is here and nowhere else that *spirit* arises as infinite concentration into the self. If soul is the form of the body, spirit is the sublation or the sublimation (or perhaps the repression?) of any form of bodies in the revealed essence of the sense of the body—of the body of sense.[12] The *spirit* of Christianity is incorporated here in full. *Hoc est enim corpus meum* . . .

But here there arises yet another way of exhausting the body and the sense of the body. It is the deported, massacred, tortured bodies, exterminated by the millions, piled up in charnel houses. Here too, the body loses its form and its sense—and sense has lost all body. These bodies are not even signs any longer, nor are they at the origin of any sign. These bodies are no longer bodies: spiritualized into smoke, as an exact reversal of and response to those who evaporate into spirit. Similar, even though different, are the bodies of misery, the bodies of starvation, battered bodies, prostituted bodies, mangled bodies, infected bodies, as well as bloated bodies, bodies that are too well nourished, too "body-built," too erotic, too orgasmic. All those are only signs of themselves; they are the being-itself of the sign where nothing offers any sign to anything.

Such are the sacrificed bodies, but sacrificed to nothing. Or rather, they are not even sacrificed. "Sacrifice" is a word that says too much, or not enough, to designate what we have done and what we do to bodies, and with bodies. "Sacrifice" designates a body's passage to a limit where it becomes the body of a community, the spirit of a communion of which it is the effectiveness, the material symbol, the absolute relationship to itself of sense pervading blood, of blood making sense. But sacrifice is no more.[13] The blood that is spilled, is spilled atrociously, and only atrociously. There was a spirituality of Christ's wounds. But since then, a wound is just a wound—and the body is nothing but a wound, even when it protects itself and oils itself, dresses itself as if to render itself inaccessible to any lesion.

The body is but a wound. None of our wounds, in a sense, is new, regardless of the economic, military, police, psychological techniques that inflict them. But from now on, the wound is just a sign of itself, signifying nothing other than this suffering, a forbidden body, deprived of its body. It is not simply a misfortune or a malediction, for these things still offer a sign (those tragic signs that have become indecipherable); and it is not simply illness (as if we knew what we suffer from and where health is), but it is pain [*le mal*], a wound open onto itself, a sign resorbed into itself, until finally it is neither sign nor itself. "Eye without an eyelid, exhausted with seeing and with being seen": this is what Marcel Henaff says of our Western body when he reaches the end of a project first outlined by the Marquis de Sade.[14] Or in the words of Elaine Scarry: "the world, the I, the voice are lost in the intensity of the suffering of torture"; "dissolution of the world, de-creation of the created world."[15] We must understand this "created" world as a world of bodies, a world in which bodies come to presence. That is, a world in which bodies are the bodies they are.

But what is this *being*? What do we know of the being-being of the body, and of the being-body of being? Perhaps nothing yet. Philosophy is certainly not the one to tell us.

In the meantime, there are five billion human bodies. Soon, there will be eight billion. Not to say anything of the other bodies. Humanity is becoming *tangible*, and also tangible in its inhumanity. What is the space opened between eight billion bodies? What is the space in which they touch or draw apart, without any of them or their totality being resorbed into a pure and nil sign of itself? Sixteen billion eyes, eighty billion fingers: to see what, to touch what? Since we know that it is all for nothing, for no other purpose than to exist, and to be *those bodies*, what will we be able to do to celebrate their number?

To the extent that the body is a wound, the sign is also nothing but a wound. Are we still capable, are we already capable of confronting the wound of the sign, this flaying where sense gets lost? Sense is lost in this pure sense that is also the wound. The wound closes the body. It multiplies its sense, and sense gets lost in it.

Everything is possible. Bodies resist. The community of bodies resists. The grace of a body offering itself is always possible. The pain of a body suffering is always available. Bodies call again for their creation. Not the kind of creation that blows into them the spiritual life of the sign. But birth, the separation and sharing of bodies [*le partage des corps*].

No longer bodies that make sense, but sense that engenders and shares bodies. No longer the semiological, symptomatological, mythological, or phenomenological pillage of bodies, but thought and writing given, given over to bodies. The writing of a *corpus* as a separation and sharing of bodies, sharing their being-body, shared out by it, and thus divided from itself and from its sense, exscribed all along its own inscription. This is indeed what writing is: the body of a sense that will never tell the signification of bodies, nor ever reduce the body to its sign.

To write the sign of oneself that does not offer a sign, that is not a sign. This is: *writing*, finally to stop discoursing. To cut into discourse. Corpus, anatomy. One must not consider the anatomy of dissection, the dialectical dismembering of organs and functions, but rather the anatomy of configurations, of shapes—one should call them states of the body, ways of being in the world, demeanors, respirations, gaits, pelts, curlings, masses. Bodies are first to be touched. Bodies are first masses, masses offered without anything to articulate, without anything to discourse about, without anything to add to them.

Discharges of writing, rather than surfaces to be covered by writings. Discharges, abandonments, retreats. No "written bodies," no writing on the body, nor any of this graphosomatology into which the mystery of the Incarnation and of the body as pure sign of itself is sometimes converted, "modern style." For indeed, the body is not a locus of writing. No doubt one writes, but it is absolutely not where one writes, nor is it what one writes—it is always what writing exscribes. In all writing, a body is traced, is the tracing and the trace—is the letter, yet never the letter, a literality or rather a lettericity that is no longer legible. A body is what cannot be read in a writing.

(Or one has to understand reading as something other than decipherment. Rather, as touching, as being touched. Writing, reading: matters of tact.)

I repeat: we ask for the body of a sense that would not give signification of the body, and that would not reduce it to being its sign. I repeat and I ask again, asking first of myself, a tact of writing, a tact of reading that I know discourse is unable to provide. The body insists, resists, weighs on the demand: for it is after all the body that requests, demands this anatomical and catalogical writing, the kind of writing that would enable it not to signify (not to turn into either a signifier, a signified, or self-signification). The contrary, or more than the contrary, of an incarnation. In incarnation, the spirit *becomes flesh*. But here we are talking about a body that no spirit *has become*. Not a body produced by the self-production or reproduction of the spirit, but a body given, always already given, abandoned, and withdrawn from all the plays of signs. A body touched, touching, and the tract of this tact.

Corpus of tact: to touch lightly, to brush against, to squeeze, to penetrate, to hold tight, to polish, to scratch, to rub, to stroke, to palpitate, to
handle, to knead, to hug, to embrace, to strike, to pinch, to bite, to suck,
to hold, to let go, to lick, to carry, to weigh . . .

A body always weighs; it lets itself weigh, be weighed. A body does not
have a weight, it is a weight. It weighs, it presses against other bodies, onto
other bodies. All bodies weigh against one another: celestial bodies and
callous bodies, vitreous bodies, and all others. This is not a matter of me-
chanics or gravity. Bodies weigh lightly. Their weight is the rising of their
mass to their surface. Endlessly, the mass rises to the surface, and peels off
as a surface [*s'enleve en surface*]. Mass is density, the consistency concentrated in itself: but this concentration in itself is not that of spirit, for here
the "self" is the surface whereby mass is exposed. Massive substance is
supported only by a spreading, not by interiority or by a foundation. So,
as Freud remarks, "Psyche is spread out"—adding "she knows nothing
about it."

This non-knowledge is the very body of Psyche, or rather, it is the body
that Psyche herself *is*. This non-knowledge is not negative knowledge or
the negation of knowledge; it is simply the absence of knowledge, the absence of the very relation of knowledge, whatever its content. Using a certain vocabulary, one could say: knowledge wants an object [*de l'objet*], but
with bodies there is only subject [*du sujet*]; with bodies, there are only subjects. But one might say that in the absence of an object there is no subject
either, no transcendental ground, and that what remains is precisely the
body, bodies. *The "body" is grounds for not having any object* (grounds
for not being a subject, subjected to not being subject, as one says "subject
to bouts of fever"). The substance that only touches on other substances.
A touch, a tact, as "subject" before any subject. Uninscribable, exscribing
everything, starting with itself.

The body does not know; but it is not ignorant either. Quite simply, it
is elsewhere. It is from elsewhere, another place, another regime, another
register, which is not even that of an "obscure" knowledge, or a "pre-
conceptual" knowledge, or a "global," "immanent," or "immediate"
knowledge. The philosophical objection to what philosophy calls "body"
presupposes the determination of something like an authority of "immediate knowledge"—a contradiction in terms, which inevitably becomes
"mediated" (as "sensation," "perception," synaesthesia, and as immense
reconstitutions of a presupposed "representation"). But what if one could
presuppose nothing of the kind? What if the body was simply there, given,
abandoned, without presupposition, simply posited, weighed, weighty?

Body would then first be the experience of *its own weight* (of its matter,

its mass, its pulp, its grain, its gaping, its mole, its molecule, its turf, its
turgidity, its fiber, its juice, its invagination, its volume, its fall, its meat, its
coagulation, its dough, its crystallinity, its twitching, its spasm, its unknot-
ting, its tissue, its dwelling, its disorder, its promiscuity, its smell, its taste,
its resonance, its resolution, its reason).

But here the *experience* would be the weighing itself, the weighing that
weighs without weighing itself, without being weighed or measured by
anything. *Experitur*: it tries, attempts, risks itself, and risks itself right
away, all the way to its own limits—it consists in nothing other than these
limits, borders and ends, new beginnings of itself, where it touches itself
or lets itself be touched, a weighing, a pondering, a fall, a funeral, a lifting,
a lip, a lung, an exhalation of breath in which it hardly touches itself, in
which it runs the risk of being at its end, of exhausting itself before being
itself. An experience of freedom: a body is delivered, born, it is born at its
weighing, it is nothing but its weighing, this minute expenditure of a few
grams delivered over to quivering on contact with so many common extremities of other foreign bodies, bodies that are so close, so intimate with
this body in their own freedom.

There is no experience *of* the body in the same way that there is no
experience *of* freedom. But freedom itself is experience, and the body itself
is experience. It is insofar as their essential structure (the structure of each
of them, and the double structure that folds and unfolds them into one another) resembles precisely the structure of the sign-of-itself and the being-
itself of the sign. *The body has the same structure as spirit*, but it has that
structure *without presupposing itself as the reason for the structure*. Consequently, it is not self-concentration, but rather the ex-centration of existence. Existence does not presuppose itself and does not presuppose anything: it is posited, imposed, weighed, laid down, exposed.

Thus, the body does not have any way of knowing, and there is no lack
here, because the body does not belong to the domain in which "knowledge" or "non-knowledge" is at stake, any more than knowledge itself belongs to the domain of bodies. If one agrees to say, and if it is fitting to say,
that thought does not belong to the order of knowledge either, then it might
no longer be impossible to say that the body thinks and also, consequently,
that thought is itself a body. This comes down to saying only that thought
is here taken back to "matter," to its matter—thought *is* itself this renewal
that does not come *back*, but that comes, properly speaking, to this existence—posited, suspended, confined in this very block, this network of tis-
sues, bones, minerals, and fluids out of which it does not go, because, if it
did exit it, it would no longer think.

One must think thought here, one must weigh it as a word not yet uttered, not yet escaped from a mouth, still in the larynx, on the tongue, the teeth that will instantly make it resound, if it is spoken. A word pronounced but not said, posed, as slippery as spittle, itself saliva, a minute flow, an ex-perspiration of the mouth in itself, in its fissure, in its bowels. A swallowed, unspoken word, not choked back, not retracted,[16] but swallowed in the stolen instant of being spoken, swallowed with this bare taste of saliva, barely foaming, barely viscous, a distinct dissolution, impregnation without the immanence of a blandness where what is given is the taste of the swallowed word, washed away before being uttered. This savor is not *savoir*, whatever the etymological link. This voice is not language, and what is more, this voice remains without vocabulary, without vocalization, and without vocalics. It thus resembles the "dialogue of the soul with itself," which is merely another form of the being-itself of the sign, but it engages neither in dialogue nor in monologue. It distances itself from any "logic." It resonates, nonetheless; it is its own echo: that is, a reverberation of the weighing of a body, a reverberation without verb where what is not "in itself" vibrates "for itself." A body is always the imminence of such a voice; it is its trace, the dull, grating noise of a weighing of a thought [*d'une pesée d'une pensée*].

One must think the thought of the body thus. A double genitive: the thought that is the body itself, and the thought we think, we seek to think, on the subject of the body. This body here—mine, yours—which attempts to think the body and where the body attempts to be thought, cannot do so rigorously. That is, it cannot give up signifying the body, assigning signs to it—except by allowing itself to be brought back to its own thinking matter, to the very place from which it thoughtlessly springs.

Here is the hard point of this thing "thought," nodule or synapse, acid or enzyme, a gram of cortex. A *gram* of thought: a minimum weight, the weight of a little stone, called a scruple, the weight of an almost-nothing that disconcerts and that forces one to ask why there is not nothing, but rather some things, some bodies. A gram of thought: trace of this pebble [*caillou*], of this calculus [*calcul*, also "stone"], engraving, tiny incision, notch, cut, hard point of a tip, engraver's stylus [*poinçon*], body of the first cut, breached body, body separated [*partagé*] by *being this body* that it is and by existing it. The cortex is not an organ, it is this corpus of points, of tips, of traces, engravings, stripes, lines, folds, marks, incisions, schisms, decisions, letters, numbers, figures, writings "engrammed" [*engrammées*] in one another, decoupled one from the other, smooth and striated, even and granular. A corpus of the grains of thought in a body—which is neither a "thinking body" nor a "speaking body"—granite of the cortex, telling the beads of experience.

Of course, there is violence and pain in this thought. It never stops banging into itself, hard, resistant, impenetrable, being destined to think its hardness by means of that hardness itself, impenetrable by dint of essence and of method. To think at the point of the thinking body is to think without knowing anything, without articulating anything, without intuiting anything. It is thinking withdrawn from thinking. It is touching this gram, this series, this range, it is an indefinite corpus of grams. Thought itself touches itself; but it does so without being *itself*, without making its way back to itself. Here (but where is this "here"? It is in no place that can be pinpointed, since it is at the point where place first becomes a place, is occupied by a body, is occupied itself as the body of the place: for if there is no body *there*, there is no place), here, then, it is not a matter of reuniting with untouched matter, nor dissolving into its massive and naive intimacy. There is no "intact matter"; if there were, there would be nothing, not one single thing. But here, at the body, there is the sense of touch, the touch of the thing, which touches "itself" without an "itself" where it can get at itself, and which is touched and moved in this unbound sense of touch, and so separated from itself, shared out of itself [*partagé de lui-même*].

The body enjoys being touched. It enjoys being squeezed, weighed, thought by other bodies, and being what squeezes, weighs, and thinks other bodies. *Body*, because drawn out of the undivided totality that does not *exist*, and a body that *enjoys*, because it is touched in this very withdrawal, through it and thanks to it. Touching one another with their mutual weights, bodies do not become undone, nor do they dissolve into other bodies, nor do they fuse with a spirit—this is what makes them, properly speaking, bodies.

This joy is senseless. It is not even the sign of itself. This very joy is a mass, a volume offered on its surface, and it is a corpus of points, traces, grams, skins, folds, grains. Within this corpus, there is no signifying body, but there is no dissolution either. There is only this other corpus: touching, tasting, feeling, hearing, seeing, being a grain, savor, smell, noise, figure, and color—a random series, as open-ended as it is closed, as infinite as it is finite. This body no longer has any members,[17] if members are the functional parts of a whole. Here, each part is the whole, and there is never any whole. Nothing ever becomes the sum or the system of the corpus. A lip, a finger, a breast, a strand of hair are the temporary and agitated whole of a joy that is each time temporary, agitated, in a hurry to enjoy again and elsewhere. This elsewhere is all over the body, in the corpus of the parts of all the body, in the body of all the parts, and in all other bodies, which each can be a part for another, in an indefinitely ectopic corpus.

Joy does not come back to itself: this is precisely what makes it joy. However, it enjoys nothing but "itself." It rejoices in *itself*.[18] This is how the body rejoices in itself: it enjoys an "ipseity" that consists in not possessing the Self of subjectivity, and in not being the sign of its own sense. *Ipseity* itself, this body itself, this very body, in its very self enjoys, but this enjoying or this joy takes place as the very ex-position of this body. This joy is its birth, its coming into presence, outside of sense, in the place of sense, taking the place of sense, and making a place for sense.

This does not mean that the body comes before sense, as its obscure prehistory or as its pre-ontological attestation. No, it gives sense a place, absolutely. Coming neither before nor after, the sense of the body is given as the place of sense, as its circumscription and its exscription, as its end and its birth, its limit and its outcome, its aim and its obstacle, its being and its abyss. One could say, the *finitude* of sense. But since one often misunderstands this term, since one inevitably turns it into the starting point of a mediation in which the "finite" body must be converted, once again, into the incarnation of an infinite (into the being-self of a Sense or a Non-Sense), it might be better to say that the body is the *absolute* of sense. The ab-solute is what is detached, what is placed or set apart, what is shared out [*partagé*]. This sharing is itself ab-solution. A body allows for a place of absolute, inalienable, unsacrificable sense.

That this absolute place of sense is itself always ectopic changes nothing in the absolute nature of its sense. It is by touching the other that the body is a body, absolutely separated and shared [*partagé*]. The absoluteness [*l'absoluité*] of its sense, and the absoluteness of sense "in general" (if there is any such thing), is not kept "within" it, since it is itself nothing but the being-exposed, the being-touched of this "inside." As body, the absolute is common, it is the community of bodies. "As body": but that is all there is; that is, there is nothing other than this separation and sharing [*ce partage*]. We are not invoking "materialism" against "spiritualism": we are calling on being as absolutely partitioned [*partagé*] from and by sense as such. A single body—if it is possible to isolate such a thing—exposes itself as the sharing [*le partage*] of its separate senses.

Neither signification, nor manifestation, nor incarnation, and not revelation, either. The body exposes—the body; bodies expose each other. A naked body gives no sign and reveals nothing, nothing other than this: that there is nothing to reveal, that everything is there, exposed, the texture of the skin, which says no more than the texture of a voice. The voice again brought back to the mouth, a lip of voice, a skin of thought. Lip, throat, belly, which have nothing to deliver, to liberate, which are themselves liberation.

Only the body fulfills the concept of the words "exposition," "being exposed." And since the body is not a concept (since therefore there is no "body"), such a filling in is both nil and infinite, providing always both more and less than what a conceptual logic demands.

Being exposed, exposing: it is the skin, all the various types of skin, here and there open and turned into membranes, mucous, poured out inside of itself, or rather without either an inside or an outside, absolutely, continually passing from one to the other, always coming back to itself without either a locus or a place where it can establish a self, and so always coming back to the world, to other bodies to which it is exposed, in the same gesture that exposes them to itself. Al Lingis calls the skin "an exorbitant, shapeless, mute, inoperative, unexpressive materiality," which "when stroked, deploys a lascivious and exhibitionist nakedness."[19] But the skin is always exhibition, exposition, and the minutest look is a touching that brushes against it and exposes it once more.

Injury, the wound, closes the body, gives it the function of a sign. But the wounded body is still meant to be touched, it is still offered to the sense of touch, which restores its absoluteness. Thus, the body has been turned into nothing but a wound. We have not simply tried to dominate it through struggle, or hurt, or even kill it; we have tried to take away its absoluteness from it.

What stands "behind" a face—but also behind a hand, a belly, a buttock, a breast, a knee—the "he" or "she" who hides behind a face stands entirely outside of this face, and this is why, first of all, there is no face. There is, first, skin detaching itself from the world, from other skins, but detaching itself only while remaining attached, attached and exposed, attached by its detachment from the body. Absolute skin. What is a body if not a certain detachment of the skin, of bark, of surface, if not a carrying off and setting aside of a limit that is exposed and exposes itself? The gesture of the limit, the gesture at the limit, is touch—or rather: touching is the thought of the limit. To touch is to be at the limit, touching is *being* at the limit—and this is indeed being itself, absolute being. If there is something rather than nothing, it is because there is this limit made body, these bodies made limit, and exposed by their limits. Absolutely. Thought must touch on this.

Limits of matter (gases, liquids, solids), limits of kingdoms (mineral, vegetable, animal), limits of the sexes, limits of bodies, limits where sense becomes impossible, absolutely exposed, poured out, removed from any mystery, offered as the infinitely folded and unfolded line of all the bodies that make up a world. This world is their exhibition, that is, also their risk. Bodies run the risk of resisting one another in an impenetrable fashion, but they also run the risk of meeting and dissolving into one another. This double risk comes down to the same thing: abolishing the limit, the touch, the absolute, becoming substance, becoming God, becoming the Subject of speculative subjectivity. This is no longer the ab-solute, but saturated totality. But as long as there is *something*, there is also something else, other bodies whose limits expose them to each other's touch, between repulsion and dissolution.

Of course, *there is never* any "touching" as such, nor is there ever any "limit" as such: but this is why there is something, all things, as absolute, separated and shared out [*partagés*] bodies. Consequently, neither substance nor subject, but *corpus*, a catalogue without a logos, which is "logos" itself, bodily entries, entries that would be exposed, touched, one after the other, exposing one another, touching one another, detaching from one another, penetrating one another, withdrawing from one another—entries without any order or system, making neither sign nor sense, but exposing all the entries of sense.

No continuity, no immanence of sense to sense. Sense is body: it is exposed, detached, touched. And not the continuity of transcendance either, between signs and sense, between sign and what is beyond the sign, between sign of self and the self of sign. But a *corpus*, an ectopic topography, serial somatography, local geography. Stains, nails, veins, hairs, spurts, cheeks, sides, bones, wrinkles, creases, hips, throats. The parts of the corpus do not combine into a whole, are not means to it or ends of it. Each part can suddenly take over the whole, can spread out over it, can become it, a whole—that never takes place. There is no whole, no totality of the body—but its absolute separation and sharing out [*partage*]. There is no such thing as *the* body. There is no body.

Instead, there are patient and fervent recitations of numerous corpuses. Ribs, skulls, pelvises, irritations, shells, diamonds, drops, foams, mosses, excavations, fingernail moons, minerals, acids, feathers, thoughts, claws, slates, pollens, sweat, shoulders, domes, suns, anuses, eyelashes, dribbles, liqueurs, slits, blocks, slicing, squeezing, removing, bellowing, smashing, burrowing, spoiling, piling up, sliding, exhaling, leaving, flowing——

TRANSLATED BY CLAUDETTE SARTILIOT

Response to Jean-Luc Nancy

Gayatri Chakravorty Spivak

*J*ean-Luc Nancy was absent when this response was presented. Perhaps this merely made visible the nature of staged responses. All
such responses are attempts to appropriate the other and thus make the
other, already absent as such, absent as "other," the person to whom I respond. I make as if to enter a space when the other's text is not yet there
and ask, if I were to write that text and no other, what problems would I
encounter? As if I were not responding, but rather asking the interminable
question: what spaces would I leave open for a respondent I cannot imagine, whose burden I carry? It is an echo chamber whose task is to give shape
to Narcissus as respondent—one another's differance.

The "problems" of Nancy's texts came to me by way of such an effort,
the conjuring of a reflecting pool sponsored by Echo. And the contractual
conventions of the academic response, speaker and respondent neatly separated in person—Nancy's admirable delicate gravity—yet "engaging in
debate," did not come in to cover the phantom of Echo's voice and Narcissus's carapace. The problems, then, of that phantom paper: (1) the desire
to philosophize; (2) ignoring the institution; (3) the desire to remember
others; (4) not knowing how to.

The Desire to Philosophize

Candace Vogler, when she was a graduate student, described affirmative
deconstruction as trying to privilege the ontic in the ontico-ontological difference and to perform that privilege, with all its attendant difficulties and
enablements, in as many ways as there are occasions.

A shrewd description, no doubt reflecting some of the problems with my own understanding of deconstruction. Let us gloss it a little: deconstruction reads and rereads the ontico-ontological difference, necessarily insufficiently, as ontico-ontological differance. The ontic is different from and pushes away the ontological, and the ontological does the same, but differently; and both do so in the interest of the event of living and the task of making sense. In the event, the insufficient performance of this task, the invocation of the "trace" in "context," may look like, be a simulacrum of, such a giving of privilege. If this is so, the performance would involve, among other things, acting in that "space of prior interrogation, a vague average understanding of being . . . [which] up close, we cannot grasp at all."[1] It would involve, among other things, acting the limits of philosophy in the average, giving up to chance, using, among other things, the chanciness of the pedagogic instance, the average, familiar, everyday formula for which is: "I will let you follow this up."

Echoing Nancy's absent Narcissus, insufficiently in the manner of Echo, produces, for this cluster of high-risk gestures, the highly serious *statement* of abdication: "But, what is this *being*? [A p]hilosophy is certainly not the one to tell us," combined with the acting out of the desire precisely to philosophize in the tiny gap between "saturated totality" *and* the skinniest skin, not even a face, "removed from any mystery, offered as the infinitely folded and unfolded line of all the bodies that make up a world."[2]

This desire to catch the limit *for a philosophizing* that is not a philosophy takes me through to a refusal to acknowledge that this particular project (a lecture, a book) could be described within the ontico-ontological differance, although, in terms of the specifically political project, a version of this differance is recited: "it is both sense and the sign of its own sense— but as soon as it's the one, it loses the other." Nancy would place his project beyond Levinas's: "What stands 'behind' a face . . . stands entirely outside of this face, and this is why, first of all, there is no face." This may contain a brilliant way-down retake on the mind-body barrier (no use dismissing it as merely Cartesian, *the* bad word)—*literally* the echoic "inside" of the narcissistic carapace exposed outside in Echo. The desire to philosophize at the limit inserts this retake into the history of philosophy: Merleau-Ponty, in writing "'what we call the flesh . . . has no name in any philosophy,' offers," albeit "[p]aradoxically," nothing more than "a response to the decomposed corpse of Tertullian."

I think it is the desire to grab the limit that gives rise to the *il faut*'s— the "we [philosophers?] shoulds"—in the text. "But since one regularly [*regulièrement*] misunderstands th[e] term [finitude], since one inevitably

turns it into the starting point of a mediation . . . it might be better to say
that the body is the *absolute* of sense." Might it not, also and at the same
time, be better to give in, to mark the slipping away cheerfully with regret
rather than deflect it into so dangerous a word as "absolute," to acknowledge that misunderstanding is still to understand, to leave the body to
chance as well, for it is in chance anyway. To be able to *state* a problem is
not to perform the solution, may indeed be the opposite. And that, of
course, is all I am doing: stating some problems. Echo and Narcissus are
both caught *and* launched by statements, necessarily of problems, even as
questions.

This philosopher knows that "misunderstanding is still understanding," which is rather different from "all understanding is misunderstanding." Thus he writes: "[N]either substance nor subject, therefore [*par con-
séquent*], but *corpus*, a catalogue without a logos, which is 'logos' itself
. . ." To misunderstand is still to understand, the cata-logon is the "logos."
And therefore, here and there, he gives in to catalogues, makes lists. And
he does change an ordinary-language word for "prior"—*d'abord*—into a
kind of word for "touching." "Les corps, d'abord—c'est-à-dire, à abor-
der—sont masses [Bodies are first—that is to say, to be touched—are
masses]." This is a good gift of a philosophical performative. Every time I
read *d'abord* in the text, I have to remember that the word means, for the
time being, not just "first" but also "to be touched, for touching"—and
. . . think the consequences through, of course.

The desire to philosophize wrestles us to the ground, and there we lie,
embraced.

Ignoring the Institution

If affirmative deconstruction is understood, by way of the insufficiency of
its transgressions, as, among other things, to embrace the familiar, the average, the daily, the chancy, as enabling limits, it also involves the acquisition of knowledge in order to suspend knowledge. There is a nice line in
Glas. Believe me, it's hard to act it, to put it to work in a *mise-en-oeuvre*:
"If we did not read, we would have, ourselves, the imprudence to comment
on this wearing of the grape cluster."[3] This is a good pedagogic position in
the human sciences in the university. It stands up against uncritical know-
nothingism as well as pedantic vanguardism. I know from experience that
power play in the classroom *can* bite the dust on this one. Yet the suspension of something acquired *can* also serve as a technique outside the uni-

versity, if one at least attempts to give up the idea of its correct understanding in the name of its authors, of a "body of work." The differantial relationship—one different from and pushing off the other, yet as "the same"—between the proletariat and capitalism, communism and nationalism, feminism and imperialism, science and superstition—I cannot get off on this list now; a catalogue is too much the logos. My point, however, is that *if* we do not take into account what kind of technique the here and now calls for, we tend to forget the most familiar staging of our own speaking. And privileging the ontic, if that is what it is, becomes like playing at milkmaids. After all, the body has no problem unfolding and folding, almost-being, more-than-being, as it always has. That part is as easy as living, thinking, and dying. The problem posed here is to think it right, the academic problem as it is the differance of the socius.

Think of all the moves that had been made to think this easy thing right, for presentation at an institutional conference: the condition of possibility of international and national telephone systems with a sufficiency of circuits, the condition of possibility of state university systems with their statutory relationships with state legislatures and the principle of electronic facsimile-transfer, the condition of possibility of air travel, of international hotel chains with convention facilities. We had all agreed, one way or another, to be sustained by the efficient functioning of these systems, those of us who had come to speak against the abuse of power, those of us who had come to speak against exclusion, and those of us who had written papers about how hard it was to catch the easiest thing, kept away, grimly, by diseases of the body that taught us the desire to philosophize at the body's limit, whose hardship is only too easy to grasp in our familiar everyday.

The Desire to Remember Others and
Not Knowing How To

All of us had given our prior assent to the efficient functioning of a telematic society and all that it entails in order to take *whatever* stand we took at the conference. Echo echoes everything. I hope, therefore, that I will not be misunderstood if I say that one of the *hardest* things about performing the privileging of the ontic within the performance of a discipline or *any* politics is that the ontic is never yet articulated into the ethical as it is calculated in the moral and the political. (I also knew that at a meeting of the International Association for Philosophy and Literature, where this exchange was first staged, I would at least not hear the dominant complaint of U.S. pragmatism, that this was necessarily an ahistorical transcendental theory from above in the *disguise* of the inaccessible ungrounded below: that we must assume and learn, over and over again, its being-there as a craft not yet or ever to be graduated into prescriptive or inspirational practice-talk.)

The hardest thing about this position, then, is that it is not yet articulated into the ethical, and calculated into the moral and the political. Yet we are not caught up in the desire to philosophize alone; we must also want to be good, within our limits. I could read Nancy's invocation of the Holocaust and the teeming millions within that wanting. But again, Nancy is too good a philosopher not to know that, in the space where he would philosophize, there is not much difference among those bodies in the *corpus*: "Similar, even though different, are the bodies of misery . . . [and] bodies that are too well nourished." And as for the "five billion human bodies" that we are . . . "since we know that it is all for nothing, for no other purpose than to exist, and to be *those bodies*, what will we be able to do to celebrate their number?"

The answer is really nothing or everything by just hanging around as bodies, where bodies are something like a writing without a writer-agent or the possibility of reading. But, of course, we don't hang around *only* as bodies. As important as guarding the ungrounded memory-event of bodiedness is the provisionally grounded practice that that memory-event suspends as it makes it possible. Indeed, it is possible to trace the itinerary of the discontinuous yet concurrent memory-event of bodiedness as a limit/ condition to rational political practice in Marx. The crisis in international communism has something like a relationship with a forgetfulness of the ungrounded body. I am not for a moment suggesting that Marx trafficked in ontico-ontological difference. But, if this is the early difference between species life and species being, where the limit to practice is conceived of as the place where knowledge is impossible, where nature is "the great body without organs of the human being," where human life and death are but nature relating to itself, then the later Marx restaged this intuition as the Realm of Freedom, also a beyond for which political practice can only prepare discontinuous facilitation.[4] Nancy too shuttles between thought as hylograph and statements like "[t]here is no experience *of* the body in the same way that there is no experience *of* freedom." I do not think this concern is trivial. I think the memory-event of the *corpus* is critical to all practice. But I must also insist that that memory-event cannot usurp the place of practice, even in the name of the most careful catalogical philosophizing.

And in that nontrivializing yet critical spirit I will make a suggestion: why remember others as teeming millions or starving bodies? Why not imagine them as other subjects of knowledge caught in the same sort of but not the same bind?

I will proceed slowly here, once again. Incarnation, *Theologica*, the death of God, the gas ovens, and the teeming millions are not the only story, even if "our West" is mentioned once. How do contemporary polytheism and animism fall into or out of the ungrounded memory-event of the body when it is not the Latin word *corpus*? What do we substitute there?

Jean-Luc Nancy and Gayatri Spivak are two middle-class people born around the same time, one in Europe, one in Asia, both to grow up to become university teachers, brought together almost face-to-face by the chance of having come into contact with Derrida's texts, responsible to each other on the West Coast of the United States, where the conference took place. It is, then, with our common friend as intermediary that I will attempt to face the question: what do we substitute there? In this move I transgress the Narcissus-Echo mime, for the effort to substitute is more calculating, and you need a third party, so that "another 'subjectivity' comes again [*vient encore*]," to guarantee the substitution, to make sure that it is as just as possible, under the circumstances.[5]

I have by now read all of *Corpus* (the book) and I see that the points I raised in my response, and indeed the part of the book that I responded to, have all been "situated," many times over.[6] Not specifically as *my* questions, of course. The paper I responded to has been deflected within a broader frame, and the occasion has been described as follows:

A small section of *Corpus*, in a quite different version, had originally been given as a paper at the conference "Bodies, Technologies" at the International Association for Comparative Literature [*sic*], University of California at Irvine, April 1990. Translated by Claudine Sartiliot, Avital Ronell, and Brian Holmes, this text appears in English in the Proceedings of the Conference. [That, I believe, is the present volume.] It is reprinted also in Jean-Luc Nancy, *The Birth to Presence*, Stanford University Press, 1993. (*Corpus*, p. 106)

It is then within the broader frame of that book, of which the text I responded to was a "quite different" fragment (Echo echoes everything and in fragments), that I will reframe, by way of Derrida, the two or three general issues that closed that unique occasion.

In 1968, in a famous paper presented before the Société Française de Philosophie (perhaps a rather more serious event for the young Jacques Derrida than the IAPL was for the mature Jean-Luc Nancy), Derrida wrote as follows:

[The] differences [in/of language] . . . are produced effects, but they are effects which do not have [*qui n'ont pas*] as cause in a subject or a substance, in a thing in general, an existent [*étant*] that is somewhere present, and itself [*et lui-même*] escaping the play of differance. If such a presence were implied in the concept of cause in general, in the most classical fashion, we then would have to speak of an effect without a cause, which very quickly would lead to speaking of no effect at all. I have tried to indicate the direction [*visée*] of the way out of the closure of this framework via the "trace," which is no more an effect than it has a cause but which by itself cannot suffice [*ne peut suffire à elle seule*], outside the text, to operate the necessary transgression.[7]

The "trace" is not sufficient for the full transgression of thinking an effect without a cause that is necessary to fulfill the desire to philosophize. The book *Corpus* is an attempt not to fall short of but rather to exceed the transgression by marking a multitude of "traces," a kaleidoscope of (con)texts, perhaps to see if the error assigned to "classical" method can be avoided in this maximal way. The supertextuality of these traces, always above, beyond, and beside their texts (the "trace" is never outside), generates the logorrhea of the catalogue, leaving an embarrassment of *Spuren*.

I had missed the mark of this in the shorter version. And I believe that, within the institution, where the student, the reader, the listener, the colleague will not have been taught to read slowly, to circle around these catalogues as it were, the maximal overpresentation of the body runs the risk of being celebrated as effects without a cause, the "absolute," "which would very quickly lead to speaking of no effect at all."

"The space of bodies does not know death," Nancy writes, "but knows each body as a death. . . . Not the discourse of a being-for-death" (*Corpus*, p. 49). To be sure, this body inhabits a particular space between the Heideggerian *Dasein* (being-for-death) and the Heideggerian animal (world-poor being), since this too is a "tracing." "Un corps ne cesse pas de *se*" (p. 98), almost untranslatably "a body does not cease to transit."[8] Yet, because of the insistence upon there being something that is susceptible to all these tracings, the question that Derrida teaches us to ask about the animal in Heidegger keeps coming back to this reader: "Compromised, rather, by a *thesis* [a book between covers is *also* a thesis] on animality which presupposes—this is the irreducible and I believe dogmatic hypothesis of the thesis—that there is one thing, one domain, one homogeneous type of entity, which is called animality *in general* [or called *corpus*], for which any example would do the job."[9]

The embarrassment of catalogues, the maximalization of the trace, too often makes it seem that "any example will do the job," especially in the transaction of institutional readings that will not "let [them]selves be approached by the resistance which [*corpus*] may offer thought"—and the rhetorical conduct of the book does not attempt to teach us to do it, does not "call for and comprise [*comporte*], in its turn, a force of auto-effacement."[10]

That there is a *corpus* is the force of *hoc est enim corpus meum* as the arkhe and telos. Is *Corpus* able to cross it out? In my substitutive and mediated reading, "Hoquet"—the hack of the cough—the French echo of the Latin *hoc est*, caught between two namable languages, is a mention rather than a use of the *Durchstreichung*. And the substitutive gesture of "it is our *Om mani padne* [*sic*, the book's only typo]" (*Corpus*, p. 7) will not necessarily suffice. Any example will not necessarily suffice or too easily "suffice to operate the necessary transgression."

For why is "the jewel is in the lotus" substitutable (to mark a difference, of course) for "this is my body"? And are the People of the Book (the other two formulas are from Islam and Judaism) the only people? Do women share the last supper? This is where I had brought in polytheism, in the original echo.[11]

Here, I embed what I too have inserted in another place: . . . a letter arrived from Jean-Luc Nancy, in which he quite appropriately reminded me that "polytheism is a completely Western, Greek, word and there would be a lot to say about that."[12] There was also a reminder that *poly*theism was, therefore, too Cartesian. And an unacknowledged, precomprehended monotheist point of departure which might as well be an origin? To honor my friend's good critique, here is a first quotation from an exchange with a loving friend, now dead:

> Whatever the philosophers say, I think it is important that mono- as well as poly- would be mistranslations of *advaita* or *dvaita* that would take away the agility of the popular ethical mind-set that makes nothing of this undecidability. Mono is "un-two-ed," a strange way of saying One! Omni- (science or potence) does not fit into this too well. And the "two-ed," without a precise authority of a One to stand guard over it, can stand in for an indefinite swarm. Translation of *advaita* and *dvaita* as monism (non-dualism) and dualism has a lot to answer for. These intuitions cannot be reasonably *verified*, but they are a coherent way of repeatedly taking a distance from the inflexible principle of reason (*dharma* as code, *karma* as determinism) in the everyday performance of the sense that the type case of the ethical predicament is the dilemma. What reason plots as an asymptote is founded by an epistemic shuffle where god and man are indeterminately in each other's corner. It is also no less plausible as a description of something as tenuous as a "mind-set" than the structural orientalism of a *homo hierarchicus*.[13] As you have repeatedly pointed out, the "West" is not without its discomforts about the inconsistencies in the omniscient-omnipotent God. I have worked my way away from the question of om-

nipotence to Indic performative ethics by starting where you end. My subtext has of course been that the question of God is too monotheist. Over
against it is not polytheism but the *dvaita-advaita* habit of mind. Hence my
questions earlier: in these Sanskrit texts we are reading, is there an invari-
able word for God? Is it at least vestigially susceptible to a noncompetitive
one-person model?

Within this predictable and repeated staging, an unbelieving, middle-class, contemporary *dvaitin* might beg leave to invoke that other staging of an "origin." She
might crave for that invocation a singular space on the agenda because the March
of History that some of you recalled is not quite the March of her History. The
Second World War, much on the mind of our conference [a conference with Derrida
in New York], brought in for her kind, in a circuitous way, not all at once, not as
a cause leading to a consequence, a certain kind of freedom, which then demanded
an imagination of a world other than the old *European* monotheist world, which
in turn led to a near total loss of ethical authority, partly because the old *European*
monotheist time had miraculated into the new secular time of ethics. It is indeed
the resurgence of polytheist violence against the forcibly justified violence of the
state that places on her this responsibility: to ask, in an assembly such as this, if it
is possible to think of an unromanticized, contemporary, hegemonic, corrupt polytheism in the house of ethics.

I turn and return now to the original echo: I was brought up as a
middle-class "polytheist" child. Although I am irreligious and politically
absolutely against the Hindu communalist majority in India, I am of course
at ease in that other loose, average polytheist idiom, haunted as it is by the
possibility of communalism. Let's put it this way: there is an average polytheist everyday available to me without actively engaging the question of
belief.[14] Now if I want to twist and turn with it in order to see its relationship to the ungrounded body (*corpus?*), I have nothing to work it with but
the Semitized near-monotheist high-Hindu discourse of the nineteenth
century, developed under the auspices of a species of nationalism and the
discourse reactive to it.[15] It is almost as if colonialism staged the catalogon-
logos dividing embrace, the ontico-ontological differance, yet another way.
Theoretical access to contemporary polytheism and animism even as objects of a critical symptomatology by their practitioners suffers from this
imperialist *clinamen*. I am not talking about access to theory but *theoretical* access to the average for use as philosophical critique rather than mention as scholarly accumulation. This is no different in indigenous universities. And any Eurocentric *corpus*-talk is haunted by the Judeo-Christian
story, with its own *clinamen* toward a domesticated high-European polytheist past (the Greeks, the saints of Catholicism as the condition and effect
of the conversion of the barbarians) as the only story, the ontic caught in

the compromised space of the indigenous, the ontological in the equally compromised discourse of imperialist education.

The word "polytheism," with its uneasy burden of paleonymy, called forth a "response" from Jean-Luc Nancy. It played out its provocative responsibility upon an anonymous reader as well, so much so that I will recite it in my text, playing out my response between its lines:

"I think Spivak owes us something more in the way of showing what a polytheist everyday would feel like." "Showing an everyday"—"ontologizing the ontic"—is this not precisely the rock on which Jean-Luc Nancy and I are both hitting our skulls, with a difference? Is the removal of this rock—in a more magisterial discourse called the ontico-ontological *difference*—the discharging of a debt? To whom do I owe this debt and why? Is it because, having accepted an invitation to respond, and subsequently to publish, I owe it to the anonymous reader who will validate it for a certain public? Or do I owe it as the migrant who wants in—the Chinese-American cardiologist will make his appearance soon—a displaced native informant whose "anecdotes" the anthropologist will transcode for public consumption? Do I owe this debt because the old colonial subject gets hyphenated as the new and well-placed migrant? "I disagree with her about the difficulty of finding such alternatives [substitutes?]. (As she knows perfectly well, even within the Western tradition, one need only look at the polytheist function classical myth serves in medieval and Renaissance vernacular literature), though I do agree with her about the problem of staging alternatives on the same level, at the same conference, as Western philosophy." Is there no difference between the *function* of "classical mythology" *even* within the Western tradition as it is made "to serve" in historically distant European "period"s, and *contemporary* Hinduism—whatever it is—for a *contemporary* "Hindu" in a hyphenated situation? What are the subject-positions being conflated here? In the interest of what? Am I not asking Nancy to imagine here the anguish of being muscle-bound by "*knowing* perfectly well"? "A simple anecdote would suffice." For what? to consolidate the distinction between "high" and "low" discourse that the Reader "questions" at the beginning of the next paragraph of her Report? Is it not my contention that from "the polytheist everyday" we seem to be able to offer nothing but anecdotes? "A Chinese-American cardiologist's commenting . . . how folk notions of karma, as represented by childhood memories of his mother saying 'If you don't eat your peas, you'll come back as a chicken next time,' have affected his sense of causality in trying to recommend preventative measures for heart disease." I have no criticism of the doctor's heuristic device. My concern, however, is not to use childhood folkloric "cultural" material in the service of adult "scientific" rational or theoretical practices. Indeed, I have elsewhere attempted to indicate the problem with reading a conversational exchange between my mother and myself that began a decade ago and is continuing—not by way of folkloric material but the ethical discourse of the *Upanisads*—as "an echo from elsewhere."[16] It is on this level that the *dvaitin-advaitin* habit (the "polytheist everyday") intervenes. In these pages I am speaking, by contrast, of a determining and constant "everyday" that cannot emerge into theoretical discourse except betrayed by way of a Europeanized idiom, *even when speaking of polytheisms and everydays.* If I should say, in response to this bit of Reader's Report, আমাদের দে শা পাগল করে (with Kāli in it) or, in reaction to my fatal attraction for *Corpus*-style denegated phallocracy ঘরের বার করন বাঁশী আমারে (with Rādhā in it), the translation and transcoding footnote for those who do not share this compromised everyday would transform breakfast eggs into "unfertilized ova of domesticated poultry." At any rate, the doctrine of *karma*, a Hindu/Buddhist bit of "culture," is at one end a rationalization of the caste system (part of much theological debate over the centuries) and at the other a common noun meaning "work" on the near-colloquial level of most North Indian languages. The use of it by the doctor might belong as much to the second half of his hyphenated identity, Chinese-*American*, where "karma" is a sixties-hip jocular word for which an earlier generation of Americans might have substituted "kismet." The Reader is quite right in surmising that "Spivak's appeal runs the risk of sounding like nostalgia for something that just might not exist." That is exactly my fear, and I have no *theoretical* access to check it out as a variation of the level on which Nancy's *corpus* might not exist either. It does not seem nostalgia, but anguish, for it is a broken counterpoint of the "now" as differantiated memory-*event*, not some irretrievable past. And indeed, "[Spivak's appeal] . . . might not ['cannot' is my problem] be *significantly* different after all" (emphasis mine).

What makes the Reader think I am speaking in defense of "the Hindu case [being] different"? The fact, I think, that he has decided that I am "the [not even 'an'!] outraged cry of particularity." I am speaking of getting out of the dominant monotheist narratives in thinking *Corpus*. I am not talking of identity politics. On this level of trivialization, my feeling is that the forbidding prudence of a Derrida is less troubling than Nancy's "maximal tracing."

Benevolent reprimands and "belittling befriendings" such as the above have something like a relationship with, are indeed reinforced by, those "postcolonial" colleagues who take Dr. Johnson's way out, kick the stone hard and say, Gayatri Spivak may not have access to her polytheist everyday for investigation of its traffic with the body, but we do. This may well be true. But I beg such postcolonial colleagues to show me how, in the academic discourse that they and I process/profess, they manage not just to state the problem (or solution) in a scholarly or polemically inspirational way, but to perform it, not only as a staged cultural other, but as the dominant instrument of philosophizing, when the intellectuals in the ex-colonies that they have left are not capable or willing to do it institutionally. (There is magic in the air of the U.S. university; you can't dine out on being "postcolonial" in the ex-colonies.) Otherwise they are with me, however unwillingly, joined in a common struggle, asking Jean-Luc Nancy to see that his problem is shared by us with a difference, not only as teeming millions but as constituted "subjects" of knowledge.

I have spoken of "polytheism" rather than "animism"—whatever these labels might distinguish—because I do not have access to an "everyday" in "animism," did not pass through the performative ethics of parenting into the politics of the social mode there, am "irresponsible" in it.[17] On a totally public register (as distinguished from the everyday—by what differance?)—I have called for an "animist" liberation theology—celebrating the alterity of space—as opposed to the masculist humanism of individual-transcendence monotheist liberation theology. That is my "response to Jean-Luc Nancy" in the uncertain domain of "the public use of reason." The monotheist must trace space by the Book (*Corpus*, p. 73). "The sacredness of animist space can prove a liberation theology, but not if it is museumized (catalogued?) from above, only if we learn space as a name of absolute alterity, an alterity that is effaced as it is disclosed in the difference between Gross National Product and Gross Natural Product."[18] The difference of the specifically Hindu case is, as they say, "not my karrma." I hold no brief for communalist identity politics.

This is such a grave misunderstanding, with such widespread consequences, that I append below another example of my respect for other "everydays" where I have not been "responsible"—a circumstance to be rigorously distinguished from crying outragedly for my own in a travestied idiom. This example will also allow me to slip out of the Reader's Response into *Corpus*.

At a certain point in *Corpus*, as an example of how "*concentration* (initials: *KZ*) will have been the mark of the birth of *our* world: the concentration of the mind [*l'esprit*], the incandescent SELF—and the concentration of bodies, masses, gathering, presses," we pass into another interminable catalogue, where "any example will do the job." At the head of the next paragraph—"[i]t is thus that the [*our* in the previous paragraph] world is produced"—a place-name called "Bangladesh" (or rather, as I notice now, "Bengladesh," perhaps I am wrong in my typo-count) appears in another catalogue, in parentheses. The parenthesis runs as follows: "(a cyclone in Bangladesh, with its hundreds of thousands dead, tens of millions victims, is indissociable from demography, from the economy, from the relationships between North and South, etc.): or again, on another level . . ." (p. 69).

What Nancy writes in the parenthesis is correct and good, of course. The problem is that in a parenthesis, in a chain of alternative examples ("or again," and he goes on to talk about AIDS), concluding with the inevitable "etc.," it becomes no more than a pious litany for trivializing readers for whom a *Chinese*-American and a Resident Alien Indian become part of a "polytheist(!)" lump. This sort of gesture must be incessantly supplemented by attempts to break into the experience of the impossibility of the one-on-one ethical relationship, not where "they" produce "our" world, but where we try to enter theirs, responsibly, responding—where we "let ourselves be approached by the resistance ['Bangladesh'] offers to thought."[19]

"*Concentration* will have been the mark of the birth of our world," Nancy writes, in opening the paragraph that leads on to the name of Bangladesh in parenthesis. The German word *Konzentration* is included beside the French. Had he in mind the use of that word by our intermediary quoting Paul Celan quoting Walter Benjamin? If so, I commemorate that passage here as an example of minimal tracing, which will not suffice to bring about the necessary transgression—of the *de facto* invocation of a grounding uncaused cause—before I register my respect for Bangladesh, opening a question.

Rather than opening out something of comparable Judaic stature as the Christian *hoc est enim corpus meum*, Derrida becomes uncomfortably situational in the very opening line of his essay on Celan: "One time alone: circumcision takes place but once. Such, at least, is the appearance we receive. . . . We will have to circle around this appearance. Not so much in order to circumscribe or circumvent some *truth* of circumcision . . . [b]ut rather to let ourselves be approached by the resistance which 'once' may offer thought." It is along the lines of this modest program that he comes to Celan's recommendation of concentration as the best mode of reading. I cannot here retrace the steps in the text that have given these words layers of meaning that cannot be wrenched from a reading of Celan, whose parents were both shot by the SS, citing Benjamin, a self-deleted casualty of the Second World War: "Attention is the natural prayer of the soul."[20] Celan is addressing a German audience fifteen years after the war, accepting the Georg Büchner Prize, saying: "I am looking for [*suche*] the region from which come [*kommen*] Reinhold Lenz and Karl Emil Franzos whom I have met on my way here and in Büchner's work. I am also . . . searching for my own place of descent [*Herkunft*]."[21] It is within this frame of entwining the "self" and the murderous "other" that Celan offers "Concentration"— *Konzentration*—as the irreducible ingredient of the attention that is another name for the kind of reading that marks the limit of the public use of reason even as it requires it. It is to Derrida's comment that I draw attention here: "The word [concentration] can become a terrible word for memory. But one can understand it *at once* in that register in which one speaks of the gathering of the soul, or of the heart." Although I read this passage carefully rather recently, I believe it was the lesson of this transformative attention to the other that leaned over my encounter with the so-called victims of the cyclone. A lesson that unites the maximizing project with the paradoxical ethical power of the obstinate acknowledgment of the context: "Enlarge art [here philosophy]? No. On the contrary, take [philosophy] with you into your ownmost [*allereigenste*] narrowness. And set yourself free."[22] This narrowing, circling effort must focus even as *Corpus* expands. I cite myself in that supplementing spirit:

I was on the edge of the armpit of the Bay of Bengal, the waterlogged islands of Kutubdia and Maheshkhali and the town of Cox's Bazaar, the places hit by the cyclone and tidal wave of 29 April 1991. Every act of life there is a major effort. I did not think *of* these efforts and encounters while I was there except to reflect repeatedly and bitterly upon the contrast between the cheerful relief and rehabilitation efforts of grassroots workers, mostly women, in the area, and the hyperreal videographic image of the absolutely abject and dependent victim. These places are not outside of globality; in another context I could tell the story of the presence there of the U.S. task force and its tremendous *popular* critique as one episode in a serial narrative. When I returned to the capital city of Dhaka, Farhad Mazhar, a male activist, a pharmacist-poet who knows his Marx and Hegel, asked me: "What did you see?" I had not thought of this yet. But, since a question generates an answer, I scrambled to legitimize myself to this man of work. Beside me were sitting a woman, a high school graduate from a country town who is a teacher at a barefoot school (not a player in the culture of the coastal islands), and a woman law graduate, considerably more articulate but less of a worker, just beginning to worry about the problems of Bangladeshi rape law. I had seen, I said, that life and death are in the rhythm of water and land for these coastal peoples—I implore the U.S. reader not to confuse this with an identikit for all Bangladeshis—and not only for the very poor among them. They build in the expectation of obliteration, planned obsolescence at the other end. *Everyone*, including the health and relief workers from other parts of Bangladesh, sometimes no more than half a notch above the lowest of them in class, remarks on the fact that loss of land and kin seems to leave a noticeably impermanent mark on the inhabitants of this area. Yet they are not "fatalists," they grieve and want relief, to rebuild in the face of certain loss, yet again. This is an eco-logical sense of being-in-the-world. . . . In the understanding of history as sequence, knowing how to help [these victims] presumed knowing what should be wanted, easier within a more scientific vision of the formation of class, but not possible on this coastline. Here the cultural rather than the class subject was repeatedly being instituted, or instituting itself in an eco-logy, a logic of a greater household or *oikos*, where the subject of the logic is not necessarily "worlded" as human in the common individualist sense. For my interlocutor Mazhar, this was *proof* that, after the critique of consciousness as appropriation, Marx had not theorized property adequately, and that the *task* of alternative strategies of development that respected subaltern agencies of the institution of culture is to learn to rethink property. I had no such confidence; I was stalled at "what is it to learn" and offered a contradiction that I had also seen. If this was an eco-logic where the unlikely material subject was the pulse of the tide and the rhythm of the waterlogging of wind, I was in no way ready, daily encountering these very people's savvy discussion of the U.S. task force—that had taken its helicopters back home, that had dropped supplies already available and moving "in much larger quantities" in the slow-moving trawlers, that had created more trouble in their medical facilities because they could not communicate, that had been contemptuous of the locals, all comments heard from these very people—simply to narrativize them as an earlier pre-scientific stage where the proper help was to control nature so that these people could be redefined as passive and graduate to a more or less remote commitment to, *or* critique of, capitalism. What would it be to learn otherwise, here? Better offer the contradiction: they will not move as unwilling refugees. . . . Even in this liminal culture, by religious naming Muslim-Hindu and Buddhist, women have an ironic relationship to both eco-logic and the positing of land as its postponement. In exogamy, these women shift their loyalty from father's land to husband's, quite as our female colleagues do. In reproductive culture, these girls' knees scissor in at adolescence and slowly open wider and wider as the rhythm of childbearing *in* the rhythm of tide and wind is seen as the definitive predication of gendering.[23]

The activist, the lawyer, the teacher are also Bangladeshis of course, subjects of knowledge, undone and done and done in by *corpus*.

The Death of God has not been rehearsed, then, in my space of everyday. Can *we* say, "[w]ith the death of God, *we* have lost this glorious body, this sublime body: this real symbol of his sovereign majesty, this microcosm of his immense work, and finally this visibility of the invisible, this *mimesis* of the inimitable" (emphasis on "we" mine)?

Consider Derrida now on Augustine. In the long passage in *Glas* where Derrida comments on Hegel's critique of Kant, there is a beautifully staged intervention on the fetish, which situates the Hegelian opposition of fetish to Eucharist.[24] The history of the imposition of that creolized Portuguese word to construct Africa as object is now well known.[25] Yet that history "normally" belongs to another part of the academic subdivision of labor. It does not historicize the philosopher Hegel when European philosophers use the dialectic for philosophizing. The literary-philosophical "theoretical" type looks up Marx and Freud for fetish.

Of course one hears what one is ready to hear. When I hear Derrida calling Augustine "Italo-Maghrebin," reinventing Augustine as a North African who crosses the Mediterranean to Rome, I can ask: does he have the same sort of problem that we do? Is he performing an Augustine who cannot himself undo the metalepsis of the Eucharist as counterfetish but whose text might betray the secret? I cannot tell, but the text of Nancy that I seem to be able to read would gain if that pretext to the "spiritualizing of Christ's wounds" were remembered in the breach.

If in "Shibboleth" Derrida "traces" "himself," puts himself in the text of, the Jewish male among Jewish males, and leaves himself open for the "poetic" (or ethical or responsible/responding) reader, in "The Other Heading" he "traces" himself as a hyphenated European, as in his reading of Augustine.

At the end of the latter essay, there is a long catalogue of double duties confronting the "new Europe"—in whatever interest that proper name needs to give itself an outline today. Let us consider the sentence that introduces these duties: "Hence the *duty* to respond to the call of European memory, to recall what has been promised under the name of Europe, to reidentify Europe, this *duty* is without common measure with all that is generally understood by that name [*sous ce nom*], though it could be shown that a wholly other duty supposes it [*tout autre devoir le suppose*]."[26] In Derrida's prudent and (con)textualized practice, it is "the other duty"—whatever its textualized proper catalogue would be (the "traced" same, insufficient to bring about the necessary transgression, of slipping into assuming *corpus* as universal ground, for example)—that silently "supposes" (notice that it is not a presupposition, which would assume a continuity with the "duties" actually outlined) while (? at another time and place? in another mode?) the "same" proposes duties. Assuming a responsible, poetic, ethical reading, which in our general institutionality is far from given, notice the play of supposition and presupposition in Nancy's text: "the outlines of areality along which *we are exposed together, neither, that is, presupposed by some other Subject, nor postposed in some particular and/or universal end*" (*Corpus*, p. 80; emphases Nancy's). Whatever the definition of "areality"—"the property of surfaces (*area*). By chance, the word lends itself to a lack of reality, or a tenuous, light, suspended reality" (p. 39)—this originary exposure as bodies together can coexist with a "thought" thought the following way: "A thought *does not say* 'hoc est,' but a thought *is* 'hoc est,' position without presupposition, exposition" (p. 99; emphasis Nancy's). Derrida's careful ethics of the supposing other as limit to thought is needed here, for there are bodies and there are thoughts before selving and othering. But if we, Nancy and I, say bodies and thoughts, have we escaped that difference? Or will saying make it so? This goes back to my echo-response: "desire to philosophize."

It is no surprise, then, that at the other end of the spectrum, Marxism, that most honorable attempt to implement the public use of reason, a dream more maximal than Nancy's can hope to be, yet also and globally betrayed by the absence of the attention to the impossible experience of ethical singularity that must supplement politico-philosophical effort, has been somewhat symptomatically sentimentalized by *Corpus* to the level of body-talk, in a few remarks on capital and the class struggle (p. 96). Marx's effort was rather to rationalize class formation, so that capital could be fought with its own poison. "Class struggle" against "capital" can occur when reasonable class-consciousness organizes through its realization that it is rationalized labor power, rather than suffering bodies, that produces capital—"the wealth of nations." Workers are the "agents of production." The source and legitimation of value, the irreducible unit of calculation (rather than the body as ground), is carefully kept open in a space of difference: "A thing can be a use-value without being a value."[27] It is because this appeal to the public use of reason and this theoretical sophistication were not supplemented by the "traced" singularity of ethics—the *people* in the many (con)texts of the globe rather than the masses—as the experience of the impossible that it fails. The middle way—the maximal cataloguing of heaped bodies—would like to straddle the gap. It is a desire to philosophize impossibilities rather than set them to work.

Corpus is not much marked by sexual difference. I will therefore close with the sexed body, not yet with gendering, as in the "original" response. Elizabeth Grosz has written in *Sexual Subversions* of the two bodies in Luce Irigaray's feminist philosophy.[28] Derrida, if I understand him, has wondered if sexual difference is not pre-propriative. The skin, "removed from any mystery, offered as the infinitely folded and unfolded line of all the bodies that make up a world," as in Nancy's paper for the conference, folds differently over different bumps and holes in the two different sets of bodies.

Not only the desire to philosophize, the "obsessive desire to save in un-interrupted inscription . . . what happens—or *fails to happen*," but the gendered position of the philosopher seems to rush in when I read: "From (a)phall [*(a)phalle*] to (a)cephal, a body spread, equal, plural, zoned, shad-owed, touched" (*Corpus*, p. 35).[29] I understand what the agenda is here; this is before libido-talk, where bodies are all connected in a space of bod-ies. Yet, although "one [who?] will name it neither 'woman,' nor 'man,'" and although the phallus is not—yes we know—the penis, some sort of assignment of name is surely at work when the cephalus and the phallus are the only parts of the body that have to be annulled in order to invoke this spread body. Forty pages later we read, in connection with a mass that belongs neither to physics nor to phenomenality nor yet to Freud, "the par-adigm is no doubt the womb of the woman, mass which localizes so many ectopies" (p. 75). This benevolence about the womb, combined with the relegation of the phallus and the cephalus to a post-*corpus* space, is, at least, gender-marked.

I began by speaking of giving in to the familiar. However it is written in gendering, menstruation is a familiar site of the body as something like a writing without writer-agent and, since not all women are mothers, with the structural necessity of the impossibility of reading.

Arrived here, my helpful Reader reminds me that Jean-Luc Nancy had, after all, dealt with menstruation in "*Menstruum universale* (Literary Dis-solution)."[30]

This fine essay is in fact about *Witz*/wit/*esprit* and literary dissolution. In the epigraph is a quotation from the German romantic writer Novalis that uses the Latin phrase. The final footnote gives Nancy's own gloss on the phrase. Epigraph, then, and footnote. I quote the latter:

Which [the epigraph] means that *there is no menstruum universale*, that instead universality is what dissolution excludes. Beyond the analysis of *Witz*, we would be led to the analysis of the very *particular* character of *menstruum*. And in par-ticular to that of the singular *conception* which is at the origin of the word and the thing in alchemy: *menstrue* (masculine), the dissolvant, is named by analogy with *menstrue* (feminine) menstruation, supposedly endowed with the capacity to dis-solve. It is thus linked to the negative sign of fertility; but also as a sexual taboo, which corresponds moreover to this power of dissolution; but also to one of the major differences between the sexes—and, more precisely, to the difference whose masculine counterpart Fliess, at the time of his connection with Freud, found in the "menstrual" swelling of his nose. Well the *nose*, throughout the literature of grotesque *mélanges* (and particularly in some pages of Sterne and Jean Paul), brings us back to *Witz*: "The Romans knew that *Witz* possesses a prophetic faculty; they gave it the name of nose." (F. Schlegel) Cf. our *Rhinologia*, soon to be published.[31]

It seems churlish to "respond" to a text published fourteen years ago, to take it as a "substitute" for what was not mentioned in *Corpus*, especially since I think the Nancy of *Corpus* is different from the author of this article. Yet one of my strongest intuitions against Nancy's method in his current configuration is that, although the thought of Reason as a *white* mythology prompts us to say "[a] new determination of bodies of work has to precede or accompany the elaboration of these questions," the reader as other is institutional.[32] S/he reads in the old way, is not "responsible," and treats everything written in Nancy's name as "Nancy," a body of work. My Reader represents this reader. Therefore, to repeat, "trace" minimally, acknowledge (con)text, bar the way to "the required transgression" (the author as authority) as best you can, though it will not always suffice.

My apologies made, then, I proceed to show how the final footnote in "*Menstruum universale*" is not a substitute for the gap in *Corpus*.

Just as the essay proper is enclosed in epigraph and footnote, menstruation in the footnote is situated in *Witz*—leading from *Witz* in the second sentence and going back to it in the last. The "beyond" of the second sentence culminates in a *Glanz auf der Nase*, occluded in the proper name of a bit of one's own (collaborative, and therefore allowing a "we"—the others being Novalis, Fliess, Freud, Sterne, Jean-Paul, Schlegel, and Roman men) body of work. That alchemico/female menstruation is a particularity does not necessarily prove that "there is no *menstruum universale*," but that perhaps all (provisional) universals ("the required transgression") are at least bifurcated. (I spoke of it in the original response by way of Luce Irigaray and will do so again.) Indeed, the "*conception . . .* at the origin of the word" is itself bifurcated in sexual difference, between alchemy and the female body. "Conception" is bifurcated between thought and physical reproduction. Within this abyssal frame, menstruation is "conceived" in a gendered way, as the dissolution of "conception," and (therefore?) a "[hetero]sexual[sexist?] taboo." Thus the "menstrual swelling of the nose" is not a "male counterpart" but a catachresis forced into an "analogy" whose force of figuration lies in gender-dominant appropriation. When I write of "menstruation . . . as something *like a writing* (in the "original" response, included here), I am not claiming the female body as ground. I am simply not looking at it from the point of view of heterosexual reproduction, but in terms of its entwining with the Latin word for "measure," so that we speak of our bodies as marking "periods," "monthlies." There is a catachresis here too, for the sun's movement gives us the months, and though menstruation is not accurate with the periodic computation of months we measure the sun, or the moon, "monthly," in our "periods," the body figured in writing, the female body as lunatic heliotrope. *Phainesthai* "means" both "bringing to light" and "giving birth," after all.[33]

In all the multifarious catalogues of *Corpus* there is no mention of a queer body. Reading specifically Irigaray and Foucault, I have felt that, historically, the homosexual can undo our banishment of Eros from the ethical field. In the context-"tracing" of the bifurcated universal, then, here is Irigaray. What is needed here is not bio-logy as cata-logon, but the distance of ad-miration. Irigaray rereads Descartes on wonder: "Who or what the other is, I never know. But this unknowable other is that which differs sexually from me. This feeling of wonder, surprise and admiration [*admiration*] in the face of the unknowable ought to come back to its place: that of [*revenir à son lieu; celui de*] sexual difference."[34]

Nancy is too good a philosopher not to know this at all. "As long as there is *something* there is also something else, other bodies that the latter's limits expose to touch, between repulsion and dissolution" ("Corpus," forthcoming).

Between repulsion and dissolution. Is this a veiled invocation of another difference—between same sex and same gender? I cannot know. But if it is, and here I add an *il faut*—it should be—then I come back to my refrain. There is no escaping the merely post-posed social, to philosophize at the limit. The body is free in its bindings in the world, or no place at all. And "from ['free body'] to ['incarnated liberty'] a *world* is opened whose most proper possibility requires that 'body' and 'liberty' *are neither homogeneous nor heterogeneous to one another*" (p. 90).

Jean-Luc Nancy and
the Corpus of Philosophy

Gary Shapiro

*H*ow to touch, tactfully, the corpus of Jean-Luc Nancy? How can this corpus be shared and divided (*partagé*)? How can these words or thoughts be weighed? This text seems to set itself vigilantly and rigorously in opposition to the mystery of the incarnation and urges us to demystify the discourses of the body. The very translatability of the paper—to whatever degree translation is possible—and its presentation—in whatever way presence is possible—are modalities closely linked to the question of what body and corpus are and can be. The text "Corpus" is exscripted, to speak with Nancy, written out, that is, in a way that distances it from the breath and the tongue. It is already divided, shared. Here is my body, take it and eat, even in my absence, especially in my absence, in remembrance of me, it seems to say. Is there not a whiff of the incarnation here? But then as Jacques Derrida asks, in the text "Ellipsis"—on which Nancy writes elsewhere, or more precisely which he reinscribes— "how can the phantom of the center not call to us?"[1] How can we not ask what sense is to be given to translation in the new "corpuscular philosophy" (deforming the sense of a good seventeenth-century term), to the substitution of one set of sounds and gestures for another? If we can summon up the proper tact, will we then make (con)tact with this embodied and disembodied thought? Or is contact to be scrupulously avoided as it is omitted, along with consensus and consent from Nancy's set of entries, his anatomy, his "catalogue without a logos"?

I want to inquire concerning Nancy's relation to philosophy. That will require an interrogation of his relation to the *body* of philosophy, both in the sense that the body appears as an unavoidable philosopheme and in the sense that philosophy itself may be said to be or consist in a body (of texts, thoughts, questions, and so on). So it will be to question, as Nancy does, philosophy's specular or imaginary conception of itself, that self-conception in which philosophy views itself as having transcended or absorbed the body without remainder. Philosophy in its mirror phase gazes at the body or at its own spoken or written embodiments and sees something that is apparently integral and mastered by the soul, thought, or the logos. We will have to raise the question of how philosophy would have to be deformed and transformed if it thinks *corpus* and not body, if it is seen as having a *corpus* and not the docile body that it imagines.

If we knew only this one text of Nancy's, which whispers, cries, and insinuates in its incantatory rhythms that philosophy cannot tell us of the body, we might all too hastily conclude that he is an antiphilosophical thinker. Yet in fact he is always working at the edge—at the extremities, entries, apertures, disruptions, prostheses—of philosophy, at those places where its body (or corpus) consorts with nonphilosophy. Now surely it is the case that Nancy's corpus means to solicit or shake the body of philosophy and philosophy's body. In his extended corpus, that is, in all of his writings, as well as in the one we have just read, he is exploring and testing the limits of philosophy; these texts are oriented toward that corporeal edge of philosophy where empiricism is risked (in a deeper sense than allowed by self-described philosophies of experience) so that the risk of empiricism becomes the experience of risk.[2] This working at the edge can be recognized in the way that Nancy has been recently incorporated into the canon of anticanonical philosophy in a collection entitled *Transforming the Hermeneutic Context: Nietzsche to Nancy*. (Why Nietzsche? Nietzsche wrote of the bodies [not "*the* body"] that form the horizons and contexts of all meaning and interpreting; bodies for Nietzsche, *corpus* for Nancy, are what always must transform the hermeneutic contexts.) That collection ends with Nancy's "Le partage des voix," which argues that the "hermeneutic circle" all too facilely invoked these days is a logocentric reduction of the more radically plural and open *hermeneia* that forms the condition of all meaning.[3]

Corpus, then, is not just a concept (nor is it an anticoncept) but the body of work, the body that works, a *corpus* that works on philosophy by letting it appear as *corpus*, which is neither the body of tradition nor the tradition of the body. The corpus, in every sense, of Nancy's work aims at rethinking community not as an enclosed and finished circle of meanings in which there is always a mediated return to the origin, but as the sharing of words, senses, and voices and, as he now makes explicit, the sharing of corpus or the corporeal. In *The Inoperative Community* Nancy explores a spectrum of possible forms of sharing and dividing (*partager*). In love, he argues, we are captive to the contradiction between the desire to enlarge and complete the self by merging with or appropriating the other and the need to maintain desire itself, which requires a condition of separation and distance.[4] That impossible condition of desire is like philosophy's double wish to embody itself completely and to free itself from the body. Something similar happens with respect to the voice in Nancy's corpus—and note how these questions about the voice and love are also questions about the body; the voice that he explores is always one at the limits of articulation, rather than the voice that would make thought present without intrusion, the voice that sings, howls, complains, growls, or moans as in Nancy's dialogue "Vox Clamans in Deserto."[5] Here the voices of Rousseau, Kristeva, Derrida, Saussure, Hegel, and others (including assorted animals) constitute an exacerbated and irreducible polyphonic meditation on voicing. That text, like Nietzsche's *Zarathustra* (think of *Zarathustra* IV), should perhaps be described as the libretto for an opera, a staging of possibilities of the voice that are ex-centric and ec-static. These philosophical music-dramas remind us not of Wagner, who, when all is said and done, remained within the traditional melocentric confines of character and integral utterance, but of a work like Arnold Schönberg's *Moses und Aaron*. This opera must orchestrate the voice of God despite the prohibition on representing him, and does so by pluralizing that speech and song into many voices so that there is no one representation; and it must focus our interest on a stuttering hero, whose every choked utterance reinforces rather than obliterates the contingent and ectopic dimensions of speech and song. These are voices in which interruption and the bodily base of the voice have become operative principles.

This corresponds to Nancy's most extended exemplum in "Corpus" of how one should think the thought of the body by weighing one's words. Think of *penser* (or of our English "thinking" for that matter) as "a word not yet uttered, not yet escaped from a mouth, still in the larynx, on the tongue" (see "Corpus," reprinted in this volume). Language, even before it reaches what we call "audible expression," is secreted in the throat, the chest, the tongue. Words, as at the beginning of Aeschylus's *Agamemnon*, may resist utterance through a terrible inertia ("an ox stands huge upon my tongue," says the watchman on the roof of the palace). And it is fitting that the uncanniest voice in the Nietzschean opera belongs to the Ugliest Man, the man of exorbitant and excessive body, who killed God because he could not bear the gaze of the witness, that is, could not endure to be measured by the standard of the whole or complete body that, as Nancy tells us, is indeed a theological notion. As he suggests at the beginning of "Corpus," the death of God may mean the death of all bodies; it is not only God's body that is decomposing, as Nietzsche's madman says, but any body (or anybody?) that is conceived as centered and integral, the sort of thing in which God might be incarnate or that reflects the image of the Creator.[6]

The theological tendency in the philosophical conception of the body is confirmed by an analysis of Kant's discussion of the ideal body in the *Critique of Judgment* and of Hegel's account of the symbolic, classic, and romantic forms of the body in his *Aesthetics*. For Kant the ideal body is not of this or that race or stature; it is a norm that expresses the suitability of a bodily being of this type to carry out the purposes of reason. In other words it is the general possibility of the word (or reason) become flesh. In Hegel's philosophy of art this incarnation is no longer merely possible but actualizes itself. It does this first through a series of symbolic hints in bodies of mixed animal and human form (like the sphinx or Hindu deities), then takes on its most beautiful and restful expression in Greek sculpture, and finally goes beyond the limits of the visible in romantic art, in which the body is shown undergoing a total loss of meaning (as God dies and is crucified and humiliated) before spirit manages to emerge through and from the body, effecting its resurrection and *Aufhebung*.

It is thought-provoking, then, that at the wake of God staged by Nietzsche, the Ugliest Man alone affirms the thought of eternal recurrence (an uncanny thought, a thought at the limits that must explode all the philosophical appropriations of the body because it disallows and displaces any centering tendency), and he does so in a voice hardly distinguishable from noise, a voice that hardly vocalizes at all: "for something welled up from the ground, gurgling and rattling [*gurgelnd und röchelnd*] as water gurgles and rattles by night in clogged waterpipes."[7] Nancy undertakes another testing of the limits of philosophy and body in the essay "Wild Laughter in the Throat of Death," where he says that philosophy, despite all of its theories of wit, comedy, and irony, has never been able to subsume laughter, this corporeal convulsion, this unmasterable bodily transformation that exposes the limits of meaning (transforming the hermeneutic context).[8] This is the laughter invoked by Nietzsche and Bataille as the other side of nausea. Laughter is verbal entropy; it is one of the points at which we can no longer maintain the illusion that language is a self-contained structure of meanings, but are forced to acknowledge its corporeality, as bodies shake manically and uncontrollably.[9]

Is there a body then, or only a corpus? Is there a body now? In his essay

on Derrida's "Ellipsis" Nancy writes of the lost body (*corps perdu*) that is
the ellipsis, the absent center, of Derrida's writing. *The* body does not exist,
Nancy repeats. Has something happened to what once was the body,
something analogous to what has happened to the words "corps" and
"corpus," which once enjoyed a rich and multifaceted life in English but
which have now been reduced to the forms of "corpse" and military
"corps" (the last denoting the artificial and imposed uniformity of death
in life)?[10] In *corpus* there is an extra sound to trip over, a parasitic con-
sonant to give us pause, to interrupt the stream of vocalization (Michel
Serres says that the consonants have a parasitic function, intervening in the
spontaneous flow of the sound of vowels).[11] We are forced to weigh our
words differently.

Certainly Nancy wants to evoke a certain history of the complex relations and incestuous intercourse of philosophy and the body. What is the
deep structure of these gestures of inclusion and exclusion of the bodies
that philosophy is destined to incorporate or discorporate? What if philosophy and its discourse, Nancy asks in effect, were determined from the
beginning by this struggle with the bodily? I select for the time being just
part of one sentence from Nancy's sketch of this *agon*: "The body was born
in Plato's cave . . ." *Is* there a body before the correlative notion of the soul,
the immaterial, indissoluble animating principle? The body was born out
of the need to distinguish the soul from its other. It is coeval with philosophy, as Nancy suggests that love and philosophy are coeval. We might
speculate, as did Bruno Snell some years ago in *The Discovery of the Mind*,
that before philosophy, if such a form of speech is allowed, the psyche was
just another part of the anatomy or corpus, the breath that went down to
Hades when one's limbs were left behind, and that perhaps those prephi-
losophical Greeks, having no notion to contrast with that of the corpus,
had no concept of the body as integral, whole, and totalized. They had a
corpus and an anatomy but not a body. What Plato did in simultaneously
inventing body and soul was to introduce a set of categories that would
henceforth provide the matrix within which all valorizations and permutations of these thoughts would be played out. Rather than say with recent
fashion that philosophy has just begun to think the body (since Nietzsche
or since Merleau-Ponty), we should say that it has *necessarily* been thinking the body from the beginning. Let me now cite the entire sentence: "The
body was born in Plato's cave, or rather it was conceived and shaped in the
form of the cave: as a prison or tomb of the soul, and the body first was
thought *from the inside*, as buried darkness into which light only pene-

trates in the form of reflections, and reality only in the form of shadows." The cave or *hystera* of Plato is indeed a womb, a matrix in the fullest sense, as Luce Irigaray has reminded us, so the body is indeed "born" there.

Once these initial binary distinctions have been generated—the inside and the outside, the prison and the prisoner, the light and the dark, true meaning and its simulacra—the machinery of all philosophical discourse concerning the body is in place. Which is the signifier and which the signified? The machinery lumbers on, producing all possible variations on these themes and exhausting all the options for valorization and all the permutations of separation and fusion. At its limits this discourse performs its miracle of incarnation, death, and resurrection, demonstrating that the body is the necessary, if fortunate, fall of the soul so that the integrity of both is attained by a dying unto the body that wins it back again. The high and the low change places; the body becomes full of meaning rather than the obstacle to meaning.

The structure is embodied in Hegel's discussion of the crucifixion, to which Nancy constantly alludes, and in his famous saying "The wounds of the spirit heal without leaving a scar behind." Hegel plays with such a dizzying exchange of signs in a passage to which Nancy glancingly refers. After a critical review of physiognomy and phrenology, the two great reductive sciences of the body in his time and the forerunners of speculative neuroscience, Hegel says that a better example of the supposed identity of the high and the low can be found on the level of bodily activity and function rather than in static structure: "The infinite judgment, qua infinite, would be the fulfillment of life that comprehends itself; the consciousness of the infinite judgment that remains at the level of picture-thinking behaves as pissing."[12] In this all too facile philosophical joke, a *Witz* devoid of "wild laughter," all the signs are still in their proper places. Genuine speculation is represented by phallic generation, just as Plato in the *Symposium* had identified the longing for immortality by which men generate children with the dialectical ascent to the eternal and unchanging. Hegel doesn't discuss wounds here, and he would no doubt consider circumcision as one of those symbolic deformations of the body in which a culture is still desperately searching for its true meaning.

Even Merleau-Ponty, the philosopher of the body and of the flesh, simply inverts the structure of sign and meaning established by Plato, according to Nancy's matrix. The principles of Nancy's dissection or anatomy of philosophy here are very close to those deployed by Nietzsche, Heidegger, and Derrida in their diagnosis of the metaphysical malady. When Nietzsche describes the history of metaphysics as culminating in the claim that the apparent world (of nineteenth-century naturalism) is the only world, to be awarded all of the positive characteristics previously reserved for the world behind the scenes, he is preparing the way for Nancy's claim that the body of phenomenology is just the inverted form of the meaningful soul to which the body was once opposed.[13] Similarly, Heidegger wants to say that Nietzsche's thought of eternal recurrence is nothing but an inversion of Platonism, affixing the sign of eternity to the flux of the moment. And Derrida adds that the call and the voice in Heidegger retain the appeal to presence that Heidegger had sought to erase from his thought. In each case the point of the analysis is to show the complicity of the contrasted terms; to praise the wisdom of the body is still to speak of *the* body, as the valorization of the "apparent" world still moves within the limits of metaphysics because the apparent world has been constructed from the beginning in terms of its relations with the "real" world.

But beyond the reversal of signs something else occurs, something that Nietzsche (in *Twilight of the Idols*) names "Zarathustra's beginning," that Heidegger terms the thinking of Being, and that Derrida calls *différance*. Nancy will call this thing or *monstrum* that comes: *corpus*. It emerges out of a repetition that "carries with it an unlimited power of perversion and subversion."[14] Now Nancy follows Derrida's reading of Heidegger's story closely enough to be able to say (although he does not do so here) that these philosophies from Plato to Merleau-Ponty have their own textual and thinking bodies and that once the inevitability of the matrix described is no longer taken for granted they can speak and touch beyond the limits it establishes. So we can now rewrite Nancy's statement that philosophy is not the one to tell us of the body. Although he says "philosophy will not help us," this holds only of philosophy as the thought of the body, not of philosophy insofar as it becomes *corpus*. As one of the many voices asks in "Vox Clamans in Deserto," isn't a great voice always more than one voice?[15] The philosophers can now appear as bodies of thought, embodied thought, and not only as theories of bodies; but this is possible only because of a certain event whose consequences Nancy relentlessly traces without regard to sensitive noses and stomachs: namely the decomposition of God's body after his death. Nietzsche's madman says of this decaying body, "Do we not hear anything yet of the noise of the gravediggers who are burying God? Do we not smell anything yet of God's decomposition?—gods too decompose."[16]

It is this Nietzschean moment that Nancy also invokes in his *L'oubli de la philosophie*, which anatomizes the reactive will to meaning of that form of contemporary philosophy that seeks a return to meaning (*sens*) under the signs of liberty, communication, and the subject. In that polemic Nancy demonstrates that reactive philosophy is fueled by the impossible desire of appropriating a meaning that must yet always remain at a distance.[17] The critique is reminiscent of Hegel's depiction of Kantian ethics as a series of dissemblances or displacements (*Verstellungen*) in which the unity of freedom and nature and their eternal separation are two sides of the same desire. In "Corpus" we're told that "the body is the last signifier" after the death of God, and we're provided with an anatomy of the inversions, perversions, and diversions—from bodybuilding to genocide—by means of which we are rapidly exhausting the possibilities of this matrix of signification. The technologized, prosthetic, electronic body is simply an extension of this will to meaning. None of these variations hears the force of Nietzsche's question "Now that God is dead, who is speaking?" The alternatives posed by the will to meaning are all too simple: either a stand-in speaks—if not God, then the glorified body, the idealized subject, or the state—or nobody speaks. Either willful repetition, a repetition blind to its perversity, or the nihilism of the no-body. But the body might speak and think. Zarathustra says that the honest ego "speaks of the body and still wants the body, even when it poetizes and raves and flutters with broken wings."[18] (This orgasmic "fluttering with broken wings" belongs in Nancy's catalogue too. It is an active, frantic movement, one that can reach no goal outside itself, one in which all the bodily powers are ectopically evoked and focused. It is a joy, an expenditure that makes no sense, as Nancy says; it is simply transformation, or as Nietzsche orchestrates it, metamorphosis, or becoming-animal.)

Has philosophy always and only spoken of the body within the totalizing framework that Nancy delineates so well and that is so clearly at work in the canonical thinkers from Plato to Hegel? Let me suggest that philosophy exists as *corpus* and not only within the dialectic of the body, and that as *corpus* philosophy sometimes offers anatomies. As far back as Aristotle, "anatomy" is used to designate the laying out or articulation of a subject matter in thought or writing, but for Aristotle this is fundamentally a preliminary operation prior to the structuring of the logos. If the tradition itself is a *corpus* and not merely the narcissistic mirroring of the will to meaning of the speculative subject (a phrase that must now appear pleonastic), then we should be able to find resources there for the "new thresholds, new anatomies" (Hart Crane's words) that Nancy envisions.

One begins to encounter anatomies and catalogues of experience and excess in those interstices of the grand, official tradition that appears to Hegel as the self-development of the logos or to Heidegger as the tragic destiny of the metaphysics of presence in all its hubris. One key, like *corpus* and its derivatives, is linguistic and is to be found in "experience" in the experimental sense that it had before it was captured by official empiricism, a sense that is still partially retained in the Hegelian sense of *Er-fahrung*, wandering or journeying. (*Erfahrung* can be opposed to *Erlebnis* as *Körper* to *Leib* or as, in Nancy, *corpus* to "body.")

For example, between Scholasticism and Cartesianism the program of anatomizing, which as Nancy says has always been around, is actively pursued and thematized. After the decline of neo-Aristotelian accounts of human beings as ensouled matter and before the extravagant constructions of Cartesian medicine and the artificial body politic of the Hobbesian Leviathan—two bodies that may be taken as having instituted modernity—there are other ways of writing about the body or of allowing the body to write. Montaigne's *Essays*, or "experiments," test the limits of philosophy by juxtaposing its corpus and the narcissism of neo-Platonizing humanism with the body of "Experience," the body that suffers from the stone, sees the decline of its powers and the approach of death, worries about eating and defecation. Like Nancy's text, Montaigne's must be read as a motivated confrontation of the philosophical and the anatomical, and it is for these reasons that Nietzsche recurs to Montaigne's example, especially in *Ecce Homo*, where he relates that in order to become what one is (the body one is) one must not have the slightest idea who one is. For the same reasons Barthes adopts the models of Montaigne and Nietzsche (Montaigne mediated through Nietzsche) in his later *corpus*, praising the style of the aphorism as a form of writing that manifests its contingent, written, embodied nature rather than masking itself as discourse, encyclopedia, or system. In English there is of course the great work of Robert Burton, *The Anatomy of Melancholy*, which is an anatomy in a double sense. It is both a catalogue without a logos and an exploration of the body as the site of the "indefinitely ectopic" displacement of the melancholy passion itself. Melancholy, the superfluity of black bile, is seen at first as a disruption of the presumed totalizing and integral body of health; as the catalogue continues, it becomes clear that this passion is not one thing but many, infinitely productive of excesses of love, madness of every sort, rapture, nausea, dejection, ecstasy, jealousy, abjection. The radical empiricism of these pre- and non-Cartesian thinkers has been all too often forgotten or repressed, but they offer some paths that could be explored by a philosophy oriented to *corpus* rather than to the body. They provide *entrées* into the writing of the body. But one can go further, and Nancy does, when he explores the corporeality of the writing of Descartes, who cannot maintain the dualism that is all too easily attributed to him. "While I am writing," writes Descartes in his *Rules for the Direction of the Mind*, as he implicates an entire apparatus and instrumentality by which he realizes himself as the one whose thoughts are embodied by being written and being read. In "Dum Scribo" Nancy traces how far Descartes (who perhaps should not be called a Cartesian here) "mind and body take form together—in writing which is imprinted."[19] Descartes's word for body, of course, is *corpus*. Descartes can be reread and rewritten in his corporeality, as a thinker who fantasized his body as a pen and for whom the prosthetic language in which he describes his bodily activity is not a mere metaphor.[20] And Descartes is not alone. Philosophy is a corpus, which also means that it is a plurality of corpora, and what Nancy provokes us to do is to read that corpus anatomically.

I would like to recall the first sentence of "Corpus," "A *corpus* is not a discourse: however, what we need here is a corpus." The *corpus* is and must be needed in many senses, subject to the double bind that Nancy, just a bit later, says must overtake any project of presenting the unpresentable. There can be no *corpus* as such, itself, but the *corpus* can be catalogued, anatomized, and seismographed. As Heidegger spoke of the ontological difference of *das Sein* and *das seiende*, Being and beings, so Nancy has written of the difference between bodies as they become present in philosophy (for example) and *corpus* as what comes, what emerges, yet what cannot be fully here. When Nancy says that a body is needed "here," where is the "here"? Mustn't we read this "here" as a "here, now"? Nancy wants to say both that the need for a *corpus has arisen*, that it is an event, and also that the need can never be fulfilled, except in the modes of writing-out, of cataloguing, of anatomizing.

It is something uncannily close to and distant from this structure that he has himself sketched in the essay "Elliptical Sense," which repeats Derrida's "Ellipsis." There Nancy describes Derrida's thought as the passion for a lost or absent center, as the passion to "touch and tamper with the center." Derrida, he says, "endlessly inscribe[s] this presence of the lost body" and also speaks of "[t]he foreign body which is the body of our foreignness." And he denominates Derrida's writing as taking place *à corps perdu*—in reference not just to a lost body but also to a writing with abandon, a nonreflective (nonspecular) passion for the limits. Nancy would

seem to be alluding to one of Hegel's exemplary programmatic pronounce-
ments on the nature of philosophy here. In his early essay on Fichte and
Schelling, Hegel had written:

The essence of philosophy . . . is a bottomless abyss for personal idiosyncracy. In
order to reach philosophy it is necessary to throw oneself into it *à corps perdu*—
meaning by "body" here the sum of one's personal idiosyncracies. For reason, finding consciousness caught in peculiarities, only becomes philosophical speculation
by raising itself to itself, putting its trust only in itself and the absolute which at
that moment becomes its object.[21]

This hurling oneself *à corps perdu*, Nancy says, constitutes a "material" movement in philosophy, "the moving of a lost body presented on the
limits of language."[22] Philosophy has not merely "budged," or moved its
body, it has become *corpus*. We can now attempt to name the nature of
this movement and to suggest that the *corps perdu* and the emerging corpus are two foci of an ellipse: the disappearance of the body, the coming
of the *corpus*. This is not a hermeneutical circle, and it is not the integral
figure of a new program; it is a structure that doubles gaps and distances
while intensifying tact and touch. One might think here of that scene in
Jean-Luc Godard's *Hail Mary* where Joseph discovers that the proper tact
in touching Mary's miraculously pregnant belly is not to apply the hand,
not to stroke or caress, but to withdraw the hand in love. As Zarathustra
says, "it is the smallest cleft [*Kluft*] that is most difficult to bridge."[23]

How to Give Body to a Deadlock?

Slavoj Žižek

Symbolic Beatitude

*F*ritz Lang's *noir* western *Rancho Notorious* (1950) begins where a Hollywood story usually ends: with the passionate kiss of a couple awaiting their marriage. Immediately thereupon, brutal bandits rape and kill the bride, and the desperate bridegroom (played by Arthur Kennedy) commits himself to the inevitable, inexorable revenge. His only clue to the identity of the bandits is "Chuck-a-luck," a signifying fragment whose meaning is unknown to him. After a long search, he unearths its secret: "Chuck-a-luck" designates a mysterious place whose very name is dangerous to pronounce in public, a ranch in a hidden valley beyond a narrow mountain pass, where an aged saloon singer and ex–fatal beauty (Marlene Dietrich) reigns, offering refuge to robbers for a percentage of their booty.

Wherein consists the irresistible charm of this film? Undoubtedly in the fact that, amidst the usual western plot, it stages a different mythical narrative, the one articulated in its pure form in a series of adventure novels and films whose action is usually set in Africa (*King Solomon's Mines, She, Tarzan*). These works narrate the story of an expedition into the very heart of the dark continent, where white man had never set foot. The voyagers are lured into this risky trip by some incomprehensible or ambiguous signifying fragment—a message in a bottle, a scrap of burned paper, or the babbling of some madman hinting that beyond a certain frontier, wonderful and/or horrible things are taking place. On the way, the expedition confronts diverse dangers, among them combative aborigines who, while threatening, also strive desperately to make the foreigners understand that they should not trespass on a certain frontier (river, mountain pass, abyss), since beyond it lies a damned place from which nobody has yet returned. After a series of adventures, the expedition goes beyond this frontier and finds itself in the Other Place, in the space of pure fantasy—a mighty black kingdom (*King Solomon's Mines*), the realm of a beautiful and mysterious queen (*She*), the domain where man lives in full harmony with nature and speaks with animals (*Tarzan*). Another mythical landscape of this kind was, of course, Tibet: the Tibetan theocracy served as a model for the most famous image of the idyllic world of wisdom and balance, Shangri-la (in *The Lost Horizon*), which can be reached only through a narrow mountain passage; nobody is allowed to return from it, and the one person who does escape pays for his success by madness, so that nobody believes him when he prattles about the peaceful country ruled by wise monks.[1] The mysterious "Chuck-a-luck" from *Rancho Notorious* is the same forbidden place: it is by no means accidental that all the crucial confrontations in the film take place at the narrow mountain pass that marks the frontier separating everyday reality from the valley where "She" reigns—in other words, at the very place of *passage* between reality and the fantasy's "other place."[2]

What is crucial here is the strict formal homology between all these stories. In each case, the structure is that of a Möbius strip: if we progress far enough on the side of reality, we suddenly find ourselves on its reverse, in the domain of pure fantasy. Let us, however, pursue our line of associations: do we not encounter the same inversion in the development of a great number of artists, from Shakespeare to Mozart, where the gradual descent into despair all of a sudden, when it reaches its nadir, changes into a kind of heavenly bliss? After a series of tragedies that mark the lowest point of his despair (*Hamlet, King Lear*, etc.), the tone of Shakespeare's plays unexpectedly changes; we enter the realm of a fairy-tale harmony where life is governed by a benevolent Fate that brings all conflicts to a happy conclusion (*Winter's Tale, Cymbeline*, etc.). After *Don Giovanni*—the ultimate monument to the *impossibility* of the sexual relationship, to the antagonism of the relation between sexes—Mozart composed *The Magic Flute*, a hymn to the harmonious couple of Man and Woman (note the paradox of the criticism's *preceding* the panegyric!).[3]

The horrifying, lethal, and at the same time fascinating borderline that we approach when the reversal into bliss is imminent is what Lacan, apropos of Sophocles' *Antigone*, endeavors to indicate by means of the Greek word *ate*.[4] There is a fundamental ambiguity to this term. *Ate* simultaneously denotes a horrifying limit that cannot ever be reached—that is, the touch of which means death—and *the space beyond it*. The crucial point here is the primacy of the limit over the space: we do not have two spheres (that of reality and that of pure fantasy) that are divided by a certain limit; what we have is just reality and its limit, the abyss, the void around which it is structured. The fantasy-space is therefore strictly secondary, it "gives body," it materializes a certain limit, or, more precisely, it changes the *impossible* into the *prohibited*. The limit marks a certain fundamental impossibility (it cannot be transgressed: if we come too close to it, we die), while its Beyond is prohibited (whoever enters it is forbidden to return, etc.). Thereby we have already produced the formula of the mysterious reversal of horror into bliss: by means of the reversal, the *impossible limit* changes into the *forbidden place*. In other words, the logic of this reversal is that of the transmutation of Real into Symbolic: the impossible-real changes into an object of symbolic prohibition. The paradox (and perhaps the very function of the prohibition as such) consists, of course, in the fact that, as soon as the real-impossible is conceived as prohibited, it changes into something *possible*, that is, into something that may not be reached; not something that cannot be reached, barred by an external prohibition. Therein lies, after all, the logic of the most fundamental of all prohibitions, that of incest. Incest is inherently impossible (even if a man "really" sleeps with his mother, "this is not *that*," the incestuous object is by definition lacking), and its symbolic prohibition is nothing but an attempt to resolve this deadlock by a transmutation of impossibility into prohibition—*there is One* who is the prohibited object of incest (mother), and the prohibition of this object renders accessible all other objects.[5] The trespassing of the frontier in the above-mentioned series of adventure films follows the same logic: the forbidden space beyond *ate* is again constituted by the transmutation of impossibility into prohibition. On another level, the same paradoxical reversal characterizes "national revival" in the conditions of colonial repression: it is the colonial repression itself ("prohibition") that stirs up resistance and thus renders the "national revival" possible. The "spontaneous" idea that we are salvaging the remains of a previous tradition from the yoke of colonial repression corresponds precisely to what Hegel calls "the illusion of (external) reflection": What we overlook insofar as we are victims of this illusion is that Nation, national identity, *comes to be* through the experience of the threat to its existence; prior to this experience, it did not exist at all. This goes not only for the classical anticolonial struggle but also for the present national tensions in the former Soviet Union: although the nations experience themselves as a return to the precommunist tradition, it was the communist "repression" itself that, by means of prohibition, *opened up their space*, that is, posited them as *possible*.

Thus through the reversal of (impossible) limit into (prohibited) space, of *Don Giovanni* into *Magic Flute*, we elude the real *qua* impossible: once we enter the domain of fantasy, the trauma of inherent impossibility is replaced by a fairy beatitude. Mozart's *Magic Flute*, its image of the amorous couple forming a harmonious Whole, exemplifies perfectly the Lacanian thesis that fantasy is ultimately always the fantasy of a successful sexual relationship: after the couple Tamino and Pamina successfully undergoes the ordeal of Fire and Water—that is, surpasses the Limit—the two of them enter symbolic bliss. Reference to the anticolonial national revival enables us to locate more precisely the dreamlike character of this beatitude: the agents of the anticolonialist national-liberation struggle necessarily fall prey to the illusion that, by means of their struggle, they "realize the ancient dreams of their oppressed ancestors." Therein consists one of the fundamental mechanisms of ideological legitimization: we legitimize the existing order by presenting it as a realization of a dream—*not of our dream, but of the Other's, the Dead Ancestor's dream*, the dream of previous generations.

This was, for example, the reference that determined the warm regard of many Westerners for the Soviet Union in the 1920's and 1930's. In spite of the poverty and wrongs, numerous Western visitors were fascinated by this very drab Soviet reality. Why? Because it appeared to them a kind of palpable materialization of the dream of millions of past and present workers from all around the world. Any doubts about Soviet reality thus entailed instant culpability: "True, we in the Soviet Union make numerous mistakes, but when you criticize our efforts with ironic disdain, you are ridiculing and betraying the dream of millions who suffered and risked their lives for what we are realizing now!"[6] The situation here is not unlike that of Zhuang Zi, who dreamt of being a butterfly, and after his awakening posed a question to himself: How do I know that I am not *now* a butterfly dreaming of being Zhuang Zi?[7] In the same way, postrevolutionary ideology endeavors to make us understand that what we live now is a dream of our ancestors come true. The worker in the Soviet Union of the 1930's, for example, is a prerevolutionary fighter dreaming of being a worker in the socialist paradise; if we complain too much, we might disturb his dream. This detour through the dead Other is necessary for the ideological legitimization of the present to take effect. On another level, the fantasy of the harmonious couple from Mozart's *Magic Flute* follows the same logic: dreary, bourgeois, everyday reality undergoes a kind of transubstantiation and acquires a sublime dimension as soon as it is conceived as the actualization of a prerevolutionary dream of a free couple.

Wherein does the logic of this reversal consist? A further formal homology might set us on the right track: Do we not encounter the same matrix in Freud's most famous dream, that of Irma's injection?[8] Do not the three stages of this dream correspond to the imaginary dual-relationship, its "aggravation" into an unbearable antagonism that announces the encounter of the Real, and the final "appeasement" *via* the advent of the symbolic order? In the first phase of the dream, Freud is "playing with his patient";[9] his dialogue with Irma is "totally stuck within the imaginary conditions which limit it."[10] This dual, specular relationship culminates in a look into her open mouth:

> There's a horrendous discovery here, that of the flesh one never sees, the foundation of things, the other side of the head, of the face, the secretory glands *par excellence*, the flesh from which everything exudes, at the very heart of the mystery, the flesh in as much as it is suffering, is formless, in as much as its form in itself is something which provokes anxiety. Spectre of anxiety, identification of anxiety, the final revelation of *you are this—You are this, which is so far from you, this which is the ultimate formlessness.*[11]

Suddenly, this horror changes miraculously into "a sort of ataraxia," defined by Lacan precisely as "the coming into operation of the symbolic function,"[12] as exemplified by the production of the formula of trimethylamin. The subject floats freely in symbolic bliss—as soon as the dreamer (Freud) renounces his narcissistic perspective. Editor Jacques-Alain Miller was quite right to subtitle this chapter of Lacan's *Seminar II* simply "The Imaginary, the Real and the Symbolic."[13] The trap to be avoided here is of course to oppose this symbolic bliss to "hard reality": the fundamental thesis of Lacanian psychoanalysis is, on the contrary, that what we call "reality" constitutes itself against the background of such "bliss," that is, such an exclusion of some traumatic Real. This is precisely what Lacan has in mind when he says that fantasy is the ultimate support of reality: "reality" stabilizes itself when some fantasy-frame of a "symbolic bliss" forecloses the view into the abyss of the Real. What strikes the eye here is the parallel between the dream of Irma's injection and another famous Freudian dream, that of the dead son who appears to his father and addresses him with the reproach, "Father, can't you see that I'm burning?" In his interpretation of the dream of Irma's injection, Lacan draws our attention to the appropriate remark by Eric Erikson that after the look into Irma's throat, after this encounter with the Real, Freud *should have awakened—* like the dreamer of the dream of the burning son who awakens when he encounters this horrifying apparition. When confronted with the Real in all its unbearable horror, the dreamer awakens, that is, escapes into "reality." One has to draw a radical conclusion from this parallel between the two dreams: *what we call "reality" is constituted exactly upon the model of the asinine "symbolic bliss" that enables Freud to continue to sleep after the horrifying look into Irma's throat.* The anonymous dreamer who awakens into reality in order to avoid the traumatic Real of the burning son's reproach proceeds the same way as Freud, who, after the look into Irma's throat, "changes the register," that is, escapes into the fantasy that veils the Real.

The Triad and Its Discontents

At this point, one is tempted to extend the formal homology a step further: does not this reversal of horror into symbolic bliss procure also the matrix of the Hegelian "triad"? A homologous shift that changes impasse into "pass" occurs at the very beginning of the Hegelian system, namely in the passage of Being into Nothing. What does it mean, precisely, that Nothing is to be conceived as the "truth" of Being? Being is first posited as the subject (in the grammatical sense), and one endeavors to accord it some predicate, to determine it in any way possible. Yet every attempt at it fails; one cannot say anything determinate on Being; one cannot attribute to it any predicate; and Nothing *qua* the truth of Being is *a positivization, a "substantialization," of this impasse.* Such a positivization of an impossibility is at work in every Hegelian passage of a category into another that functions as its "truth." The Hegelian development is never simply a descent toward a more profound and concrete essence; the logic of the notional passage is by definition that of a reflective positivization of a failure, that is, of the impossibility of the passage itself. Let us take a moment X: all attempts to grasp its concealed essence, to determine it more concretely, end in failure, and the subsequent moment only positivizes this failure; in it, failure as such assumes positive existence. In short, one fails to determine the truth of X, and this failure *is* the truth of X. Herein lies the accent of Hegel's interpretation of the nonexistence of movement in Zeno's philosophy. Zeno strives to prove the existence of self-identical, immovable Being beyond the false appearance of Movement. Yet this Being is in itself empty, so the passage beyond the appearance of Movement fails; one can only describe the self-sublation of Movement, that is, the notional movement of self-suppression of Movement, which is why the Heraclitic movement is the truth of Eleatic Being.[14]

As a rule, one overlooks how closely the elementary Lacanian triad *need-demand-desire* follows the inner logic of the Hegelian "negation of negation." First, we have a mythical, quasi-natural starting point of an immediate *need*—the point that is always already *presupposed*, never given, "posited," experienced "as such." The subject needs "natural," "real" objects to satisfy his needs: if we are thirsty, we need water, and so forth. However, as soon as the need is articulated in the symbolic medium (and it always already *is* articulated in it), it starts to function as a *demand*: a call to the Other, originally to the Mother *qua* primordial figure of the Other. That is to say, the Other is originally experienced as he or she who can satisfy our need, who can give us the object of satisfaction or deprive us of it. This intermediary role of the Other subverts the entire economy of our relationship to the object. On the literal level, the demand aims at the object supposed to satisfy our need; its true aim, however, is the love of the Other in whose power it is to procure the object. If the Other complies with our demand and provides the object, this object is not simply something that satisfies our need but also, at the same time, the assertion, the testimony, of the Other's love for us. When, for example, a baby cries for milk, the true aim of its demand is that its mother should display her love for it by providing milk. The proof of this is that if the mother complies with the demand in a cold, indifferent way, the baby will remain unsatisfied; if, however, she bypasses the literal level of the demand and simply hugs the baby, the most likely result is the child's momentary complacency.

It is in no way accidental that, to denote this inversion, Lacan resorts to the Hegelian notion of *Aufhebung* (sublation): "the demand sublates [*aufhebt*] the particularity of everything that can be granted by transmuting it into a proof of love."[15] By means of the transformation of a need into a demand, that is, into a signifier addressed to the Other, the particular, material object of the need is "sublated": it is annulled in its immediacy and posited as something "mediated," as a medium through which a dimension transcendent to its immediate reality—the dimension of love— finds its expression. This reversal is strictly homologous to that described by Marx apropos of the commodity-form: as soon as a product of human labor assumes the form of a commodity, its immediate particularity (its "use-value," the effective, actual properties by means of which it satisfies certain human needs) starts to function as the form of appearance of its "exchange-value," that is, the form of a nonmaterial intersubjective relationship—just as in the passage from need to demand whereby the particular object of need starts to function as the form of appearance of the Other's love.

This, then, is the first moment, the moment of "negation," which necessarily culminates in a deadlock, in the unsolvable antagonistic relationship between need and demand: every time the subject gets the object he has demanded, he undergoes the experience of "This is not *that!*" Although the subject "got what he asked for," the demand is not fully satisfied since its true aim was the Other's love, not the object as such, in its immediate particularity. This vicious circle of need and demand finds its ultimate expression in the nursling's anorexia ("pathological" refusal of food): the baby's "message" is precisely that the true aim of its demand for food was not food itself but Mother's love. The only way open to it for pointing out this difference is the *refusal* of food, that is, the object of demand in its particular materiality.

This impasse, where a demand for the Other's love can only be articulated through the demand for an object of need (which, however, is never "that"), is resolved by means of the introduction of a *third* element that adds itself to need and demand: *desire.* According to Lacan's precise definition, "desire is neither the appetite for satisfaction, nor the demand for love, but the difference that results from the subtraction of the first from the second" (*Ecrits*, p. 287). Desire is what in demand is irreducible to need: if we subtract need from demand, we get desire. In a formulation typical of the anti-Hegelian attitude of his late teaching, Lacan speaks here of "a reversal that is not simply a negation of the negation" (ibid.)—that still *is*, in other words, a kind of "negation of the negation" but not a "simple" one (as if, with Hegel himself, the "negation of the negation" is ever "simple"!). This "reversal" is a "negation of the negation" insofar as it entails a *return to the object* annulled by the passage from need to demand: it produces a new object that replaces the lost/sublated object of need— *objet petit a*, the object-cause of desire. This paradoxical object "gives body" to the dimension because of which demand cannot be reduced to need: it is as if the surplus of the demand over its (literal) object—over what the demand immediately and literally demands—again embodies itself in an object. *Objet a* is a kind of "positivization," a filling out, of the void we encounter every time we are struck by the experience of "This is not *that!*" In it, the very inadequacy of every positive object assumes positive existence, that is, becomes an object.

The crucial moment here is the effect of "appeasement" that results from the reversal of demand into desire: the emergence of the object-cause of desire resolves the mortifying deadlock of the antagonistic tension between need and demand. This *solution of the antagonistic deadlock by means of symbolic "appeasement"* gives us also the elementary functioning of the ill-famed triad "thesis-antithesis-synthesis."[16] Its *imaginary* starting point is the complementary relationship of the opposed poles. Thereupon follows the outbreak of the *real* of their antagonism;[17] the illusion of their mutual completion evaporates; each pole passes immediately into its opposite. This extreme tension is finally resolved by means of *symbolization* when the relationship of the opposites is posited as differential, that is, when the two poles are again united, but this time against the background of their common lack.

The notion that "thesis" contains "antithesis" somewhere deep in its interior and that, consequently, one has somehow to "extract" the latter from its "implicit" state within "thesis" is wholly erroneous. The "antithesis" is, on the contrary, what the "thesis" *lacks* in order to "concretize" itself, that is, in order to actualize its notional content. In other words, the "thesis" is in itself *abstract*: it presupposes its "mediation" by the "antithesis," it can attain its ontological consistency only by means of its opposition to the "antithesis." This, however, in no way implies that "synthesis" denotes a mutual completion, a complementary relationship between the two opposed poles, that is to say, a conjunction of the type "no X without Y" (there is no man without woman, no love without hate, no harmony without chaos, etc.). What Hegel calls "the unity of the opposites" subverts precisely the false appearance of such a complementary relationship: the position of an extreme is not simply the negation of its other; Hegel's point is rather that *the first extreme is, in its very abstraction from the other, this other itself.* An extreme "passes over" into its other at the very moment when it radically opposes itself to this other. The "unity" of Being and Nothing, for example, does not consist in the fact that they presuppose each other, that there is no Being without Nothing and *vice versa*; rather, Being reveals itself as Nothing at the very moment when we endeavor to grasp it in its pureness, as radically opposed to Nothing. Or, to refer to a more "concrete" example from the domain of politics: the "unity" of universal and particular Will consists not in their co-dependence but in the dialectical reversal of the universal Will into its opposite. Insofar as the universal Will is opposed to the multitude of particular Wills, it turns into the utmost particular Will of those who pretend to embody it (since it *excludes* the wealth of particular Wills). In this way, we are caught in an "immediate exchange" between extremes or opposite poles: pure love turns into the supreme form of hate; pure Good into supreme Evil; radical anarchy coincides with the utmost terror; and so forth. By means of this immediate passage of an extreme into its opposite, we surpass the level of *external* negativity: each of the extremes is not only the negation of the other but *a negation that refers to itself*, its own negation. The impasse of this "immediate exchange" between thesis and antithesis is resolved by the advent of *synthesis*.

What defines the imaginary order is the appearance of a complementary relationship between thesis and antithesis, the illusion that they form a harmonious Whole, filling out each other's lack: what the thesis lacks is provided by the antithesis and vice versa (the idea that Man and Woman form a harmonious Whole, for example). This false appearance of a mutual completion is shattered by the immediate passage of an extreme into its opposite. How can an extreme fill out the lack of its other when it is itself, in its very opposition to its other, this other? It is only the synthesis that conveys "appeasement." In it, the imaginary opposition is *symbolized*, that is, transformed into a symbolic dyad. The flow of immediate exchange between the two extremes is suspended; they are again "posited" as distinct, but this time as "sublated," "internalized." In other words, they are posited as elements of a signifying network: if an extreme does not render to its other what this other lacks, what can it return to it if not *the lack itself*? What "holds together" the two extremes is therefore not the mutual filling out of their respective lacks but *the very lack they have in common*: the opposites of a signifying dyad "are one" against the background of some common lack that they return to each other. Therein consists as well the definition of a symbolic exchange: in it, the place of the "object of exchange" is occupied by a lack. That is, any "positive" object that circulates among the terms is nothing but the embodiment of a lack.

What is thus "internalized" by the advent of symbolization is ultimately lack itself. This is why "synthesis" does not affirm the identity of the extremes, their common ground, the space of their opposition, but affirms on the contrary *their difference as such*. What "links up" the elements of a signifying network is their very difference—within a differential order, the identity of each of the elements consists in the bundle of differential features that distinguish it from all other elements. "Synthesis" thus delivers difference from the "compulsion to identify": the contradiction is resolved when we acknowledge the "primacy of difference," that is, when we conceive identity as an effect of the tissue of differences. In other words, the immediate passage of an extreme into its opposite, this pure, utmost form of contradiction, is precisely an index of our submission to the "compulsion to identify": "Contradiction is nonidentity under the aspect of identity; the dialectical primacy of the principle of contradiction makes the thought of unity the measure of heterogeneity."[18] In this precise sense synthesis "sublates" contradiction—not by establishing a new unity encompassing both poles of a contradiction, but by retracting the very frame of identity and affirming difference as constitutive of identity. The idea that the concluding moment of a dialectical process ("synthesis") consists in the advent of an identity that encompasses difference, reducing it to its passing moment, is thus totally misleading. *It is only with "synthesis" that difference is acknowledged as such.*

The "rational kernel" of the Hegelian triad consists, therefore, in the process of symbolization of imaginary oppositions: the "aggravation" of imaginary opposition into the antagonistic relation where the two poles pass immediately one into another, and the resolution of this tension via internalization of the lack. The passage of "antithesis" into "synthesis" is the passage of external negativity (of the power that strives to negate the object from outside, in an immediate way, i.e., to destroy it in its physical reality) into the "absolute" (self-referring) negativity that "posits" the object anew, but *qua* symbolized, that is to say, against the background of a certain loss, of an incorporated, internalized negativity. This inversion of external into "absolute" negativity means that the object need no longer be negated, destroyed, annulled, since it is already its very "positive" presence, which functions as the form in which negativity assumes existence: the "symbolized" object is an object the very presence of which "gives body" to an absence; it is the "absence embodied."

Psychoanalysis and German Idealism

This symbolic bliss of floating in the space of fantasy entails, of course, a disavowal of the very fundamental feature of the Symbolic Order, namely, the fact that the "big Other" is "barred," hindered, structured around a lack, a barrier in its very heart. The Symbolic Order is by definition never "fully itself." It is an order rent by some central gap; its activity consists in an incessant effort to balance, to tame—in short to *symbolize*—some resisting traumatic kernel. "Symbolic bliss" is therefore a fantasy of the symbolic system's achieving full identity with itself and thus divesting itself of the excess in its very heart.[19] Yet far from being a kind of dreamlike cobweb that prevents us from "seeing reality as it effectively is," this fantasy is constitutive of what we call reality. The most common bodily "reality" is constituted via a detour through the cobweb of fantasy. In other words, the price we pay for access to "reality" is that something—the real of the trauma—must be "repressed." Here, one can elaborate the link that connects the psychoanalytic theory of drives and the philosophy of German idealism (Fichte, Schelling, Hegel), notably its notion of reality as something constituted, "posited" by the subject.

The dimension of psychoanalytic theory that is lost with the ascent of positivist *ego psychology* is its opposition to the common-sensical (and at

the same time scientific) approach, which accepts so-called "external reality" as such as something *given* in advance, and reduces the problem of the
"psychical apparatus" to the question of if and how this apparatus succeeds in accommodating itself to reality, in connecting, "coupling" with it.
In this perspective, the psyche is "normal" if it is an apparatus open to
reality, whereas the psyche is a "pathogen" if, instead of establishing
proper contact with reality, it builds its own "disjointed" universe. It was
of course the classical Marxist criticism of "conformist" psychoanalysis,
which opposed itself to such a notion of reality. The "reality" to which
conformist psychoanalysis refers as a norm of psychic "sanity" is not neutral reality as such but the historically specified form of *social* reality. By
offering as its ideal the subject "adjusted to reality," conformist psychoanalysis makes itself subservient to existing social reality, to its relations
of domination, devalorizing critical distance toward it as "pathological."

The scope of this criticism is, however, limited by the fact that it still
retains the notion of the harmonizing of psychic apparatus with reality,
although only as a "regulative idea" to be realized in the nonalienated society to come. A step further (or a step backward into a nonhistorical ab-
solutization of the split, if we look at it with the eyes of the above-
mentioned Marxist criticism) was already accomplished by Freud himself,
whose theoretical starting point was an original, irreducible, so to speak
constitutive *discord* between the logic of the psychic apparatus and the demands of reality: it is because of this discord that "discontent in civilization" is something that defines the *condition humaine* as such. "By its own
nature," the psychic apparatus is not adjusted to reality. Rather, it runs
after the "pleasure principle," which cares nothing for the limitations imposed by reality. Thereupon, self-preservation enforces upon the psychic
apparatus a renunciation of the absolute predominance of the "pleasure
principle" and its transformation into the "reality principle." The point not
to be missed here is that the reign of the "reality principle" is not something
that the psychic apparatus could arrive at by following the immanent,
spontaneous path of "maturation," but something imposed, extorted by
means of a series of traumatic cuts ("complexes," integrations of losses).
Our most "natural" openness to reality implies that the prohibitions that
exert pressure upon the inherent logic of the psychic apparatus have successfully broken it down and become our "second nature."

However, even such a notion of the irreducible discord between the
"spontaneous" striving of the psychic apparatus for the reign of the "pleasure principle" and the demands of reality still accepts "reality" as something simply given in advance, as a positive entity independent of the

psychic apparatus, which, *from without*, exerts its pressure and disturbs the balanced functioning of the psyche. True, with this notion we are far from any kind of preestablished harmony between the psychic apparatus and reality: the focal object of psychoanalytic theory is precisely the traumatic process by means of which the psychic apparatus is forced out of the closed circuit of the "pleasure principle" and into a connection with reality. Yet "reality" is still simply here, given in advance as that to which the psyche must adjust itself. By introducing the dimension of "beyond the pleasure principle," the later Freud accomplishes two further steps that—insofar as we think out all their consequences, as Lacan did—change completely the picture presented above. The hypothesis of a "death drive" concerns this point directly. Its implication is that the foreign body, the intruder that disturbs the harmonious circuit of the psychic apparatus run by the "pleasure principle," is not something external to it but strictly *inherent* in it: there is something in the very immanent functioning of the psyche, notwithstanding the pressure of "external reality," that resists full satisfaction. In other words, even if the psychic apparatus is entirely left to itself, it will not attain the balance for which the "pleasure principle" strives, but will continue to circulate around a traumatic intruder in its interior. The limit upon which the "pleasure principle" stumbles is internal to it.[20] The Lacanian matheme for this foreign body, for this "internal limit" is of course *objet petit a*. *Objet a* is the reef, the obstacle that interrupts the closed circuit of the "pleasure principle" and derails its balanced movement—or, to refer to Lacan's elementary scheme:

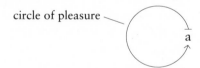

The final step to be taken is to grasp this inherent impediment in its *positive* dimension. True, the *objet a* prevents the circle of pleasure from closing, it introduces an irreducible displeasure, but the psychic apparatus finds a sort of perverse pleasure *in this displeasure itself*, in the never-ending, repeated circulation around the unattainable, always missed object. The Lacanian name for this "pleasure in pain" is of course enjoyment (*jouissance*), and the circular movement that finds satisfaction in failing again and again to attain the object, the movement whose true aim coincides therefore with its very path toward the goal, is the Freudian *drive*. The space of the drive is such a paradoxical curved space: the *objet a* is not a positive entity existing in space; it is ultimately nothing but a certain *curvature of the space itself*, which causes us to veer away precisely when we want to get directly at the object. It is for this reason that Lacan was so fascinated by the paradoxes of courtly love. The Lady is just such a paradoxical object, an object that curves the space of desire, that is, an object that offers us as the way to attain it only endless detours and ordeals. More precisely, the Lady is in herself nothing at all, a pure semblance that just materializes the curvature of the space of desire.[21] The resemblance of the depicted Lacanian scheme to the section of an eye is by no means accidental: *objet a* effectively functions as a rift in the closed circle of the psychic apparatus governed by the "pleasure principle," a rift that "derails" it and forces it to "cast a glance at the world," to take reality into account. This is how we should conceive Lacan's thesis that *objet a* serves as a support to reality: what we call "reality" is open to the subject via the rift in the closed circuit of the "pleasure principle," via the embarrassing intruder in its midst. The place of "reality" within the psychic economy is that of an "excess," a surplus that disturbs and blocks from within the autarchy of the self-contained balance of the psychic apparatus. "Reality" as the external necessity that forces the psychic apparatus to renounce the exclusive rule of the "pleasure principle" is correlative to this inner stumbling block.[22]

How should we then conceive the relationship between *objet a*, this strange body in the very heart of the psychic apparatus, and so-called "external reality"? The crucial point is that *objet a* functions as the inherent, internal "excess" that impedes *from within* the "smooth running" of the psychic apparatus, it is its immanent antagonism, whereas reality always, by definition, appears as an *external* limit. The Lacanian name for such an internal self-impediment is, of course, the *Real*. The radical conclusion to be drawn from it is that—contrary to the common-sensical external opposition of "pleasure principle" and "reality principle" (upheld also by the early Freud)—"reality" is not something given in advance but something the ontological status of which is in a way secondary, in other words, something *constituted*, in the precise sense this term acquired in German idealism. What we call "(external) reality" *constitutes* itself by means of a primordial act of "rejection": the subject "rejects," "externalizes" its immanent self-impediment, the vicious circle of the drive-antagonism, into the "external" opposition between the demands of its drives and those of the opposed reality. It is here that we find the return, within psychoanalysis, of the achievement of German idealism that was "repressed" in post-Hegelian thought, namely, the conception of the process of constitution *qua* the subject's *prehistory*, that is, what must have gone on *before* the subject could establish a relationship with "external reality." This is the process that, with Fichte, acquires the form of the I's absolute act of (self)positing (of itself as) the object, and that, with Schelling, appears as the antagonism of God's prehistory, which is resolved when God speaks out his Word.[23]

'Por causa mecánica':

The Coupling of Bodies and Machines and the Production and Reproduction of Whiteness in *Cecilia Valdés* and Nineteenth-Century Cuba

Benigno Sánchez-Eppler

*H*ow to turn slaves into citizens? How to proceed from the ideological attribution of social death in the captured and sold African body to the incorporation of the slave and his or her descendants into
the ranks of society?[1] How to shuffle—how to both mix in and thrust
aside—the black body of the slave with/in the body politic? These are just
a few ways of rephrasing the central questions of any slaveholding society
that starts to experience the crisis of its transformation from slavery to free
labor and the demand for a subsequent enfranchisement of bodies, previously regarded as things, into the capitalist order and the presumed correlative modern democratic republic.

I would like to recast those questions in a somewhat perverse yet instructive inquiry into the kinds of couplings fostered within a slaveholding
sugar-producing society.

Only as late as 1880 did the still colonial, still Spanish government of
Cuba agree to institute a process of abolition of slavery, a gradual process
that postponed final emancipation until 1886. The most summary account
of the development of Cuba's plantation economy starts with the curtail-
ment of Caribbean sugar production brought about by the Haitian Revolution of 1791. Before that moment Cuba's plantation economy could be
regarded as relatively insignificant, in terms of both its low importation of

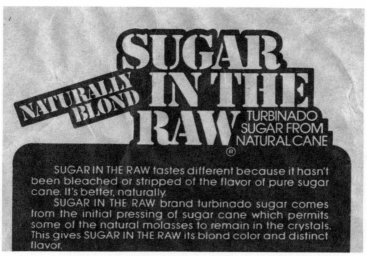

SUGAR IN THE RAW tastes different because it hasn't been bleached or stripped of the flavor of pure sugar cane. It's better, naturally.
SUGAR IN THE RAW brand turbinado sugar comes from the initial pressing of sugar cane which permits some of the natural molasses to remain in the crystals. This gives SUGAR IN THE RAW its blond color and distinct flavor.

Courtesy of the Cumberland Packing Corporation, Brooklyn, N.Y.

slaves and its low share of any of the plantation commodity markets of the day. With Haiti out of the market, Cuba's creole planter class argued for the liberalization of Spanish slave trade restrictions, and coupled the massive import of Africans with an unprecedented program of technical modernization and rationalization of most aspects of sugar production. Francisco Arango y Parreño, the leader of the Cuban planters' initiative, reduced the fear of Africanization of Cuba—and the impending doom of another Haitian denouement—with the assurance that the importation of slaves would be carefully monitored to ensure that whites would always remain in the majority. Thus the body count, the census watch, became an important component in Cuba's increasing racial-socioeconomic consciousness.[2] Throughout the 1830's and 1840's the best sugar mills operated with a mechanized manufacturing process. At these mills, the rhythms of the few machines overwhelmingly intensified the demands on slave labor. The industrial phase properly so-called came into place roughly after 1860, with the continued improvements gradually increasing production by eliminating—although never completely—the intervention of manual labor. The eighteenth century's animal-powered *trapiche* evolved into the mechanized *ingenio*, and the *ingenio* developed into the industrialized *central* of the final decades of the nineteenth century. Throughout all this the agricultural component of the production complex remained essentially what it had always been. While the developing industrial sector demanded the relative sophistication of free laborers, the cane fields could still use slaves. With regard to the census watch, the 1840's represent the height of the demographic crisis. The population figures during this decade show that the status of whites as a majority had been jeopardized by the volume of the government-condoned slave contraband—a traffic that mocked the developing Cuban resistance to the slave trade and the official Anglo-Hispanic agreements for banning it.[3]

This is the general backdrop against which Cuba's stated doctrine of *blanqueamiento*—whitening—takes shape. Cirilo Villaverde's *Cecilia Valdés* (1882) is a novelistic compendium that frames the issues of *blanqueamiento* through the incest story of Leonardo Gamboa and his lover, Cecilia, the pristine whitened *mulata*, who happens to be the illegitimate daughter of Leonardo's father.[4] Don Cándido Gamboa, the father, a Spanish-born slave trader and planter, has just acquired a steam engine to couple to their hitherto animal-powered sugar mill. To engage the voyeuristic critical engine that drives this analysis, let me say that I want to look precisely at this coupling of machine and black slaves, side by side with the succession of couplings of white men and women of color that the proponents of *blanqueamiento* hoped would lead to Cuba's whitening.

Arango y Parreño, among the most outspoken leaders of the initiative to liberalize the slave trade for Cuba back in the 1790's, provided one of the first arguments for the need to whiten the Cuban population as early as 1816:

I want to see [qualified people] discussing the timing and the plan that we must follow to whiten our negroes; that is, to identify in America the descendants of Africa with the descendants of Europe. I want, likewise, to start thinking with prudence about the destruction of slavery (to which end much has been done already), by discussing something that has not been contemplated, the erasure of its memory. Nature itself points to the easiest and most certain direction to follow. She shows that the color black yields to the white, and that it disappears if the mixtures of both races are repeated; and then we can also observe the decided inclination that the fruits of such mixtures have for white people.[5]

Arango y Parreño marshals a simple genetic argument. All that has to happen to maximize whiteness is to inhibit any woman's potential to engender children darker than herself. This kind of reasoning, together with everything else that made it repugnant in the eyes of a slave-holding society for black males to engage in sexual coupling with white women—or with any woman capable of birthing a whitened child—forms the basis for what could be seen as the ideological inhibition of the black male's capacity to reproduce. Even if individual black men were not, in fact, castrated, even

if slave marriage was practiced in some settings and ecclesiastically rec-
ommended in Cuba, nevertheless the doctrine of *blanqueamiento* depended primarily on the assertion of white male privilege[6] and the corresponding castration of blackness.

The neatly exponential decrease of blackness presumed both possible
and advisable by the ideologues of *blanqueamiento*, for the sake of erasing
the memory of slavery, for the sake of establishing a sufficient pigmenta-
tional distance from the racial marker of attributed social death, can be
best exemplified within *Cecilia Valdés* in this often quoted passage in
which the black slave María de Regla carefully charts Cecilia's pedigree for
the white Gamboa daughters and their guests:

"What I mean is that Magdalena, black like me, with a white man had seña Chepilla, brown; that seña Chepilla, with another white man, had seña Charito Alarcón, light brown; and that seña Charito had, with another white man, Cecilia
Valdés, white."[7]

In this smooth generational progression from "black like me" to the final
assignation of the highly privileged and tauntingly unqualified adjective
"white," one can detect María de Regla's own proclamation of her capacity
to participate in the program to whiten the species. It is also significant that
María de Regla, the ever-present domestic slave, controls and reveals all
the information about the succession of matings that produce the most em-
blematically whitened Cuban *mulata*.[8]

The guests of the Gamboa plantation, La Tinaja, listening to the slave's
narrative include Isabel Ilincheta, white heiress of a coffee plantation and
benevolent slave mistress within a socioeconomic order not yet so tainted
by mechanization. She has to experience the sugar plantation and its hor-
rors as a necessary preamble to her dynastically prescribed marriage with
young Gamboa. On her visit to La Tinaja, Isabel—embodying the whitest
and most feminine of sensibilities—and we through her, witness the couplings of black bodies with machinery in the *ingenio*. One such scene includes "an infernal din through which one could hear the crushing of the
bundles of cane that other half naked slaves shoved all at once and without
ceasing into the cylindric iron masses."[9] In another scene, the men talk
about runaway slaves and their recapture, while the priest wonders about
a possible correlation between the installation of faster machinery and the
rash of desertions and rebelliousness experienced throughout the plantations in the 1830's:

It is, nevertheless, a strange coincidence, that all of a sudden so many negroes have
run away and precisely from those plantations which have recently changed their

system of milling cane. Might it be that these stupid creatures figure that their work is increased because instead of milling with oxen or mules, the milling is done with the steam engine?[10]

And soon enough in the narrative we have to confront the injured body of the recaptured Pedro Briche. "If the young ladies had been asked about what they had seen at the sick bay," states the narrator in the subjunctive, they would have referred in heroic registers to an "African Hercules"; they would have dwelt on the details of physical confinement on the stocks, on the nature of the wounds; and then they would have framed the image of an "ebony Christ in the cross . . . worthy of compassion and respect."[11]

The captured runaway slave appears as a body coupled to the machinery of discipline, which would ostensibly induce in the punished a measure of consent to make possible the coupling of the alienated body with the machinery of production. The melodramatic abolitionist strategy of Villaverde turns the wounded and bound body of the slave into matter for iconographic representation. Furthermore, the elaboration of the black martyred body comes endowed with a substantial sexual charge, implicit in the grip of the feminine gaze on the nakedness of a body that is simultaneously monumental Hercules and shredded, divine Christ on the cross. Thus, the white feminine gaze, in its religious sentimental emplacement, exerts compassion, enjoys passion with passion.

With the injured black body uplifted in the young ladies' eyes, the description of the inaugural ritual to mark the coupling of the steam engine to the mill acquires an uncanny nuptial formality that points to the martyred and heroic shackled slave as the betrothed. It is Christmas day, and the following liturgical motions take place to the unwitting accompaniment of the explicitly African drumbeat from the slaves' quarters:

The curate from Quiebrahachas led the procession. . . . Two gentlemen walked by his side, each carrying a bundle of cane tied in blue and white silk ribbons with four young ladies holding the loose ends. Before the grinding mill the curate murmured a brief prayer in Latin, he sprinkled the cylinders with holy water using the silver aspergillus, the gentlemen placed the cane on the feeding rack and the first grinding with the steam engine began.[12]

Here we have another opportunity to recast the questions framed in this study: What kind of nuptials—productive and reproductive—are taking place in this moment of Cuban crisis? Looking ahead to the end of the novel, the narrative will lead to the wedding of Isabel and Leonardo, the celebration of the marriage between the coffee-producing and the sugar-producing sectors. This sacramentalization of the liaison of white interests is broken by the vengeful *mulato* justice of Cecilia and José Dolores who cannot marry as they each would like to be married. José Dolores Pimienta, brown, decent, tailor, musician, and frustrated suitor of Cecilia, kills Leonardo, Isabel's white groom, because Cecilia, frustrated in her desire to marry the white man, has insisted "that marriage must not take place!" (p. 299).

Back at the *ingenio*, the news of Pedro Briche's suicide is brought in immediately after the nuptial attention to the machinery is concluded. The news corroborates, in effect, the curate's previously posited connection between mechanization and the threat of slaves' rebelliousness. This violence by which the rebellious slave kills—self-destroys—the black groom of the machine is described by the plantation doctor in technical terms that, despite their evident physiological connotation, implicate the recently installed mechanical development in the death of the slave: "The common folk would say that he swallowed his tongue, but we refer to that as asphyxiation by mechanical cause."[13]

As the slave nurse María de Regla narrates the death of Pedro Briche in all its gruesome detail (p. 222), the drumbeat that filled the air acts as the ritual agency that unites the celebration of the machine and the suicide of the slave. It simultaneously opens up in the midst of the Cuban plantation an African interstice through which the suicidal slave enacts his passage away from the consequences of coupling his body with the machinery just installed under the auspices of white religion.[14] The postnuptial penetration of cane into the grinder is contested by the slavery-diffusing penetration of tongue down the suicidal throat.[15] Furthermore the African subversion of Christian iconography yields the following realignment of signification: on Christmas day 1830, one "ebony Christ" dies on his way to the negation of social death, reincorporated amidst evident manifestations of his African community, surrounded by the black drumbeat and by the black arms of María (de Regla).

In the plantation we are in the middle of the Nativity season, yet the iconographic deployment of the slave's black body—the most evident Christ marker, victimized in relation to mechanization—has explicitly evoked the crucifixion. The only thing resembling a Nativity narrative is a secret suppressed by María de Regla as she chronicles the already discussed genealogy of Cecilia Valdés: the nurse could have corroborated the exponential whitening proposed by the doctrine of *blanqueamiento* by mentioning one more generation, for Cecilia Valdés, white, had already conceived, with yet another white man, a nameless baby girl, presumably so dazzling white as to mock the Immaculate. María de Regla's two narra-

tives construct a preeminently Cuban iconic medallion, with the Passion of
the male black body back to back with the Nativity of the whitened female.

To what extent can the project of coupling black bodies with machines
for the production of whiter and whiter sugar be collapsed—beyond meta-
phorization—into the project of coupling white men with women of color
for the reproduction of a whiter and whiter society? To what extent is the
sugar mill a body sexual, and the *mulata* a machine? Metaphor usually
operates by establishing similarities out of difference, contiguities at a distance, but in the case of the Cuban discourse of couplings I have discussed,
the difference or distance can hardly be sustained.

From two other Caribbean representations of bodily fusion of miscegenation and economic activity I get the nod to engage—critically—in a
sexual and power fantasy that collapses these couplings. The Cuban es-
sayist and novelist Antonio Benítez Rojo, in his recent book-length study
of postmodernity in the Caribbean, in a section entitled "From Columbus's
Machine to the Sugar-Making Machine," frames a fabulously sexualized
macro-objectification of a body of water in the following terms:

Let's be realistic: The Atlantic is today the Atlantic (with all its seaports) because
at sometime in the past it was the product of the copulation of Europe—that in-
satiable bull—with the coasts of the Caribbean; the Atlantic is today the Atlantic—
the umbilicus of capitalism—because Europe, in its mercantilist laboratory, conceived the project of inseminating the Caribbean womb with African blood.[16]

In turn, the Puerto Rican poet Luis Pales Matos, in a poem written in 1934,
provides for us the corresponding micro-objectification:

> Culipandeando la Reina avanza
> y de su inmensa grupa resbalan
> meneos cachondos que el gongo cuaja
> en ríos de azúcar y de melaza.
> Prieto trapiche de sensual zafra,
> el caderamen, masa con masa,
> exprime ritmos, suda que sangra,
> y la molienda culmina en danza.[17]

The "Black Majesty" of the title advances with her ass swanking (*culipan-
deando*). Her rump (*grupa*) oozes with the movement, the oscillations,
pendulations (*meneos cachondos*) of an animal in heat. The drum (*gongo*)
coalesces, gels, these *meneos* in rivers of molasses and sugar. The products
of all this feminine bodily ostentation are the crystallized white sugar and
the viscous black by-product of sugar processing. The grammatical subject
of the last four lines is *caderamen*, not just "hips," which would be *cadera*,

but the whole bodily compendium elevated to the status of system, to the status of machinery for the satisfaction of desire. That *caderamen*, despite its evident rear-endedness, includes simultaneously hips, pelvis, buttocks, womb, sphincters, vulva, vagina, and so on. The *caderamen* then functions as the "dark grinding mill"—literally "mass against mass" (*masa con masa*), but in less ambiguous English both "cylinder against cylinder" and "flesh against flesh"—which squeezes out rhythms that culminate in a dance. The "Dance of the Millions," as the periods of exorbitant payoff in the sugar world market were called? Maybe, but in any case, a dance at the climax of a "suda que sangra," not just sweating a lot (*suda que suda*), nor just bleeding a lot (*sangra que sangra*), but more confusingly bloodsweating and sweatbleeding . . . a lot.

That's outrageous, and it should make us want to ask who is after all fantasizing the collapsed sexual and mechanical couplings, and why. Men like the Gamboas in their nineteenth-century Cuba were not just fantasizing. They actually satisfied their excess privilege and desire in the simultaneous exploitation of slave labor and women of color. Cirilo Villaverde, on the other hand, frames the fantasy of collapsing couplings to engage within the representational strategies of abolitionist discourse the monstrosity that these couplings entail. When a representation sexualizes a machine or system of production, when it mechanizes or systematizes the gratification produced by a sexual object, when it appears to engage in both operations simultaneously, such a representation installs our gaze at a very busy intersection, in the middle of a traffic that exemplifies the inseparability of the exercise of power and desire. With the "monstrous" bodily-mechanical composites in *Cecilia Valdés*, Villaverde makes available interconnected images of privilege and abuse that are inextricably racial, productive, and reproductive.

The network of couplings, the graphic composite of coupled Cuban bodies and machines, extends from the plantation and its big house, barracks, and sugar mill, to the city with its mansions, its *mulato* social and labor circles, and its docks for the importation of slaves and exportation of sugar. A multiplicity of genetic and economic relationships is referenced in the simultaneity of one panoramic mural of sexual/power fantasies. Thus the main exponent of nineteenth-century Cuban narrative realism reads like a mechanically sexualized and a sexually mechanized Bosch garden or Ernst continuum, a colony of intercoupled Haraway cyborgs. Let me close by suggesting that in dealing with either trenchant or residual racism, sexism, and classicism it may be useful to inquire into the nature of these monstrous composite fantasies. Not so much because they need to be censured, but rather because the clarity of the embeddedness of the sexual with the racial and the economic in these fantasies allows us to recognize our otherwise masked complicity with ostensibly distinct modes of oppression.

Finitude's Score

Avital Ronell

.01 Mixed Media

*I*f he said it once, he said it twice. Friedrich Nietzsche understood opera to be the genre *par excellence* of contamination. In fact, it was not until he was a DJ that N. started working on a reel-to-reel, scratching and popping, going with the disjunctive flow of sampling. That's when he began to like what he saw. In the meantime, trouble was opera's middle name. It would be lodged in the irony of the eternal return, showing signs of negativity and disease. As if it still owed us something—if only an account of itself—opera has an outstanding debt. For the record, Nietzsche once felt that the choice of opera indicates a kind of vampirism, a depletion of musical purity's essential resources. Music used to be pure and strong, an accomplice to will. Where the *Genealogy of Morals* conceived music as the "superior language," as the independent art as such, set apart from all other arts in that it does not offer up images of phenomenality as do the other arts but speaks rather the language of the will itself, directly out of the "abyss" as its most authentic, elemental, nonderivative revelation— and where the musician "became a kind of telephone from the beyond, a ventriloquist of God"—the *Genealogy* argues that opera, which places music at the service of a text, is bad music.[1] Of course this means that Nietzsche must have suppressed the inscription of music, its status as text, in favor of a kind of demagnetized hookup that we shall have to consider.

In itself, music remains intelligible to the servant of Dionysus, while opera merely offers a remedy against pessimism. Indeed, its side effects induce life-despising symptoms, for it marks the triumph of Socrates or Christ over Dionysus, of nihilism over life.[2] To the extent that it operates on the wrong side of the sound tracks, opera itself cannot, strictly speaking,

be understood in Nietzschean terms, that is, under the conditions of affirmative action. Its form as artwork is inscribed in what Nietzsche calls the
history of *ressentiment*.

This history unconsciously constitutes the discovery made by Catherine Clément in her provocative book on opera.[3] Opera somehow offers ressentimental utterances against its own feminine figurations. But the case is
possibly more difficult than Clément allows, and, as Nietzsche has shown,
resentment is not external or extraneous to opera, it cannot be regarded
as a mere theme or detachable syntagma of the operatic desire. *Ressentiment* is the very articulation of the suffering, separation, and death-
machine that opera puts in gear.

Clément casts opera as the repression of the feminine without, however,
reading the ideology of phantasms in which opera continues to be invested.
By repeating the separation of which opera stands accused (male *versus*
female, music *versus* text, in-house *versus* outdoors, etc.), and by trying to
get even with the tradition through a mere reversal of priorities, her book
is acting out the very symptoms of opera that Nietzsche had scrupulously
reviewed. Where opera offers up the drama of self-severance, Clément
presses a theoretical reinscription of the couple that comes to be asserted
in an unreflected mode. Rather than handling the constitutive falling apart
of the couple, Clément prefers to go steady and thus remains absorbed by
the ressentimental structures that opera is constantly trying to throw up.
The irreconcilable difference of the couple (Zarastro and the Queen, Wo-
tan and Brunhilde, Madame Butterfly and Mr. Pinkerton, Lucia and her
brother, Moses and Aaron), the lack ensuing upon its breakup, and the
fundamental untranslatability of its couples into sameness (music and language, music and drama)—this open wound of double or nothing—may
well constitute opera's most serious legacy. Opera is the gathering place
for a couple that relentlessly transmits its otherness to itself, teaching the
nonappropriability of one term to the other within an economy of internal
alterity or absolute difference.

Indeed, if opera exhibits itself as divided species (or even as the difference of species: Papageno, and the proliferating zoomorphic signifiers of
Fledermaus), this splitting is due in part to the property holdings of text
and music, libretto and score, composer and author. Clément, however,
typically reinscribes the unity of the couple responsible for producing the
petit a opera, reminding us to recognize *Don Giovanni* as the offspring of
Mozart and Da Ponte: "yes, [Da Ponte] wrote the text of *Don Giovanni*,
attributed eternally and to the end of time, to Mozart alone. Yes, the libretto of *Pelléas et Mélisande*, and Maeterlinck's words, so naked and so

sad, heard with such pure lucidity, are an essential part of the opera" (p. 18). This peculiar feminism that wants to establish proper paternity and legitimate authorship does nothing less than slide home into the precincts of the metaphysical male subject. Rehabilitating the rule of law and copyright, Clément exposes the true couple behind the couple, the classical paradigm for the transmission of knowledge: the one on one, which is to say, the man to man. Controlling and controlled, the seed may not spill over according to a logic of dissemination. It will never go to number two, in this case, to a director, or, for that matter, a woman. Despite the theoretical discord that her book ineluctably provokes, Clément will have helped us locate the couple as the trauma zone in the being of opera. In this regard, the book opens up opera's pained readability.

Opera will never get over itself as couple, a couple that practices sadomasochism and domination rituals, constantly readjusting the terms of bond and bondage between the text and the music that sets it up. Yet, to the extent that music is said to dominate the text, it potentially reduces all language to babel, containing the language within it as a fall from the prelinguistic purity of sound. It stages the birth of language as a fall, a kind of thrownness from the musical source. It would repeat the primordial shock in the splitting of sound into language and music. The question of accompaniment, or of priority of one over the other in the drama that severs language from music, bringing it together in the bastard form of opera, requires one to think the split and the transferential activity that opera engages. Unlike acts of translation—of one linguistic idiom into another, whose singular difficulties have been elaborated in the texts of Walter Benjamin, Paul de Man, and Jacques Derrida—opera has no original, but rather originarily happens as the work of translation without origin. Opera is not about the generation of one form out of another; it cannot assert an organic totality, a kind of transcendental unity of its disparate forms. This is not to say that opera did not dream such a totality of its parts or desire an origin. You cannot establish with certainty whether the music precedes the text or whether it goes the other way around: which is why opera opens the great politics of contamination.

.02 Babel on Tour

Die Zauberflöte (*The Magic Flute*) exemplarily thematizes the self-knowledge of opera as the contaminative genre. *La voix humaine* (*The Human Voice*) deconstructs a certain reading of contamination by affirming it. The human voice comes to be supplemented by a prosthesis (a flute, a telephone) just as God has to be prosthetically reconstructed after Babel. Opera offers up a song of Babelian language, celebrating the divine union that is known to be missed. God, the promise of a universal idiom, is both the origin and victim of a crime that seeks coupling. Ever since the beginning, the couple has been made to answer for the crime (Adam and Eve, Abraham and Isaac, Moses and Aaron). I would like to make these somewhat dogmatic assertions clear. Let us start with a sort of transfer that gives opera a peculiar status within the Babelian performance.

Opera is always lifting those words that enter its thematic body like a violent infectivity. As if to underscore the otherness of language to itself, its lingering proximity to a form of musicality, some composers seek their libretti in foreign tongues. This at once retains language in an aspect of alien otherness but also absorbs its semantic dimension to the musical code. Something of an altogether different order happened when Wagner refused the foreign tongue, preparing the stages of paranoiac opera within the dream of a totality of art forms, the *Gesamtkunstwerk*. The excess that we call "Wagner" seems to incorporate a totality that places its essential bets on the exclusion of otherness. A totality without contamination is the Wagnerian dream. But something had to be sacrificed to the dream of a transparency, something had to go the way of repression. Surprisingly, the orchestra itself became the excluded negativity—the scriptural space that converts the score into sound was driven underground. The site of technicity, where music and instrument coincide, slipped into darkness. Stuff the orchestra in a darkened pit, Wagner said, under the stage, suffocate it the way you drive out the index of otherness. Collapse one of opera's lungs. The otherness of the orchestra to the living operatic body is something Wagner made explicit for us.[4] He was not the only one, but he marked the trauma of the split off. Mozart arranged the flute as magical otherness; Poulenc installed the telephone to amplify the orchestra as difference. But to the extent that all opera participates in the dream of pure transferability, of a transfer that would secure its purity, it is perhaps not an accident that opera is also the phobic art form. *The Magic Flute*, like *Otello* or the Ring cycle, runs in part like an antipollution machine trying to clean up the toxic spill of Babel. Opera is occupied at once with the commensuality of its first couple—the parasitic couple, music and language— and with trying to wipe out an internal difference. This first couple will have committed a crime that opera knows but can no longer name. It concerns the guilt of language that cannot bear music or create a genuine synthesis. In this respect, opera offers us a sidelong glance at the Babelian couple incarnate. Each calls out to the lack in the other. In the demand that their encounter make sense, opera figures the irreducible difference in language and music. Language, for its part, is left a little emptied by the encounter, for it discovers that it can never hear itself unless music plays the other of itself.

This does not mean that music scores a victory over language. Music finds in language that it has been critically denied access to saying what it means. It is like Papageno, gagged. Not understanding what opera is about can therefore not be considered simply an accident that has befallen opera. Of course, we recognize the banal themes or familiar topoi. But this is beneath understanding, or rather secondary to the "aboutness" of opera. Not understanding opera is about the confusion that ensues from its disjunctive union, the impossible recuperation of the otherness that inhabits it. "Confusion" is another name for Babel.[5]

To be sure, opera wears other masks, and hardly cares for theorizing its predicament. For the sake of appearances it is expected that opera expose its unity, somehow arranging a bridal party for two absolutely heterogeneous values. It is to follow the prescription made out by that opera of suture, *The Marriage of Figaro*. Divided, ambivalent, the ceremony nonetheless promises an effect of the universal idiom that is music's dowry. The marriage of these values reminds us that the bond or obligation implied by their accord does not pass between a donor and a donee, a position of determinable strength and one of weakness, but rather between two texts. The ring that opera offers itself circles a circumscribed space of acknowledged difference that is then more or less effaced, depending on who is writing the inscription on the ring. But to the extent that opera constitutes itself within this double indebtedness of irreconcilable difference, it is also already establishing the grounds for a divorce court. It arranges the place where, within the continuum of a ceremony, the marriage will have turned to a failed institution, one that gives itself a hearing. How could opera not name this failure to couple?

This would be the broken record of opera. Forever and again, within the irony of the eternal return, the annulus does not close upon itself but keeps open a drama of nonrelations. In this sense, by formally and thematically posing the question of belonging and breaking out, opera comments on the aesthetics of closure.[6] The operatic embrace is open-ended, like the debt parceled out by the two values. The accounts are hardly closed but tell the story of a relation of affinity that stubbornly resists transferability. The broken contract between music and language does not imply that they are not in a desiring rapport to one another. On the contrary. The infatuation was so great that it had to come to this contract. They thought they had found something more originary in each other, a lost ground— the origin, for instance, of language in music. This, however, was before Babel. After Babel, they would need what Jacques Derrida has called a "translation contract"; they needed to promise "a kingdom to the reconciliation of languages. This promise, a properly symbolic event adjoining, coupling, marrying two languages," offers to link two parts of a greater whole.[7] The symbolic complementarity or harmony between music and language is perhaps more fragile and indebted to the divine than language's scramble for comprehensibility.

.03 The Marriage of Figaro, Divorcing the Queen

In a crucial sense, Mozart's *Zauberflöte* stages its resistance to translation. Mozart finally trips on the mother tongue. Of course this will be *his* mother tongue, if such a thing there be, for opera cannot be said to command a truly native language. It is after Babel. At any event, Mozart at last produces an opera that in a sense dramatizes the loss of an originary, mother tongue. She is pressed for time and will literally go under, get pulled down from the sky. A mother brought down to earth, tumbling like the Tower of Babel, offered to systems of pollution and mutilation. This explains perhaps why Mozart had to begin with the apotropaic flute, a kind of dagger-flute that will turn against its original, female bearer. Let us start with this Magic Flute. Why is the flute magic, why must it enchant? It offers itself as a well-traveled maternal phallus on the road to exile. It sonically traces the borders of a divided realm where divorce reigns and the lunar realm of the feminine splits off from the rising regime of enlightenment. An opera whose formal levels thematize contamination and divorce, it charts the triumph of a *ressentiment* implemented by the priestly culture of Zarastro—indeed, a distant and divorced cousin of Zarathustra. Somewhat enigmatically, Mozart names his opera after an instrument he did not particularly like. This has something to do with the logic of inoculation deployed by Mozart's dying piece. Mozart was very ill and, as his letters to Constanze show, he identified with the sense of *Tod und Verzweiflung* (death and despair) expressed by the Queen. Now, read in a Nietzschean light, the Queen of the Night can be seen to figure the embodiment of immediate and originary health. This health, which is to be understood at a level of symbolization and in terms of the valuation wars raging in the opera, is, for all its exemplariness, the most fragile of conditions. The magic wand or flute secures immunity, projects a safety zone within which the provisional owner is free of foreign agents.

As it detaches itself from the Queen, the flute points to the breakdown of originary health, which, in fact, is shown to be the most vulnerable, the most exposed and "immunodeficient." Originary health, difference, cold independence falls before the spectacle of the daughter's marriage in the precincts of reason, in the groundedness of the Enlightenment Father. Health has had to separate itself from itself in order to guarantee the victory of reason, that is, in Nietzsche's terms, of *ressentiment*. When it ceases to be the property of the original figure, the Magic Flute (health) becomes a mere *instrument* of increasingly failing strength. In another context I have tried to interpret the text of this opera in a way that would privilege a notion of impaired host defense within a movement marked by infectivity, parasitical inclusion, immunosuppression.[8] In a word, the *Magic Flute* would expose the drama of opera, an oeuvre knowingly caught up in syndromes of defenselessness and deficiency; but, in the first place, it presents the misinterpretation of a foreign substance or disease-causing agent that enters the operatic body itself. The Queen, Mozart's last antibody and guardian of the Magic Flute, will have had her forces steadily annulled. She gives away the gift of immunity to an exogenous invader who is headed straight for priesthood. He will become a monster of Enlightenment and rather more pernicious than the worm by which he is pursued at the outset. The discourse of reason eventually assimilates the invader into its culture. Mozart calls this invader Tamino. I prefer to call him Contamino.

The *Zauberflöte*, as title of the opera and immunocompetent object, is Mozart's gift to himself. If such a claim for Mozart's *Gift* can be made in the mood of a Babelian conjugation of the English and German, it is in part because Mozart disliked the very instrument that was to name the remedy, the milieu of sonic shelter for his work. Thus the flute itself, the object and the name of the object, had to undergo an immunological treatment of sorts. It had to be de-demonized, disinfected, cleansed—made *Sauber*—or enchanted, *Zauber*. In short, it had to *become* the inoculating instrument, the *Zauberflöte*, the very stylus of immunization. (The monstrous quality of this shaft is reflected in the opera's other coded monster, the figure of Monostatos, whose name means single-stemmed or single-legged.) Handed the phallic syringe, Contamino becomes what he is. He eventually proves injurious to the noble host, nurse and nourisher, causing infection more by his exploitation of host susceptibility than by his own powers of pathogenicity. This of course strips the plot to the bare bones of an immunopathological action.

.04 The Orchestra Pit

Just as the *Zauberflöte* was Mozart's last opera, *La voix humaine* was to be Francis Poulenc's final opera. Both works can be said to perform the anguish of being cut down or cut off. They both singularize an instrument, the one ostensibly coming from the inside of an orchestral pit (the flute), the other belonging to a presumed outside of orchestrality (the telephone). But is this so? Are we absolutely secure in thinking that the telephone is not an instrument? Where can we locate it? The telephone hooks up with the conductor's baton as s/he operates the orchestra. It is not only a transmitter of musical signals but also a receiver. Entire orchestras have been heard to buzz within the labyrinthine cup of the telephone receiver. In *The Castle*, Kafka alerts us to the *Gesang*, the children's chorus haunting the telephone. When they put you on hold, the telephone starts singing Muzak. In this way it is not only an instrument but an entire opera house that attends your ear. The telephone, then, cannot be asserted to exist in a simple relation of exteriority to music. It plays the position of an internal alterity. This brings us back to the trauma that Wagner introduced into music. When he wanted to incorporate the orchestra as exterior, when he rearranged the topography of production, Wagner himself turned the orchestra into a telephonic structure by driving it out of the range of visibility, making it remote to the scene—by changing the orchestra into a long-distance call.

As parasitical inclusion, the telephone engineers the noise that music suppresses, marking the disruption of musical closure or interiority. It is the locus *par excellence* where voice, language, and instrumentality share a common residence. The telephone marks the place where instrument and voice contaminate one another; it is the opera house of technology. Its click anticipates the curtain call.

In order to understand the politics of contamination practiced by Francis Poulenc when he installs the telephone in the interstices between voice and instrument, conjuring a condensed doubling of operatic logic—the phantom of the opera—it is necessary to rewind to the point where Nietzsche names the purity of a music that would not yet be pulled into the districts of opera's hysterical inmixation.

A direct hit from the abyss, on the side of the most authentic, elemental, nonderivative revelation, the place most resistant to images of phenomenality: music is said to emerge as the language of the will itself. No problem so far. What seems particularly noteworthy, however, is that Nietzsche installs the telephone at a precontaminated site, prior to music's infection by opera. Telephone cables are set up in diaphanous heights, putting through calls that outdistance the Kantian aesthetic of castration. Kant is out of line, Nietzsche has decided, because he doesn't cut it with the figure of the artist. This is why Kant's take on art is stained with an essentially effeminate aesthetics. The other aesthetic, over the boundary of a marked masculinity, skips the gender gap altogether to technologize or at least complicate the itinerary of the individual: the musician becomes a kind of telephone.

What this means essentially is that Nietzsche, anticipating Poulenc, scrambles the codes of what properly belongs to musicality. The telephone, while extending a cord outside classical notions of musical closure, is the connection itself between music and a kind of transcendental touch-tone of meaning: "a kind of telephone from the beyond, a ventriloquist of God." It is not clear whether God's requiem has yet been sung or if the telephone is all that is left, a delay call-forwarding system of the divine. Nonetheless, the emphasis is placed on the line to the beyond, the other end whose virtual presence is signaled by sheer instrumentality. As instrument, however, the musician, telephonically constellated, becomes the body through which an absent alterity—"God," the Other, the undead, you name It— speaks. Be that as it may, Nietzsche will have evoked the telephone as a transcendental Sprint to the beyond in the *Genealogy*. But already in the stages of foreplay that figure "the seduction of the ear," Nietzsche, in *The Birth of Tragedy*, starts wiring his texts telephonically. In the competition between phenomenal image and the sonic blaze, who would be so petty as to deny the possibility that Dionysus is a telephone? "The Dionysian musician is, without any images, himself pure primordial pain and its primordial re-echoing" (p. 50).

The intersection between the imageless musician and God's mediated mode of absence, their relation to opera, rarely passes the scanner without showing up Moses and Aaron, the telephonically structured couple. The ear of Moses is affixed to Aaron's transmitting mouth. There is something prompting the couple, a figure of thirdness, which is why Catherine Clément's gender gaping does not suffice to explain the genealogy of musical desire. Consider the difference between the way Nietzsche clears the abyss of gender and the way Clément spins her wheels in a peculiar heterosexist pit:

Often the men are the musicians or the musicologists. One of them plays a piano. The piano has almost a physical attraction for him; he caresses it, makes it glow like a woman brought to climax. He shines its black frame and golden insides, he manhandles it. He represents all those for whom the music comes first, as the invincible giantess, the supreme mistress, love in the absolute. And for him opera is perversion itself. . . . This perfect musician is a Don Juan who has invested the enveloping nature of music with the fantasy of an ever elusive, inviolate woman. Impenetrable; that is why he loves and protects her. (p. 13)

Clément is much more penetrating when she stops settling the sexist score. (Her sexism is no doubt inadvertent; still, why must so many forms of feminism be channeled through resentment? What would happen if one considered this: "Often the women are the musicians or the musicologists [Alicia de Larrocha, for instance, and Susan McClary, who introduced Clément's book]. One of them plays a piano. The piano has almost a physical attraction for her; she caresses it, makes it glow like a woman brought to climax . . ." Well, she would possibly have to rethink the rest of the libretto to liberate it.) When Clément leaps from one male fantasy to the other, she makes a surprise landing on the Golden Calf (p. 14), which, likened to opera, pits itself against Moses.

Now, Moses, the censor, essentially tries to supplant a televisual metaphysic with a telephonic logic; he wants to smash the image, even the phonetic image. He is in a restricted sense a servant of Dionysus, resisting the Apollonian mask. But more importantly, Moses is the partial headset of a speaking apparatus: receiving messages from the beyond, he requires another part, a transmitter. Aaron is the mouthpiece of the stutterer, Moses. Receiving and transmitting, the telephonic couple "by a perfect coincidence" happens to figure "one of the last operas in history (which) is called *Moses and Aaron*"; Clément names this a "borderline opera" (pp. 14–15). Destabilizing the image and thematizing voice, speech, and song, *Moses and Aaron* never reaches completion according to her; it collapses as the impossibility of opera, an allegory of its deconstitution. Unfortunately, Clément has shot her wad in fixing this opera as the last of a genre, but her unreflected opposition between singing and speaking and what constitutes the "best part" do not contribute to theorizing opera. Locating the culmination of a certain history of opera in *Moses and Aaron* may not be original with Clément, but it nonetheless serves to emphasize a break-off point in the conceptualization of the art form, which is to say, the moment when opera confronts itself as its own double in vertiginous specularity: the meeting of language and its other, their union contracted by God, their breakup and irreconcilable separation all played out within a reflective narcissism and absolute synchrony of two brothers. Opera will have resolved itself into a stereophonic couple organized according to transmitting and receiving ends, cut off by the static on a singular line to the beyond of opera.

.05 The Severed Silence

A few years prior to *The Undoing of Women*, Jean-François Lyotard devoted several pages in "Several Silences" to Schönberg's couple. In a somewhat psychedelic admixture, Schönberg is made to signal both the position of Luther and the return of Judaism as device. To the extent that serialism was his Reformed Church, Schönberg, asserts Lyotard, is the Luther of new music (Lyotard is the Luther of citation: "just as Deleuze and Guattari say that Freud was the Luther of the unconscious; just as Engels says that Adam Smith was the Luther of modern political economy within the confines of private property").[9] At the same time, *qua* Luther, Schönberg is truly Moses. This news seems to have been released by his press agent, Theodor Adorno: "Schoenberg, as Adorno rightly points out, wants to destroy appearances; Schoenberg's exodus is far from musical Egypt, from continuous Wagnerian modulation, from expressionism, from *musica ficta*, in the direction of the desert: voluntary impoverishment of means, the series, the two operations—inversion and retrogradation, the four positions" (*Driftworks*, p. 104). The desert mapped out by Lyotard is along the way to the signifier to be shared by composer and analyst. Yet the desert constitutes a new mode of immobility, folding back upon its concept by denying the straying or drifting movement that titles Lyotard's book (*Driftworks*). The sounds emitted by the desert violate its concept, suspending the auditory mirage and repressing the labyrinthine structure of the ear: "To extend the principle of dissonance universally is *to stop misleading the ear*: the principle of *Immobilization*, the same one that Cézanne's eye obeyed twenty-five years earlier in the Aix landscape and the one by means of which this Moses of new painting also wanted to stop misleading the eye" (p. 105). It is extremely difficult to follow the trajectory of an unseduced ear; perhaps there is little to follow since the ear will stay fixed to one locus, frozen in the desert by the rule of the immobile. In this desired predicament of immobility, where stray shots of sonority are said to be quieted, music splits off from history and the salutary epiphany: "Now one will stay in place," writes Lyotard; "there will be no resolution in the vanishing point, where the multiple gathers itself together, there will be no history, no salutary epiphany, there is a language without intention that requires not religion but faith" (p. 105). Schönberg has taken music via this new route, offering a critique of "music as an edifying recital," and turned it into "a *discourse*, produced by a language that is an arbitrary system, yet developed in all of its consequences (the language of Jehovah) and thus always experienced as unacceptable and tragic: something like the unconscious according to Lacan" (p. 105).

Now, in order to establish the essentially tragic, unacceptable dimension of music, Lyotard must paradoxically deny the split. No longer "edifying" as such, music gets swallowed up and neutralized (which is what, I suppose, its transformation into the effect of "a language that is an arbitrary system" points up)—something that is in turn reinforced by "the unconscious according to Lacan," which, we recall, is structured like language. Music has abandoned its locus of otherness in regard to language and joins a procession of absorptions into discourse. This is how Schönberg stops misleading the ear, in fact—by turning music out, exiling its crucial alterity. Although music no longer survives Babel, losing as it does in this passage its edification, it also continues to be assimilated to a certain metaphysical desire, what Lyotard calls "a new transcendence." No seduction, no castration: music is shown at once cutting into the edifice and fortifying itself in a new transcendence, in other words, in a new coupling with language. Where opera, including that of Schönberg, continually remixes Babel, always reintroducing the trauma of separating off from itself, Lyotard tends to want to remake the marriage ceremony. No running around, no being on the loose, cruising or straying, the ear sticks to a singular position of following truly. Assimilated to a language that, no longer requiring religion, withdraws the promise of a salutary epiphany, music secularizes and institutionalizes itself. This may in part explain the insistence on the Reformed Church in Lyotard's essay, the erection of an institution that created static on the simultaneous line to Moses, breaker of institution. Opera is lodged on this borderline tracing institution and its breakup.

To a certain extent, Lyotard wants to deny the loss that opera continually reinscribes by situating Schönberg within a movement of tragic intensity. From this point to his recent essay titled "Heidegger and 'the Jews,'" a difficulty articulates itself around "the jews" for Lyotard. This will have to be taken up elsewhere but cannot be left simply unmarked here. Why would opera be thought to smash itself on the rock of Judaism? (Freud, Adorno, Schönberg . . . but one should resist repeating the lineup mentality.) This is an explicit issue for Clément as well. Let us limit our discussion to the understanding of Judaism as device, as what introduces static and discontinuity, a certain rite of circumcision to which music submits.

.06 Schönberg and Freud

We are still driftworking. In a crucial way, Lyotard starts jamming on technology when he turns Judaism into a "device," which, underlying both
works, is also a figure of the unconscious. Citing Adorno on Schönberg,
Lyotard engages a Judaism that introduces a critical function in relation
to acritical society and ideology, "but probably not where Adorno expected it." Here's why:

> The desensitization of the material cannot be attributed to industrial society and
> its techniques of mechanical reproduction (which, as we know, can just as well
> produce the opposite, i.e., hypersensitization; just listen to the music of Kagel,
> Cage, Xenakis, Zappa, Hendrix). Neither can the Benjaminian concept of the de-
> struction of *aura*, which also belongs to the negative thinking of the lost *chef
> d'oeuvre*, of modern technology as alienation, be of any use to us here. (p. 132)

Desensitization arises rather from the field that Lyotard attributes to therapeutics, "which haunts Schoenberg's work as much as it does Freud's:
therapeutics through a reinforcement of discourse, discontinuity, ratio-
nality, law, silence-law, negativity, not at all in the spirit of positivism but
in that of tragic negativism, fate, the unconscious, dispossession" (p. 133).

Returning to Freud, in particular to *Moses and Monotheism*, "the ultimate text," Lyotard outlines precisely in what tragic negativism consists:

> . . . the mapping back of the cure apparatus, controlled transference, onto the pri-
> mary process: reconstituting a critical theater in the doctor's office (after dismissal
> of the supposedly precritical theater of the parental chambers and the visual phan-
> tasy); blocking out the vertiginous discovery of libidinal displaceability of primary
> work, nomadism. And this mapping back, this restoration, go unrecognized by
> Freud himself, *ignored* in their arbitrary nature, in their unjustifiable madness as
> device. (p. 118)

It is now becoming clear why Lyotard deploys Judaism as device, linking
the Freudian project to Schönberg's innovation ("technique"), what he describes as the predominance of the written, the law, "which destroys illusion: no apparent surface on which to inscribe a text, because no effect of
depth, no background. Instead of idols, the Torah, a discourse without a
third dimension" (p. 121). Schönberg and Freud form a war-machine couple that attacks the visual fantasy, the realm of idols and Apollonian drawing power. Resisting illusion, deterring representation as ideology and fantasy, they align themselves with the signifier. "No longer is there a resolution into surface chords, no more appearance, but there is a reserve in
the silence of composition; like the analyst, the composer is on the side of

the signifier" (p. 123). In order to marry music off to psychoanalysis, Lyotard has slipped unobtrusively from "music" to "composition." I have
nothing against this collapse except that it is the price to be paid for denying and foreclosing the split between music and its other. Each term in
the cited statement deserves careful scrutiny, including, of course, Lyotard's decision to couple analyst and composer in an economy that suspends the place of the musician. Lyotard neutralizes both music and language in order to squeeze them into the signifier. But why has psychoanalysis been called to the rescue—what about this marriage couch?

Psychoanalysis is credited with having severed the couple audio/visual,
and this is where, according to Lyotard, it has been espoused by Schönberg.
Lyotard anchors the Freudo-Schönbergian project within a kind of transmission system that canalizes the auditory libido. It is perhaps not entirely
beside the point that the "last opera in history," *Moses and Aaron*, dis-
connects the whole operatic machine and lies there like a dead telephone
surviving its memory of performance in silence, or even, to keep with Lyotard, in "several silences."

One of Lyotard's express purposes is to liberate music from a form of
constraint that he understands in terms of tragic negativism. The music of
anarchy hits the pages as he allows his text to theorize with a hammer ("No
need for us to cry over that, we do not want more order, a music that is
more tonal, more unified, or more rich and elegant. We want less order,
more circulation by chance, by free wandering: the abolition of the law of
value, which constitutes the body of *kapital* as a surface to puncture, as
appearance," p. 109). Still, it seems to me that Lyotard gets sucked in by
the very apparatus of restoration that he sees Freud ignoring. Freud has
failed, he argues, to recognize the mapping back of the cure apparatus onto
the primary process. Having more or less dismissed the "precritical" theater of the parental scene, which Lyotard seems to want to restore through
a certain value of primordiality, Freud has reconstituted a critical theater,
primarily an aural space of representation, in the doctor's office. This aural
space—which Freud explicitly structures according to a strict telephonic
logic—is felt to displace the visual fantasy. The relation, therefore, that
Freud promotes hooks up the analyst to the analysand, the receiver to the
transmitter (in a multipath mode and not a simple recapitulation of the
sender-receiver polarity), and the transmitter to a thinking of technology
that supersedes, I would think, the orchestra pit of a parental chamber. The
penis that the child saw disappear into the mother returns by other channels of transmission to the ear. But Lyotard seems to want to accord the

"supposedly precritical theater of the parental chambers and the visual phantasy" (p. 124) a higher status than it apparently enjoys in the switch from the visual to the audio, from the parental to the psychoanalytic precincts of attendance.

It is perhaps not an accident that Lyotard wishes to keep this fusion-bound (parental) couple intact where the analyst-analysand couple might be said to inhabit the scene of a nonrelation—or to stay with the metaphorology of Freud, the scene of disconnection. There is nothing more nomadically invested than the switchboard that Freud sets up at the base of his critical theater. This switchboard takes all sorts of calls, transfers others, and keeps still others on hold. It welcomes the arbitrary, linguistic pollutants and the free association that gave the access code to the talking cure. This is not to bill Freud as the one who relinquished the controls. But he routed the human subject through certain technological filters that complicate an understanding of simple repression.

Lyotard's own restorative mood discloses itself in this essay when he attaches music and language to sameness and the signifier, absorbing music into discourse. The denial of the divorce court to which opera is summoned itself belongs to the registers of remapping and reconstitution. His motivation remains fully intelligible, however, and ought to be commented on.

The figure invisibly operating the essay was Adorno—he put Lyotard through to Schönberg. Or, if you prefer, it was to his radiophonic commentary that Lyotard was tuned when setting up the match of dissonance. Lyotard has approached the negative theology of Adorno in order to pluralize its silence; hence the pointed silence of his essay: several silences. To accomplish his goal without a penalty, Lyotard has had to turn the transcendence of silence into music and language so that the object of music could become discourse. But the kind of pantheistic silence he establishes functions (here I shift channels and games) like a sacrifice bunt, which is to say that this movement of silence is bought at the price of reducing the silences of music. In this thinking, Judaism would perhaps install a bar between noise and the phenomenological reduction of sound to sense.

.07 Interruption

In the interruption something makes itself heard, namely, what remains after the interruption has taken place. . . . . When a voice, or music, is suddenly interrupted, one hears just at that instant something else, a mixture or a betwixt of various silences and noises that had been covered over by the sound, but in this something else one hears again the voice or the music which have become in a way the voice or the music of their own interruption: a kind of echo, but one that does not repeat that of which it would be the reverberation.[10]

.08 Answering Machine

Returning to Nietzsche's insight, where the figure of the telephone and that of the musician form a singular couple: offering a new package deal of the invisible, both are seen to be inhabited by a rhetoric of the departed. The telephone, while not reducible to any level of brute instrumentality, is nonetheless instrumental in linking up with absence; it thereby marks a gap that tenuously joins what it separates. The telephone catches stray shots coming from any being of low visibility. It takes calls from street corners and bedrooms (something the Puritans tried to fight), from unidentified callers and from the voice within. The telephone comes at you to caress you, or it can be used like a weapon, an arm without traces, a gun pointed to your head. You can use its strangulating radius to measure your oedipal leash ("call home"), or, like Joyce, retap its umbilicus into your navel. There are perhaps other uses for the telephone.

Francis Poulenc always had a fascination with street noises. He developed a peculiar appreciation for Maurice Chevalier. His first choral piece rooted itself in the gutter of *Gerede*; it was a drinking song. Composed under the guidance of Charles Koechlin, *Chanson à boire* (1922) was written for the Harvard glee club. His anti-Wagnerian musideology, his marked "antisnobbism," canonic defiance, and predilection for the atmosphere of the popular café earned Poulenc the title of "guttersnipe." A telepath receptor of hard noise, he was into random transmissions, cruising the streets. At the intersection between Debussy, Mozart, and Stravinsky, he started revving his engine, getting ready to pick up the frequencies of sheer exteriority. He was a member of a gang, so to speak, called Les Six, whose leaders ("guiding spirits") were Jean Cocteau and Erik Satie. They had a code or aesthetic politics that obliged him to let go of Debussy, which he did between 1917 and 1922. Later he regretted this. As I said, he was hitting the streets; he did not attend any of the established music schools—the Conservatoire, the École Normale, the École Niedermeyer, or the Schola Cantorum. He hit the streets, but don't get me wrong: he was melancholic, anguished, and rich. Cocteau had had his eye on Poulenc. He liked him and Auric best of Les Nouveaux Jeunes, as they were also called, because they were the youngest, the most brash, and the most Parisian of the six.[11] Les Six, it was said, brought music down to earth. But there were limits to Poulenc's tolerance. There were certain things he wouldn't put up with, such as, for example, something that Satie and Darius Milhaud had thrown together, some live background music they called *musique d'ameublement* (furniture music), intended to be ignored by the chatting, strolling audience. The show was set for March 8, 1920, and Poulenc would have no part of it. But he did go for *Les Mariés de la Tour Eiffel*, which Cocteau and Les Six put together. It was narrated by two talking phonographs.

The technological support wasn't bad, considering that Poulenc eventually was to get backing from the Princess Edmond de Polignac, née Winaretta Singer, of Singer Sewing Machine filament. Under her patronage he composed the Concerto for Two Pianos (1932) and the Concerto for the Organ (1932). Whatever, in fact, held his pieces together, Francis Poulenc created a kind of suturing factory for technology's music. Of course, putting *La voix humaine* to music or having phonographs talk and sewing machines pay the way does not necessarily supply the sonic blaze of high-tech mutation. As a title, *La voix humaine* appears to resist the technicity of its content. The cohabitation of the human voice with its technological filtering, its long-distance instrumentality, is set on the dividing line between opera and itself. The other, severed part of any duet expands into the noise machine and semantic shredding of the French telephone lines.

Poulenc offers opera a new chance for scoring on love and transference. The telephone *qua* instrument is by no means placed in a mimetic rapport with voice; while it is not identical with the human voice—something radically intervenes between voice and its transmission—it is also not a kind of mimetic Xeroxing of the voice. The telephone says something about the rapport of music with language, instrument with voice, and the breakdown of easy identifications. Operating the quasi-dialectics of long-distance and the close call, the telephone is an instrument of transference *par excellence*. The wedding ceremony / divorce hearing collapsed into one ring, it attaches the severed umbilicus of the self to the other, the voice to its resonance in an unlocalizable beyond. Maintaining and joining, the telephone line holds together what it separates. It creates a space of asignifying breaks, producing an intersection where the lines of public diffusion cross into those of more private, inwardly turned harmonics. Isn't the telephone the place that opera, in its fundamental structure, always sought to occupy? The telephone communicates the difference between the street diffusion of the aria and the introspective echo of a great house. For Poulenc to pull the telephone line into the districts of operatic logic means that he is legislating zoning laws and boundaries that signify the chains keeping the phantom of the opera restless.[12] Wagner's conspiracy, his burial plot for the orchestra, reemerges like a crack in a crypt of long-distance. But now I feel that I may be losing my grip. Back to basics. How does the telephone in fact make itself the destination of opera? Follow the twisted cord of Poulenc's argument.

In the first place, Poulenc has slipped the operator into the logic of the opera, creating a theater of the invisible, linking all the ghosts of operatic history, the disruptors and masked voices of the beyond. From Lucia's phantom to the crackling interference run by the other side of Poulenc's switchboard, opera is hosting parasites, transmission bubbles, and a sort of scratch noise. There is no smooth transition or absolute translation that would be containable by this house. Now, what does it mean to run the question of transference by opera's switchboard? How does the telephone answer for the mixed-media desire of the most contaminated of genres?

I need to consider *La voix humaine* as a philosophical opera struggling with its own determinations. It is an opera that performs the textual allegorization of its predicament, and though we may want, as did Poulenc, to stick to the streets, it is perhaps justifiable to scuttle down the telephone wires that are holding together this opera. For the telephone is not a simple installation, not a transparent allegory of inclusion. There is something artificial about it, like the transplant of an artificial organ into the body of opera. It is an organ that functions both like an instrument and like a voice, simulating *la voix humaine* while staying resolutely on the side of artifice. First, let's record the essential strains.

La voix humaine was Poulenc's third and final opera. It comes at the end of the line, and is based on Cocteau's monodrama of 1930. The opera features one character who, though traditionally contoured as human subject, is attached to the telephone like an answering machine. This character, "Elle," paces her bedroom like a caged animal. She materializes therefore somewhere between animal and machine. She is suffering the carceral silence of an enlarged telephone booth. We neither see nor hear the man on the other end, her lover. It has been said that the telephone receiver almost becomes the second onstage character. The opera is run through with interference, the intrusions brought about by the notorious hazards of the French telephone system. Elle is cut off twice and interrupted once, refers to these break-ins on five occasions, and becomes the victim of a chronic wrong-number syndrome. Everything about the arrangement suggests that she is on a destinal call, about to be put on eternal hold. The story of a breakup, *La voix humaine* dramatizes parasitical invasions on the abstract body of the couple. The couple is held together by a stringed instrument that is about to snap.

This is the last call; at the end of the opera Elle recognizes that she and her lover will have suspended relations after an impossible duet that, indeed, never manages to relate. The modulations of anguish do not follow any linear pattern, but suggest a subject that is wired, electrified by the shock of breaking off relations. On one level of phenomenal mobility, nothing happens. Still, this is Poulenc's most dramatic stage work. The drama bears upon the innovative techniques that Poulenc applied to the conversion of Cocteau's monodrama into opera. Of the 780 measures, 186 are only for solo voice with no orchestral accompaniment whatsoever, a severing that Poulenc had introduced to a lesser degree in *Dialogues des Carmélites*. While Keith W. Daniel feels, for instance, that Poulenc is producing a vocal line imitative of proper or pure speech, it is always a speech structured by telephonic syncopation and disruption, not, I would submit, "pure speech," whatever that might be.[13] Nonetheless, music is taking a return trip to the rhythmic constraints of speech: "Unlike that in Poulenc's two previous operas, the vocal writing in *La voix humaine* does not resemble that of his art songs—here he has deliberately rejected the lyricism of his solo vocal music. Poulenc's two major concerns here are to capture the proper rhythms of speech, and to mirror the normal inflections of speech with the subtle risings and fallings of the vocal line" (*Poulenc*, p. 201).

The harmonic language of *La voix humaine* tends to underscore the ambiguous light in which the opera sees itself. It produces a kind of demystified approach to a language with which it will never be joined but toward which it is always calling. Music places a call to language as if to affirm essential disconnection. Though tonality often emerges, there is more sustained tonal ambiguity in this opera than in any other Poulenc work of comparable length. Music begins by stammering, looking for itself, being deprived of stable tonality for the first eighteen measures. As the opera establishes a relation to language in a mood of immobile terror ("la donna" is not *mobile*, as we always knew, as Verdi radically showed us), it launches the following ambiguous harmonic characteristics with some regularity: nonfunctional harmonic progressions, unresolved dissonances, an extraordinary use of diminishing structures, and progressions of chords used chromatically. Tonality makes itself heard only in the most lyric passages, or by short orchestral motives based upon functional harmonies. Yet these phrases are quickly cut off by a return to ambiguity.

Daniel's interpretation points to the exceptional quality of the opera, which is to say that it is situated on perceptibly unstable ground, about to fall apart: "The overall structure of *La voix humaine* is unusual in Poulenc's *oeuvre*. The choppy, fragmentary nature of the text, and Poulenc's declamatory setting of it (reminiscent of Satie's *Socrate*) would seem to place the opera in danger of disintegrating. Poulenc's solution was to use the orchestra as a framework for holding the work together, by entrusting it with most of the lyricism" (p. 213). It is as if opera might suffer schizonoia. At the point where opera is about to experience the disintegration of its parts, where music feels itself severed from the language that it had sought to enter, a prosthetic god perturbs the moment of narcissistic wounding and reinscribes the scene. The prosthetic god—the technicity of the jointure where music comes through to language—is how Freud describes the telephone. The thing installs itself at the site of a brisure, when something is experienced as lost or long distance, removed. The orchestra responds to the distress signal sent out by a disintegrating operatic body by reemerging as a substitute for a lost object, what we "knew" before Babel, prior to the traumatic split of music from language. The role of the orchestra must not be underestimated, warns Daniel. In addition to assuming unifying and suturing functions, it portrays the ringing of the telephone "with repeated notes on the xylophone; it expresses the singer's agitation and confusion while trying to reach her lover; it even suggests the jazz which she hears in the background through the phone. Most important, however, the orchestra fills in the voids created by the inherently dry, disjointed vocal line" (p. 221).

Like the telephone, then, the orchestra is made to connect where there is little or no relation; it closes and unifies, binding the performance like a wound. The orchestra tells time; its closural gesture opens the very wound that it is asked to conceal. This is because what, according to Daniel, stalls disintegration renders it most visible—or in the true language of psychosis, most *audible*. The mark of disintegration (for the schizonoiac) is always auditory: noise disaster hits the subject like an immense catastrophe, a sonic blaze. Poulenc allows the trauma of the split the temporal dimensions of the big bang, resonating a more originary sound-split in opera's survival of itself, this telephone that rings after a felt obliteration, say, the one performed by *Moses and Aaron*.

On the somewhat less catastrophic register that links opera to noise disaster and to fantasies of language crashing into music, there is a synecdochical statement supplied by the supplemental instrument. The telephone, as member and dismembering of the orchestra, participates in the myths of organic unity where one discerns a shelter or defense against castration. We remember that the orchestra guaranteed organic totality by Wagner's dismemberment of it; prior to that traumatic action, the magic flute dedemonized the hideous contamination that occurred after successive splits into man and woman, day and night, man and bird, music and language, and so on. The orchestra and its parts, whether or not enchanted, act as metronome and mortality timer. When they emerge on the scene, as at the end of *Don Giovanni*, trouble is in the air, the death knell appears. In the great mystifications and denials of death, technology is seen as the corruption of Being. Background music, drums in a distance, a telephone that keeps ringing, are announcements from finitude. The technology that accompanies the repetition compulsion and death drive, these instruments of Being, vacillate between appearance and disappearance, marking the boundary between singing and speaking, music and its multiplicity of silences, several of which we gather under the heading of "language."

In any event, the telephone at once perverts the orchestra and amplifies its disconnective threat. It condenses being and time into a single ring that won't stop reverberating. Here's how *La voix humaine* says it:

[L]isten, dear, I'm suffering beyond words. This line is the last line which puts me in touch with you. . . . . The night before last? . . . . . . I went to sleep. I took the telephone with me. . . . . . No, in bed with me. . . . . . . Yes, I know. I'm very silly, but I took the telephone to bed with me because, after all, we are connected by the telephone. It goes into your flat, and then there was this promise that you would give me a ring. So you can just imagine I counted the minutes and dreamt all manner of things. Then it became a different and dangerous kind of ring—a wring of the neck which strangles, a ring of a boxing match I couldn't get out of—the bell rang, you hit me and I was counted out . . . . . . or I was at the bottom of the sea—it looked like the rooms in Wigmore Street—and I was connected with you by a diver's air tube, and I was begging you not to cut it—you know, dreams that are idiotic when told, but at the time terribly real. Because you're speaking to me. . . . . . [. . .] Now, I can breathe again because you are speaking to me. But my dream's not foolish. If you break the connection, you snap the air tube I'm holding onto for dear life.[14]

The telephone connects itself as artificial organ to the collapsed lung of the operatic body. Whether wind instrument or oxygen tent, voice box or atonal charm, the telephone taps back into a certain beginning where singing and language rose with the breath: "Now I can breathe again," sighs music, "because you are speaking to me." ("Maintenant, j'ai de l'air parce que tu me parles": now I have the air, the aria, because you are speaking to me.)

.09 Play It Again

And yet, Poulenc was a guttersnipe, his ears were open to the outside, he kept breaking out of the heavy walls of opera like a schizo safecracker. He hung out in music halls, in cafés, and on street corners. This is why his last opera exposes itself to the street episteme of noise and dirt, avoiding the quarantined ghettos of transcendental music. Continually running interference with itself, his rendering of the human voice is accompanied by static. The telephone connection houses the improper. Hitting the streets, it welcomes linguistic pollutants and fakes music. Still, like opera, it stages the refusal to synthesize even as it switches on the contaminating blender. There's the mix, and there's even a match, but it will go no farther.

The possibility of a telephone was never fully dissociated from musical strains. From Sir Charles Wheatstone, who called his string telephone (1819) a "magic lyre," to Kafka, on whose telephone in *The Castle* angels sing, the telephone hollowed out an eerie symphony hall for departed spirits. Around 1874, Elisha Gray, Alexander Graham Bell's rival, was occupied with a system of musical telephones, which he wished to apply to manifold telegraphic transmissions. The history of this phantasmal music hall has yet to be written. All I can say is that to this day, the telephone still houses background music, as if to deaden the pain.[15]

.10 Disintegration

On July 19, 1960, Francis Poulenc wrote to the woman who sang the lead body part in *La voix humaine*, Denise Duval. "Mon Rossignol à larmes," he began, "J'aimais ta voix joyeuse au téléphone. Comme moi, tu n'es pas faite pour la solitude." Next paragraph. "On ne parle que de toi et de *la Voix* à Aix. Le resete est un hors-d'oeuvre, dit-on. . . . A dimanche. Je t'adore. Fr."[16] His biography reaches an end. I translate: "Saturday, January 26, 1963, Francis Poulenc gave a concert in Maastricht, Holland, with Denise Duval. Francis returned to Paris the following Monday. On Tuesday, he telephoned Denise Duval to have lunch with her at her place the next day, but Wednesday morning, the 30th, he called her to say he was hoarse and could not go out. At one o'clock he died suddenly."[17]

.11 Kierkegaard

QUOTEQUOTEQUOTE"But what follows from maintaining that wherever language ceases, I encounter the musical? This is probably the most perfect expression of the idea that music everywhere limits language" QUOTEQUOTEQUOTEQUOTEQUOTEBut what follows from maintaining that wherever language ceases, I encounter the musical? This is probably the most perfect expression of the idea that music everywhere limitsQUOTE languageQUOTEQUOTEthat music everywhere limits languageQUOTE music everywhere limits languageQUOTEits language

Hiroshima in the Morning

Peter Schwenger

*E*arly on the day he was to speak at the 1966 Johns Hopkins conference on structuralism, Jacques Lacan gazed from a Baltimore hotel window and found the image of (in more senses than one) his subject.

It was not quite daylight and a neon sign indicated to me every minute the change of time, and naturally there was heavy traffic, and I remarked to myself that exactly all that I could see, except for some trees in the distance, was the result of thoughts, actively thinking thoughts where the function played by the subjects was not completely obvious. In any case the so-called *Dasein*, as a definition of the subject, was there in this rather intermittent or fading spectator. The best image to sum up the unconscious is Baltimore in the early morning.[1]

This image, assimilated into poststructuralist thought, surfaces intermittently in several scholars' later work. Notably, Lacan's meditation was the starting point for one of the first pieces of nuclear criticism, Dean MacCannell's 1984 essay entitled "Baltimore in the Morning . . . After: On the Forms of Post-Nuclear Leadership."[2] Despite the allusion to the 1983 made-for-TV movie, the essay is not about the time after a future nuclear attack, but after a past one; and the postnuclear leadership referred to is our own. Taking from Lacan the notion that a culture can have an unconscious, MacCannell examines documents relating to the problem of the "inner city"—that is, to a certain social class inhabiting the city centers—and to the corresponding move of the educated and well-to-do into country and suburban towns. His conclusion is that, unconsciously of course, the United States is preparing to sacrifice its cities to nuclear attack, along with their socially problematic populations—thus rendering the enemy strikes relatively harmless or even beneficial. The argument is similar to that of Martha Bartter's later "Nuclear War as Urban Renewal."[3] In the science fiction that Bartter studies, the annihilation of U.S. cities is followed by a return to the mythic wilderness of pastoral purification. Yet in all this talk of cities and nuclear war one city has been relegated to a place that one is tempted to call the unconscious. In Bartter's essay it appears not at all; in MacCannell's it occupies less than a page before the focus returns to contemporary urban concerns. And this liminal position is the one generally occupied in Western consciousness by that other city, city of the Other, Hiroshima.

I

Hiroshima in the morning, at 8:15 on the morning of August 6, 1945, cannot, like Baltimore, be described as an image of the unconscious. There is no such image; we are incapable of retaining one. In the words of a Hiroshima survivor, "Human emotions reach a point beyond which they cannot extend—something like a photographic process. If under certain conditions you expose a photographic plate to light, it becomes black; but if you continue to expose it, then it reaches a point where it turns white."[4] Like the white shadows burnt into the sidewalks and walls of Hiroshima, we are only a blank, the mark of an absence, where the comprehension of that morning is concerned. This white mythology is admittedly an image, but only of our inability to image—an inability that all too easily shades over into denial, and into the relegation of the whole city once more to the unconscious.

"Once more" I say because survivors' reports warrant our describing what happened to Hiroshima as a massive irruption of the unconscious. "The flash that covered the city in morning mist," one survivor has written, "was much like an instant dream" (*Death in Life*, p. 34). In his study of atomic bomb survivors Robert Jay Lifton has noted the frequent use of such terms as "nightmare," "dream," and "dream realm" (p. 34). For instance, Dr. Michihiko Hachiya writes in his *Hiroshima Diary*: "Outsiders . . . reported with amazement the spectacle of long files of people holding stolidly to a narrow, rough path when close by was a smooth easy road going in the same direction. The outsiders could not grasp the fact that they were witnessing the exodus of a people who walked in the realm of dreams."[5] Many of those walkers later described their state at that time in a significant Japanese phrase: *muga-muchu*, "without self, without center" (*Death in Life*, p. 26). Externally nothing remained of their old selves: clothing was stripped away, living bodies were swollen and burned beyond recognition. But more to the point, the instant after the blast the internal perception of its surviving victims was that absolutely nothing remained of the reality around them, not even enough to orient them to the degree of its loss. "Hiroshima didn't exist," is all that one survivor can say; "Hiroshima just didn't exist" (p. 29). What people saw instead was so incomprehensible that it had to be assigned by them to a realm other than reality, the only realm in which such scenes could possibly have been experienced before, that of dream. The effects of shock upon its victims' perceptions contributed further to the dreamlike quality. Shock results in the deadening of pain, and indeed of all physical sensation; a sense of unreality; a suspension of time or an effect of slow motion; and the unfolding of events in silence. All these characteristics are noted in survivors' accounts of their experiences. More eerie than any other is the complete silence that fell over Hiroshima after the bomb, a silence so marked as to seem a palpable presence.

To link Hiroshima with the idea of a dream is not to deny the reality of what happened there, a reality that almost immediately after became manifest in material, inescapably corporeal ways, which I will not describe. If I speak of a state of mind, it is because in this way alone there is some chance of tracing a trajectory between our state and that of the people of Hiroshima. And this can occur only at the level of the unconscious—has in one sense already occurred. For if Hiroshima in the morning, after the bomb has fallen, is like a dream, one must ask whose dream it is. Who is the dreamer? The ready answer, of course, is that the dream is the unconscious creation of those who dropped the bomb; it is their unconscious. This is not an answer that can be easily dismissed. The long debate over the decision to drop the bomb, and the subsequent debate over that debate, include too many factors that cannot be accounted for by military strategy alone. Both Japanese and Americans have felt that race was probably a factor, making it easier for the enemy to fulfill its function of an Other on which could be projected all the qualities that a nation would wish to deny in itself. War ultimately aims at validating a national self, a national ego that, according to Elaine Scarry, aspires to "the dream that one will be . . . exempt from the condition of being embodied."[6] But this dream is only realized through the violently contrasting demonstration of the Other's embodiment. The Japanese were no less involved in this dynamic than were the Americans, and no less committed to the validation of a consciously created national self.

This Japanese national self was represented and summed up by the cult of the emperor, a fact that might be suggestive to an analyst of dreams. In *The Interpretation of Dreams* Freud makes use of the Andersen tale of "The Emperor's New Clothes" in order to analyze the common dream of finding oneself naked in public. To the question of who the emperor might be, Freud answers that he is the dreamer, stripped of the power of his conscious self. The slow-moving automatons of Hiroshima, then—stripped of clothing, stripped of flesh, stripped of self—have been catapulted into an unconscious that reverses their nation's consciously held dream. They have been forced to live as reality the unmaking that validates national making and that is the price war demands for it. The victims' experience, on both sides of any war, is absorbed into the officially designated reality of the winner: the consciousness of a certain national self, and the concept of history that supports it. As for the reality of the victims' unmaking, it is systematically relegated to the unconscious. This is done, Scarry maintains, by omitting it from language, or redescribing it, or marginalizing it through metaphors that incorporate it into the scenario of national making.

It is through language, then, that war's aspect of unmaking is removed from a nation's consciousness; it could consequently be argued that language creates the unconscious to which it relegates that aspect, thus concealing it. And this may be so not only after a war but during it, and "always already": we are brought back to Lacan and his well-known dictum that the unconscious is structured as a language.

In the Johns Hopkins talk, Lacan warned his audience not to take this too literally: "I have never said that the unconscious was an assembly of words, but that the unconscious is precisely structured." In a sense the dictum is a redundancy, he continues, "because 'structured' and 'as a language' for me mean exactly the same thing" ("Inmixing," pp. 187–88). The metonymy and metaphor that for Lacan together make up language might just as well, he says, be the condensation and displacement that for Freud make up dreams: the structuring principles are the same in both versions of the unconscious. That structuration—which is to say, that unconscious—is the Other to self in Lacan's sense of the term: "The Other is the locus in which is situated the chain of the signifier that governs whatever may be made present of the subject—it is the field of that living being in which the subject has to appear."[7] As is indicated by the reference to "the chain of the signifier," the "field" here is structured "as a language." It is a field that is far wider than the subject, which, when that subject appears, does so in an "intermittent" or "fading" way, like the lights of Baltimore emerging from the dimness of early morning. And while the Other is a locus or field that is all-encompassing, omnipresent, the subject has to make do with "whatever may be made present." Whatever may *not* be made present to the subject remains unconscious.

That morning at Hiroshima the "not present" manifested itself: "Hiroshima didn't exist." The city is made to feel the full force of the unconscious, the field within which the "fading" subject has to appear. In a blinding flash that field is revealed, and inscribes itself on the bodies of Hiroshima's citizens. Some of those bodies it utterly consumes; some it brands forever with the sign of that moment, with the patterns of the kimonos worn then, with the angle of a body's posture, a face's tilt. Language, which for Lacan is equivalent to structure, is involved in this massive destructuring of the physical world; for all its abstractness it is as much the "cause" of the body's suffering at Hiroshima as is the physical fire.

Yet language, that ambiguous *pharmakon*, is remedy as well as poison. If language is structure, it can help us to make the world, to make something even of its unmaking on that August morning. And if the unconscious is structured as a language, it is language that may provide us with a road into the unconscious and some understanding of it, as happens when we read the metonym and metaphor of dream.

The psychoanalytical process does not stop at dreams, of course; Lacan heaps scorn on the formulation *life is a dream*: "the real has to be sought beyond the dream—is what the dream has enveloped, hidden from us" (*FFC*, p. 60). There is then a practical thrust to Lacanian psychoanalysis: "What is a praxis? I doubt whether this term may be regarded as inappropriate to psycho-analysis. It is the broadest term to designate a concerted human action, whatever it may be, which places man in a position to treat the real by the symbolic" (*FFC*, p. 6). The links between language and Lacan's idea of the symbolic are well known; as for the problematic term *the real*, I will refer only to one observation by Lacan: "Is it not remarkable that, at the origin of the analytic experience, the real should have presented itself in the form of that which is *unassimilable* in it—in the form of the trauma, determining all that follows, and imposing on it an apparently accidental origin?" (*FFC*, p. 55). The real to be treated here is that which is enveloped, hidden, in the dream that unexpectedly descended upon the citizens of Hiroshima. That "unassimilable" experience may be read in the classic terms of the trauma, magnified to overwhelming proportions. Indeed the bodies of Hiroshima's citizens often enact the deferral that is typical of trauma: years later, out of the body's unconscious, as it were, the trauma's effects come to the surface in the form of keloids and cancers—the scars of the unconscious, to borrow a Lacanian image, literalized and physically manifested. But the concept of deferral is not just a kind of determinism, an eternal return of the past in the present. It involves the revision of past events at a later date so that they fit into a later phase of development or understanding. In a letter to Wilhelm Fliess (Dec. 6, 1896) Freud refers to this process as a "re-transcription," thus hinting at the agency of the letter in the unconscious and at language's role in treating, in the form of the trauma, the real. Inscription, then, physical or psychical, may become transcription; scars of both kinds may be translated into new meanings; and the unconscious that is Hiroshima may emerge into a language that is adequate, if not to its impossible real, at least to us who are struggling to come to some kind of deferred terms with it.

The only language adequate to Hiroshima is the unconscious as it speaks in texts. Indeed, this may be the only language adequate to the Real of history in general, according to Fredric Jameson. He argues that "history is *not* a text, not a narrative, master or otherwise, but that, as an absent cause, it is inaccessible to us except in textual form, and that our approach to it and to the Real itself necessarily passes through its prior textualization, its narrativization in the political unconscious."[8] Jameson goes on to assert that texts themselves may have an unconscious and may be— perhaps must be—interpreted accordingly. The critic's writing is, or ought to be, a form of listening to the forces within the texts, rather like Freud's practice in *The Interpretation of Dreams*—in which, of course, he underscores the parallels between the work done by the dream and that done by literature. The praxis of treating the real by the symbolic may thus be accomplished by literary analysis as well as by psychoanalysis; the line between them is permeable.

It should be clear why I am now turning to a text that is ostensibly not about Hiroshima, a novel in which the bombing of that city is relegated to its usual place in Western literature, to the unconscious, here a textual unconscious. But I hope to show that such an unconscious is the real subject of the book, the Real enveloped within the dream that is *Gravity's Rainbow*.

II

Of the many reasons why Pynchon's novel encourages this sort of interpretation, not the least is the fact that *Gravity's Rainbow*[9] begins with an actual dream. "A screaming comes across the sky" is the novel's first sentence; that screaming of an approaching rocket "holds," in an improbable temporal distortion, during the entire slow dream evacuation that follows—holds that sequence within the arc of the descending rocket as the novel will later reveal itself to be similarly held. The sequence is extraordinarily rich in textures both physical and metaphysical. The dreamer has, this time, not missed the train that was Freud's symbol of death and that now clinks along slowly in shadow, crowded with dim faces. There is no longer any escape possible: the evacuation of the city reveals itself "not as a disentanglement from, but a progressive *knotting into*" (p. 3). The city is not only the target of the rocket but a symbol of the forces that produced it and that inescapably produce its inhabitants. An enormous decrepit hotel is the journey's goal, shabby hell and microcosm of the city itself: "Underfoot crunches the oldest of city dirt, last crystallizations of all the city had denied, threatened, lied to its children" (p. 4). And these words, with their evocation of the psychological under a geological or archeological figure, remind us that Freud's first figure for the unconscious in *Civilization and Its Discontents* is the city of Rome.

In more ways than I have time to speak of, the manifest content of Pynchon's novel may be read as that of a dream. Like a dream it has a latent content; and that latent content, I would argue, is summed up in Hiroshima. Though (with some notable exceptions) the time span of *Gravity's Rainbow* runs from December 1944 to September 1945, Hiroshima is all but absent. Aside from an ironic flicker when a Japanese speaks of returning to the peace of his hometown, the name of Hiroshima appears only once in the book, as a cryptic fragment encountered by Tyrone Slothrop, the book's wandering protagonist:

In one of the streets, in the morning fog, plastered over two slippery cobblestones, is a scrap of newspaper headline, with a wirephoto of a giant white cock, dangling in the sky straight downward out of a white pubic bush. The letters

MB DRO
ROSHI

appear above with the logo of some occupation newspaper, a grinning glamour girl riding astraddle the cannon of a tank, steel penis with slotted serpent head, 3rd Armored treads 'n' triangle on a sweater rippling across her tits. The white image has the same coherence, the hey-lookit-me smugness, as the Cross does. It is not only a sudden white genital onset in the sky—it is also, perhaps, a Tree. (pp. 693–94)

The first thing we should note is that when Slothrop encounters this scrap of paper he can have no idea of the content of the full communiqué; nor can the paper give him any. For him, and momentarily for the reader, the scrap of paper is detached from the realm of the factual; thereby both letter and image are rendered cryptic. This cryptic quality, like that of dreams, encourages a deciphering process that involves a spreading network of associations; within that net is captured more of the truth of Hiroshima than could have been presented by the full official page. That truth is an unconscious one in two senses. It is a revelation of the unconscious forces that manifest themselves at Hiroshima; and it is a revelation that takes place, for Slothrop, only at the unconscious level: "He doesn't remember sitting on the curb for so long staring at the picture. But he did" (p. 694).

And as for us, staring at another fragment, this fragment from Pynchon's novel, what can we decipher of Hiroshima? Of the passage's many associations I will analyze only the genital ones: the cloud from the explosion is not a mushroom but "a giant white cock dangling in the sky straight downward out of a white pubic bush." A simple identification of the bomb with phallic power doesn't get us very far, explaining little about the nature of that power and the reasons for its taking the form it did at Hiroshima. We get further if we approach the problem from the margins, literally. The official logo of the newspaper recapitulates the phallic element, situating it in such a way that it becomes highly charged psychologically. Moreover, the description of the logo bulks as large here as does that of the wirephoto. It is thereby implied that "official," banal, and unthinkingly accepted patterns are linked with what was soon to become known as the Unthinkable; that there is a psychopathology of everyday life that eventually manifests itself in some such form as Hiroshima.

Beneath its cartoon sexuality, the logo is as disturbing an image as any analyzed by Freud: "a grinning glamour girl riding astraddle the cannon of a tank, steel penis . . ." In terms of the castration complex, the woman has been given back that which the child originally perceived as having been taken away from her. The same image can be detected, again marginally, a little after the passage on which we are concentrating, in the narrator's description of Hiroshima on that morning: "At the instant it happened, the pale Virgin was rising in the east, head, shoulders, breasts, 17° 36' down to her maidenhead at the horizon." This curious deflection of interest onto a constellation seems to have only one purpose: to present the gigantic form of a woman, bit by bit, down to the genital area where something entirely unexpected is revealed, the phallic cloud depicted in the wirephoto. It remains ambiguous whether, "dangling in the sky straight downward," it is aimed at the virgin's maidenhead; or whether, rising from the horizon, the cloud restores to her the penis she was thought to lack. The same ambiguity is seen in the logo, where it is unclear whether the glamour girl is smugly flaunting "her" penis or enjoying the ride of her life on "his." In either case, directly or indirectly, the result is masculine empowerment. But the indirect route, the detour by way of the unconscious, takes a much more interesting form.

What is on the surface a grotesque image, calculated to terrify the male—that of a woman with a penis powerful as a steel cannon, explosive as a bomb—at another level brings to the male comfort and empowerment. For the classic castration complex depends on the apparent "evidence" that the threat of castration can be carried out, has been carried out on the female. It is this threat that gives its efficacy to the *Non du Père*, the "No!" by which the Father forbids the usurping of his sexual privileges. Now the evidence is reversed in order to deny the validity of that threat. And since the *no* of the Father, the *Non du Père*, is also the *Nom du Père*, the Name of the Father which is language, there are other consequences. The authority of language is denied, the chain of signifiers is broken, and the structured field that is our destiny is mastered—or so we hope. The sexual fantasy thus reveals itself to be the dream of full accession into the *Nom du Père*, into the power of the symbolic system.

Impossible as this dream may be, its consequences are real. The attempt to realize in the world something of which we are not even conscious leads ultimately to events such as Hiroshima. A fantasized revision of woman's body gives the power to inscribe on others' bodies—including those of women—a language from which one now feels oneself to be exempt. Indeed a hint of this can be detected in the logo, where we see the "3rd Armored treads 'n' triangle on a sweater rippling across her tits." This is partly, of course, proprietary confirmation of the phallic gaze, for whom the "hey-lookit-me smugness" is played out. But the tread marks are unsettling, evoking images of the 3rd Armored's tanks passing over the woman's body and so marking it. One recalls the somewhat sadistic ring of Lacan's language as he describes the relation of the signified to the signifier: "the signifier has an active function in determining certain effects in which the signifiable appears as submitting to its mark, by becoming through that passion the signified."[10]

The overall terms of this analysis are reinforced by their appearance throughout *Gravity's Rainbow*. There is, after all, an actual scene of castration in the novel. Though it misfires because of a case of mistaken identity, it is meant for Tyrone Slothrop. Its purpose is to undo the unique properties of Slothrop's penis, properties that were acquired by a process of Pavlovian conditioning in early childhood. His father in effect sold him to a psychologist working for the state; he now has an erection at any locale due shortly to be hit by a rocket. This affinity may in part result from a fact that links the mechanistic nature of Pavlovian psychology to the larger mechanisms of World War II: the psychologist who conducted the experiments upon young Tyrone was also the developer of Imipolex G, a plastic used in German rocketry. Slothrop's penis is then a curiously literal version of the phallus as signifier, "the signifier," according to Lacan, "intended to designate as a whole the effects of the signified, in that the signifier conditions them by its presence as a signifier" (*Ecrits*, p. 285). The reference to conditioning here allows us to distinguish Slothrop's flesh-and-blood penis, which has been conditioned, from a very different version of conditioning signified by the (conceptual) phallus. If we ask who is responsible for that conditioning we must go beyond the psychologist, beyond the father to the Father that is the entire structuring system within which (as he gradually discovers) Slothrop is bound. Searching for the secret of his childhood trauma, Slothrop finds only a widening network of connections on all levels of society, where even supposed enemies are knotted together in vast cartels. What he learns on a social level is the Lacanian truth of "his relation as a subject to the signifier" (*Ecrits*, p. 287).

Not surprisingly, Slothrop's reaction to all this is full-blown paranoia, a common effect of the castration complex. Paranoia may arise from a specific and personal trauma (such as being sold by your father and having your penis experimented upon); but it may also arise from the general nature of the human situation itself. To begin with, we must resist the tendency (a somewhat paranoid one) to make the simple distinction between "us" and "them," between the paranoid and the aggressor. Paranoia and aggressivity are recognized by psychoanalysis as two sides of the same coin. So the paranoid vision repeatedly referred to in *Gravity's Rainbow* when turned inside out is a study of aggression. In Lacanian terms, it is the inversion of the aggressivity that arises out of the futile and continually frustrated attempt at full realization of the self—first in the imaginary stage, and later through the symbolic system. We are dealing then with "a correlative tension of the narcissistic structure in the coming-into-being of the subject" (*Ecrits*, p. 22). Not a personal trauma but a universal condition is the source of paranoid aggressivity. Its recurrent expression on the national scale is war, which Lacan ironically describes as "the inevitable and necessary midwife of all progress in our organization" (*Ecrits*, p. 27). There is of course no such progress—not even, for the most part, in the understanding of war's nature. To link war to the castration complex, as I have done above; to read it as a signifying act, as the fantasy of full accession into the signifying system, as the subject *becoming* the signifier (no long subject to the signifier) if only for an other—these notions, no doubt, will seem bizarre to some. As is necessarily the case for the contents of an unconscious, before they manifest themselves through material symptoms in the world.

Whether Pynchon intended all this, whether he is a Lacanian or even a

Freudian—these questions are beside the point. If Lacan's theories partake of truth—a word he insists on—then they must be "there" in the presence defined by its absence from consciousness. And a writer's associations may then coalesce in language that hints at that other language, language of the Other, which is the unconscious. Hints are what emerge, effects at the level of the unconscious, as we look at a certain fragmentary communiqué, and look at Slothrop looking at it. Our perception, like his, is a dim one; the entire encounter takes place, after all, in "morning fog." Only, as "the fog whitens into morning" while Slothrop watches the ambiguous image of the white cloud, we sense a significance to this reiterated whiteness: the cloud that is the sign of Hiroshima is akin to the one that envelops him. The forces that manifested themselves at Hiroshima are latent in our lives. Attempting to read the unconscious through a contained text, we remain oblivious of the degree to which it continues beyond its borders, containing us in turn.

Yet momentary and cryptic flashes of insight punctuate the dimness of our apprehension, like the flickering of traffic in Baltimore's faint dawn. And these we must learn to read, for all the reasons I have stressed in this tale of two cities, which indeed are one. Hiroshima's terrible difference from Baltimore is the product of a common structuring dynamic that contains them both. And what Hiroshima was, Baltimore may yet become . . . the morning after.

Writing the Body:

The Rhetoric of Mutilation in Marguerite Duras's *L'amante anglaise*

Anne Tomiche

*A*lthough there are few descriptions of bodies in Marguerite Duras's fictions, images of corporal dismemberment, murderous mutilation, and explosion of the body recur. Her texts often deal with crimes, fragmented bodies and violence done to them: this is most explicitly the case of *Moderato cantabile* (1958), *Les viaducs de la Seine-et-Oise* (1959), *Hiroshima, mon amour* (1960), *L'amante anglaise* (1967), and *La maladie de la mort* (1982). In order to pose the question of mutilation, of fragmentation, in terms of the relation between the body and discourse, I have chosen to focus on *L'amante anglaise*. This narrative takes the form of three interviews conducted by an investigator-analyst in order to reconstitute, reconstruct, and understand the murder committed by Claire Lannes, who killed her deaf-and-dumb cousin Marie-Thérèse, cut her into pieces, and threw the different parts of the body in trains all going in different directions.[1] I want to explore how fragmentation organizes not only the representation of the body within the diegesis (since Claire Lannes literally cuts up the body of her cousin after murdering her) but also the discursive and narrative apparatus. I shall argue that, through the function of the "cut," *L'amante anglaise* suggests that the forces that (de)construct the body and the forces that (de)construct the text are the same: fragmentation (de)structures similarly both the subject and discourse. Such a focus on the fragment in Duras's text seems consistent with a certain "postmodern" concern for the broken piece and the shattered totality (for example, Lacan's *imago du corps morcelé*, Derrida's use of the metaphor of castration, and Blanchot's notion of the *fragmentaire*). The interest of Duras's text is that it suggest an intersection between a psychoanalytic (Lacanian) rethinking of the self and the contemporary rethinking of the nature of textuality (in Derrida and Blanchot's works). As we shall see, such an intersection relies on the function of a "cut" and establishes an analogy between the body and discourse.

That it is through the function of the "cut" that a link is textually established in *L'amante anglaise* between the body and discourse can be seen as early in the text as the beginning of the first interview conducted by the investigator-analyst, when he summarizes the "facts" of the crime as given in the police report. Fragments of a human body were found in a number of different locations in France, in different trains. All the fragments have been identified as belonging to the same body, which has been reconstituted, except for the head, which is missing. Because all the trains that carried the fragments went through the village of Vierne whatever their final destination was, the police concluded that the crime took place there and that the murderer threw the fragments of the body onto the different trains: "Fragments of a human body have been discovered all over France in trains. . . . The *recoupement ferroviaire* has allowed us to discover . . . that the crime took place in our village" (p. 11). "Recoupement ferroviaire," a key phrase that recurs several times in the text, points in two directions. First, it refers to the dismemberment of the dead body, which has been cut and cut again before being put in circulation throughout the railway system: the term "recoupement" inscribes both the cut (*coupe, coupure*) and the repetition (*re*) of the act of fragmenting the body. At the same time it indicates the system of clues and interpretation that leads to the identification of the victim and the circumstances of the murder, and finally to the murderer. The "recoupement" is therefore a point of intersection, a means of cross-checking the clues and sources of information essential to the reconstruction of the body and to the possibility of a complete interpretation of the murder. This interpretive gesture is the very gesture of the investigator-analyst who, throughout the novel, tries to reconstitute and understand Claire's apparently unmotivated crime. The term "recoupement" itself thus links the figure of the body (the criminal dismemberment operated on the body) and the structure of discourse (the attempt to reconstruct an interpretation).

Marguerite Duras has stated several times her fascination with crime (in an interview given to the journal *Cahiers du cinéma* in 1980 she said:

"I love crime").[2] Many of her fictions, like *L'amante anglaise*, take as their point of departure a criminal *fait divers*. In a very controversial article published in the daily newspaper *Libération* in 1985, she even went so far as to call "sublime" the murder of a child supposedly committed by his mother.[3] (Since then, the mother has been declared innocent by the French judicial system.) Not very long before Duras, another famous French intellectual—Jacques Lacan—showed a great deal of interest in apparently unmotivated crimes. His thesis published in 1932, *De la psychose paranoï-aque dans ses rapports avec la personnalité*, was an effort to understand what motivated Aimée, a young woman in full possession of her intellectual faculties and with no explicable motivation, to try to murder an actress with whom she had never had any personal contact. His 1933 article entitled "Motifs du crime paranoïaque" concerned the incomprehensible crime of the Papin sisters, who had killed and mutilated their employer and her daughter. This interest in unmotivated crime shared by Duras and Lacan is not the only reason to link them. Duras is aware of the discourse of psychoanalysis and in particular Lacan's discourse, and moreover, Lacan was aware of her discourse. He even paid her homage in a short text entitled "Hommage fait à Marguerite Duras du *Ravissement de Lol V. Stein*," where he stresses the similarities of their discourses: "Marguerite Duras shows that she knows, without me, what I teach."[4]

Without going so far as to argue that Duras's fictions are, unbeknownst to her, applications of Lacanian theory (which would be a very reductive gesture), it is possible, at least as a point of departure, to read Claire's crime in *L'amante anglaise* in terms of Lacan's notion of the *imago du corps morcelé*: the images of the fragmented body reveal the original splitting of the subject in the narcissistic structure in which the subject identifies with an imaginary "ideal." In this identification the subject alienates himself in a perpetually "opening rift" because he is caught in the permanent discordance between reality and the ideal to which he aspires. Aggressivity (the *imago* of the fragmented body) is the correlative tendency of this narcissistic mode of identification.[5] As "passage à l'acte," crime—which has to be understood as a significant representational structure and not as the result of an impoverished normality—materializes the aggressivity correlative of narcissistic identification in the constitution of subjectivity. Furthermore, crime thereby actualizes an unconscious desire for self-punishment. Via his victim the criminal strikes at an ideal of himself that has been exteriorized and, at the same time, brings upon himself society's wrath. This concept of self-punishment was, according to Lacan, the only way to explain Aimée's "cure" and the Papin sisters' tranquillity after having committed their crimes. In that sense, the criminal's "passage à l'acte" is an attempt to dissolve the imaginary construct, an attempt that liberates the criminal from his madness at the same time as it perpetuates the discrepancy between who he is and who he wants to be, which is the origin of his "madness" in the first place. The crime, paradoxically, "cures" the paranoid by liberating him from the unconscious guilt at the origin of his delirium, and at the same time renders permanently impossible the identification between the real and the ideal, revealing an absence—a split, a cut—at the heart of the ego, an absence that constitutes his subjectivity since subjectivity is only a continuous series of failed attempts to identify with an ideal.

In *L'amante anglaise* Claire's apparently unmotivated crime functions as a form of self-punishment: "They should decapitate me for what I did," she says (p. 184). Claire Lannes (née Bouquet), by decapitating Marie-Thérèse Bouquet, the woman who is "of the same flesh and blood" and "whose final name is the same" (p. 185), mutilates her imaginary double, she kills herself: "it seems that one has killed the other as one would have killed oneself" (p. 32). At the same time, the crime as self-punishment functions as a form of cure. Claire says that before the crime she had felt frightened to the point of madness (p. 135), but that once she committed the crime and the dismemberment of the body, she recovered her peace of mind (p. 139). Furthermore, Claire's crime seems to reproduce what Lacan has described as the correlative tendency of narcissistic identification. Claire's narcissistic identification with her deaf cousin Marie-Thérèse led her to stuff wax in her ears, thereby isolating herself from the symbolic domain of speech. On the other hand, Marie-Thérèse herself had taken Claire's place at home: she took care of the house, made all the decisions, was the true housewife. Moreover, Claire identifies with Alfonso, her closest friend in the story: she would cut wood for two days to mimic him (p. 91).

The network of identifications in *L'amante anglaise* extends far beyond Claire's narcissistic identification with Marie-Thérèse and Alfonso. This network creates a matrix of indistinction in which Claire is neither subject nor object. As Claire's husband, Pierre, tells the interviewer, Claire could just as well have killed him rather than Marie-Thérèse (p. 123). This association-identification between Marie-Thérèse, the cousin, and Pierre, the husband, is even inscribed in the cousin's name "Marie," homophone of *mari*, "husband" in French. Moreover Pierre, because he once dreamed that he killed Marie-Thérèse, becomes a potential murderer, and the interviewer emphasizes this identification between Claire and Pierre (p. 83).

The interviewer himself identifies with Claire: "I am trying to find out who Claire Lannes really is and why she says she committed this crime. . . . I am looking for a reason for her [*je cherche pour elle*]" (p. 62). The investigator looks for an explanation on Claire's behalf, in her place: he takes her place. In this network of identifications, Claire Lannes is neither subject nor object but a sort of boundless emptiness: "She was like a room without doors, where the wind blows and takes everything away" (p. 90). Claire's subjectivity is thus a fundamental emptiness perpetually replenished by the narcissistic identifications that try to deny that emptiness.

In fact, not only are cutting and throwing away the two operations involved in Claire's criminal act; they also are two of Claire's constant activities. As her husband says, she used to cut things, to break plates and throw them in the trash, and she once cut her blankets. Claire's general tendency to cut and cut again (*recouper*) is part of the "recoupement" of the body understood as a fragmentation, a segmentation. When asked by the investigator to explain why Claire so often cut things into pieces, Claire's husband suggests that it might be to make the disaster total and complete. The only "reason" that he can find is "so that the disaster would be complete . . . so that it would be . . . *locked up* is the word that comes to my mind" (pp. 120–21, my emphasis). In the same way, when Claire herself explains why she broke and threw away plates, she says: "I want three or four walls, an iron gate, an iron bed, windows with bars, and I want Claire Lannes to be *locked up* there. So, I open the window and I throw out plates so that someone can hear me and take me away" (p. 172, my emphasis). Cutting and throwing function as a cry meant for no specific addressee but for an anonymous "someone," a cry whose function is to lock up or enclose the disaster associated with Claire herself. Claire's desire, expressed through her acts of cutting and throwing away, is thus to produce boundaries (the boundaries of walls, of an iron door, and of windows with bars) in order to delineate a space where she could be enclosed. Cutting and fragmenting (the cousin's body, plates, blankets, things in general) thus function not only as the correlative tendency of narcissistic identifications but also and paradoxically as the enactment of Claire's desire to produce boundaries and an enclosed totality.

The literally fragmented and "disarticulated" body, which is the paradoxical product of Claire's desire to produce totality, becomes the textual emblem of Claire's discourse and writing within the diegesis and of the narrative structure itself. That writing (and reading) depends on a process of *cutting* rather than on a more conventionally conceived process of healing has been stressed by Derrida, who, in his discussion of Philippe Sollers, writes: "the operation of reading/writing goes by way of the blade of a red knife."[6] Reading and writing are operations structured by mutilation, a "cut," in which the "presence" of the text paradoxically establishes itself. In fact, aesthetics in even more general terms is the function of a cut: analyzing the feeling of the beautiful in Kant's *Analytic of the Beautiful*, Derrida notes that it is in "the pure cut [*la coupure pure*]," in the interruption, the "hiatus of the abyss" that the feeling of the beautiful arises.[7] In Kant's definition the beautiful arises as a *without*, a *sans*: it is the object of a disinterested *Wohlgefallen*, which pleases universally *without* concept, and it is the form of finality perceived *without* the representation of an end. The being cut off from the goal—absolutely cut from an end—is an absolute interruption, "a pure cut." This "pure cut" that structures the aesthetic feeling of the beautiful is the cut of a "without" ("without concept," "without the representation of an end"—*ohne Vorstellung eines Zwecks*). But this "without" is not a lack: "the *without of* the pure cut is without lack, without lack of anything" ("The *Sans*," p. 90). Beauty does not function without this *sans*—and the homophonic proximity in French with *sang* (blood) and *sens* (sense, direction) reinforces the associations among the cut, violence, and signification: it "*functions* only with *this* particular *sans*, it gives nothing to be seen, especially not itself, except with that *sans* and no other" (pp. 90–91). It is through a process of cutting that a text establishes its authority and the aesthetic feeling is the function of a cut.

This relationship between a process of cutting and the operation of writing is one of the aspects that Derrida's *Glas* emphasizes, even performs.[8] In *Glas*, Derrida links certain aspects of the Jewish tradition to writing on the subject of castration, as it relates to power. The Jewish circumcision is a symbolic castration, a simulacrum of castration that, as such, can ward off castration and establish power. In a parallel way, Derrida associates Genet's signature (the name of a flower, the broom flower) with the operation of a cut: "The flower is cuttable-culpable [*coupable*]. It is cut, castrated, guillotined" (p. 20b). Indeed Genet in his texts compares criminals with flowers: both are *coupable*, cuttable and culpable. It is in this cut that Derrida locates Genet's style, the power of Genet's discourse: "To be decapitated is to appear—banded, erect: like . . . the phallus, the rectile stem—the style—of a flower" (p. 21b). Moreover, Derrida's own text, written between two other texts, between Hegel and Genet, becomes an example of the self-castration by which the author establishes his power: "Why make a knife [*couteau*] pass between two texts? . . . to cut up [*découper*], to dominate. You are no longer allowed to know where the head of this discourse is, or where the body is, the neck [*cou*] is dissimulated. . . . If I write two texts at once, you won't be able to castrate me. If I delinearize, I erect" (pp. 64–65b, trans. modified). In this sense, a simulacrum of castration is the ruse of writing by which the text establishes its authority.

In spite of the very different perspectives, crime as analyzed by Lacan and writing as analyzed by Derrida (both in terms of his own writing and in more general terms as part of the aesthetic field defined by Kant's beautiful) are thus both structured by a cut. Through a criminal mutilation, the paranoid symbolically strikes himself, realizing an unconscious desire for self-punishment in such a way that the crime functions as the simulation of a cure. In a similar way, the author establishes the "presence" and power of his text through a symbolic self-castration that functions as a simulacrum of castration and, as such, can ward off castration. Both the concept of self-punishment and of symbolic self-castration rely on a "cut"—at the heart of the ego or of the text—that structures the psychoanalytic undermining of the rational self as well as the contemporary rethinking of the operations of reading and writing. The interest of *L'amante anglaise* is that it points to the relation between the Lacanian rethinking of subjectivity and the Derridean rethinking of writing by showing that the "cut" (de)structuring the body and the "cut" (de)structuring discourse function in a similar way. In other words, in spite of the sharp internal differences and conflicts between Lacan and Derrida, *L'amante anglaise* allows us to construct a point of intersection. *Glas* and the Papin sisters meet in Genet's *Maids*, one of whom is named Claire, like the main character of *L'amante anglaise*.[9] Furthermore, by constructing an analogy between the dismembered and fragmented body and the dismembered and fragmented discourse, *L'amante anglaise* suggests that both subjectivity and discursive communication are constituted in the space of a similar cut.

Indeed, Claire's discourse within the diegesis as well as the narrative structure itself are constituted by the function of a "cut." Not only has Claire cut off her cousin's head, but she has also hidden it, and she has withheld the name of its location from her discursive reconstruction of the crime. Withholding the name of this site thus functions on a textual level as a "decapitation" operated on the body of the text. In this second decapitation the absence of the head is at the same time the enabling factor of Claire's discourse and what makes her confession incomplete, mutilated by her refusal to reveal the missing clue. Moreover, Claire's discourse remains fragmented because of its own seriality: "I jump from one topic to another. Don't think that I don't know when it happens" (p. 178). Claire's discourse is described as being "without head or tail to it [*sans queue ni tête*]" (p. 55). Figuratively speaking, Claire's discourse, jumping from one subject to another without articulations, is thus a dismembered discourse: rhetorically Claire's discourse *is* a body, although a disarticulated one. However, Claire also tells the interviewer: "I am talking to you because you know nothing and you want to *learn everything*" (p. 180). Although she does not tell everything and although her discourse remains fragmented, Claire talks so as to satisfy the investigator's desire to learn *everything*. "To learn everything" for Claire in that context therefore does not mean revealing the missing clue, which would become the element in terms of which all the other clues would be ordered and hierarchized. Rather, in order to satisfy the investigator's desire to learn *everything*, Claire's discourse entails fragmentation and segmentation (just as we have seen that her desire for an enclosed totality was paradoxically enacted in her acts of cutting and fragmenting). Moreover, the narrative itself, in its very structure, is cut up into three different sections, three separate interviews, three different and disconnected versions of the same event. Each of those versions strives for an interpretation or explanation of the crime that would give a totalizing version of the event, but each remains in fact partial, and explicitly points to its incompleteness. When Pierre asks the interviewer if what he is telling him leads him toward an explanation of Claire's crime, the interviewer answers: "Toward several explanations, different from those that had come to my mind before listening to you. But I am not allowed to select one in the book in progress" (p. 99).

The fragmentation of the textual body in *L'amante anglaise* is therefore not simply a question of form, it is not the mere fact of writing or speaking in fragments, it does not simply substitute incompletion for totality. Fragmentation both calls for and resists totalization. The fragment calls for an "everything" (the total reconstruction of the body, the investigator's desire to learn everything, the totalizing version of the crime), but it is not self-sufficient, and it cannot be combined with the other fragments to form a self-sufficient whole. In this sense the textual fragmentation of *L'amante anglaise* functions like Blanchot's "fragmentary": "The fragment is not self-sufficient. . . . But it cannot be arranged with the other fragments to form a complete thought."[10] Indeed, the privileged mode for the fragmentary is the interrogative mode in which unanswered and unanswerable questions subvert the certainty of inquiry, opposing the logical and dialectical categories of affirmation and negation through the openness of an endless questioning. The interrogative mode is central to *L'amante anglaise*. The interviewer asks questions to Claire, and both of them also question the questions:

[Investigator:] You don't know why you killed her?
[Claire:] I wouldn't say that.
[Investigator:] What would you say?
[Claire:] It depends on the question I am asked.
[Investigator:] Nobody ever asked you the right question about this crime?
[Claire:] No. I tell you the truth. If someone had asked me the right question, I
     would have known what to answer. But this question, I cannot find it either.
     (p. 165)

The "right question" remains unanswered and unanswerable, thus preventing both the interviewer and the reader from reaching any definitive
and certain conclusion in the inquiry. Moreover, this "right question" is
unasked and even unaskable. When asked to give an example of what a
"right question" would be, Claire describes how she used to listen to her
friend, Alfonso, and her husband, Pierre, behind the door and how this
silent and hidden listening led to a better understanding. A relation of association by contiguity is thus established between the nature of a "right
question" (as the investigator asks for an example of such a "right question") and a silent listening behind doors, outside the presence of the speak-
ers. Both point to silence, to an ineffable element present in discourse,
"present" although unarticulated and unarticulable. The "right question"
remains unasked, unaskable, and the text ends with Claire's imperative address, an order to listen: "If I were you I would listen. Listen to me" (p.
194). If, in Blanchot's terms, "fragmentary speech represents a provocation
of language" (L'entretien, p. 232), the fragmentary aspect of L'amante anglaise represents a "provocation of language" inasmuch as it subverts the
categories of affirmation and negation, questions the possibility of questioning, and so "gives voice" to the "presence" of a silence in discourse and
to the necessity of a silent listening.

   Like Claire's criminal fragmentation, fragmentary writing functions at
the same time as self-punishment and "cure." Within the diegesis, writing
is present in the form of inscriptions made by Claire on the fragmented
body and on the wall of the cellar where she committed the crime. The
words inscribed on the body and on the walls are a proper name, "Alfonso," and a place name, "Cahors." Such inscriptions expose a disjunction, a "cut," between name and referent since they do not conform to the
conventional possibilities encoded in the inscription of a name on an object
(to suggest belonging; or to indicate destination, as on a package; or to
mark the source of production of goods). The disjunction between name
and referent is further complicated by the fact that the fragmented body
whose parts bear these nominal inscriptions is sent in all directions, with

no specific destination. Claire's writing on the fragmented body is an act of self-punishment since by "signing" the mutilated body she makes it possible for the police to identify her as the murderess. At the same time her writing functions as a curative substitute for an impossible appeal or call. When Claire is asked to account for the inscription of Alfonso's name on the cellar wall, she says: "Maybe I wanted to call for help? . . . I've written before to call for help when I knew at the same time that it wasn't any good" (p. 178). Writing becomes a substitute for an unarticulable cry, a call for help, an appeal.

Not only on the diegetic level is writing presented as having the function of both a "cut" and a cure. On the level of the global narrative structure in its fictive auto-generation writing is also presented as this double function of cut and cure. Indeed, at the beginning of the text the narrative is said to be constituted by three interviews conducted by the investigator, three interviews that have been recorded before being compiled into the book such as we read it. The first interview, of Robert, the bartender, is structurally the most complicated of the three since during it one tape recorder recorded the interview and at the same time another tape recorder was playing back the tape of an already recorded conversation. The latter tape, which had been made on the evening when Claire was arrested, was a recording of everything that had been said in the café where the arrest took place that evening and where Robert was working. The interviewer, by playing back this first tape during the interview, thereby recorded it again on the second tape, along with Robert's comments:

[Investigator:] Everything that is said here is recorded. . . . I have here a copy of the recording that was made in the café that evening [when Claire was arrested] without your knowledge. This tape *faithfully repeats* what was said in the café that evening but it *just repeats* the words *blindly*, opaquely. So, it is up to you to set *the book in motion*. And when what you say has given that evening its real depths and dimensions we can let the tape *recite what it remembers* and the reader can take your place.
[Robert:] How about the difference between what I know and what I say, what will you do about that?
[Investigator:] That's the part of the book that the reader has to supply for himself.
  (pp. 9–10, my emphases)

A number of elements construct a semantic field associating the tape with a human body rather than with a material object, a product of technology: the "faithfulness" of the tape (it "faithfully repeats"), its ability to "repeat," "recite," and "remember" contribute to constructing the tape as a body. Indeed, a tape is the recording of a body's voice. However, as a tape-recorded voice it is a voice speaking without a body, a voice detached from the body that constituted its source, a disembodied voice: a tape-recorded voice can thus be seen to figure a disjunction, a cut, between voice and body. Such a cut is rhetorically figured, in the above-quoted passage at the beginning of the investigator's first interview, by the description of the tape as a *mutilated* body: the tape is blind. Although the tape/body is faithful to the conversations that took place in the café, it is incomplete because it could only record what was said and not what remained unsaid, what was said but not what was seen. Outside its context and reference, the body/tape is said to be a voice (it "repeats" and "recites") and a memory ("it remembers") but without eyes ("it just repeats . . . blindly"). To "heal" the "mutilation" of this first tape the interviewer therefore introduces a second machine, which will register both the previously recorded dialogue and Robert's commentary (Robert was there, he saw, he was the seeing eye), that is, both the text and its interpretation. And the book as a whole—which consists of the recording of the three interviews, Robert's, Pierre's, and Claire's—presents itself as an attempt to make up for the limitations of the first tape, an attempt to "cure" the blindness of the disembodied voice of the tape recorder. Thus "cured," the book/body will be able to walk and move ("the book in motion"), whereas the static (because blind) tape/voice could only recite. The interviewer's attempt to produce a total-izing account of the crime is thus rhetorically articulated as an attempt to produce a "whole" body—a body that not only speaks but also moves and sees.

However, the second tape, which records everything (both the first tape and Robert's comments about it), will fail to give a total account of the crime just as the first tape did, since it will still require a reader to supple-ment it. The second tape (and consequently the whole book also) remains an inevitably fragmented account, a mutilated body. And the place of the reader ("the part of the book that the reader has to supply for himself") is precisely in the space between what is known and what is said ("the dif-ference between what I know and what I say"), a space between what is not recorded and what is recorded, a space between what is seen and what is said, a space between the eye and the voice, a space that figures both Claire's discursive strategy and the fictional narrative project of the inves-tigator, who seeks to measure and eventually close this indefinable dis-tance. In fact, the place of the reader *is* Robert's place ("when what you say has given that evening its real depths . . . *the reader can take your place*"): since Robert's role is to enable the blind and static first tape to become a book/body that can move, the fact that the reader will have to take Robert's place suggests that the reader's relation to the second tape is the same as Robert's relation to the first tape. Indeed, during this first interview, Robert's comments, which punctuate the first tape's account and supply a frame for the taped event, install the written text in an analogical relation to the disembodied and blind voice of the first tape recorder. Robert's comments may "set the [body of the] book in motion," but this moving body is just as mutilated as the first tape-recorded voice that speaks not from the body of its origin but from elsewhere since his comments are caught in a peculiar relationship to their own moment of enunciation. In the absence of citational marks, the two enunciations begin to collapse temporal distance and to confuse the referents and the utterances. The blurring of the two moments of enunciation makes it difficult to identify where the voice comes from, whether it is from the blind and disembodied tape recorder or from the eyewitness. The effect of this slippage is thus to render problematic the status of the *récit*, and to call into question the possibility of bridging the gap between the voice and the eye, hence the possibility of reunifying the body. Robert's comments thus repeat and double the tension, the split, the cut between body and voice, and between eye and voice figured by the first tape-recorded voice—a cut that the book that is set in motion "embodies."

The interest of *L'amante anglaise* is that it points to an intersection— a "cut" not in the sense of a separation or a fragmentation but in the second sense of the "recoupement"—between a psychoanalytic rethinking of the conception of the self and a rethinking of the functioning of discourse. Such an intersection consists in the function of what I have called the "cut"—a rhetoric of mutilation—which structures both subjectivity and language, writing and the body. The recurrence of images of fragmented bodies in Duras's texts and her interest in crime can be read in terms of a "deconstruction" of the concept of the stable self and in terms of a "deconstruction" of the structure of discourse. Both are marked by the function of the "cut" that structures the concept of self-punishment as well as that of symbolic castration. In *L'amante anglaise* this double deconstruction operates on the structure of discourse, as well as on the figure of the body, establishing an analogy between the forces that structure subjectivity and the forces that organize the text itself.

Writing (as) the Perverse Body in Friedrich Schlegel's *Lucinde*

Jeffrey S. Librett

I

*L*acan: "The written is not at all on the same register, or of the same genre [tobacco: *tabac*], if you will allow me this expression, as the signifier."[1] Friedrich Schlegel: "The doctrine of the spirit and the letter is so interesting because, among other things, it also puts philosophy in touch with philology" (*Athenaeum Fragments*, 93; 29, 179).[2]

To approach the question of the writing of perversity in *Lucinde*, it is perhaps "useful" to begin with the famous Schlegelian fragment, "It is just as deadly to the spirit [*Geist*] to have a system as to have none. Spirit will therefore apparently have to resolve itself [*sich . . . entschließen müssen*] to combining both [*beides zu verbinden*] (*Athenaeum Fragments*, 53; 24, 173). Despite the fact that he does not thematize the letter (or writing) explicitly, Schlegel can be seen as determining its status here insofar as he is determining in a quasi-dialectical manner what it is that kills spirit.[3] If, according to Saint Paul, the letter kills while the spirit gives life, then what kills the spirit here, too, is evidently *writing*, which, bizarrely, imposes at once systematization (the fixation of a dead form) and desystematization (the multiplicity and dispersion that inevitably result from the struggle over an apparently inaccessible meaning the letter seems to hide). Because, according to Schlegel here, the spirit is always killed by the letter in these two ways at once, its life is to be understood as both systematicity and nonsystematicity and neither. It follows that as both systematicity and nonsystematicity, spirit, in its life, is both the other of writing and writing itself. The life of the spirit is (not) the life of writing. This determination of the relation between spirit and letter is not dialectical but only quasi-dialectical. In the first place, although the spirit must "resolve itself" to "combining" systematicity and nonsystematicity, the fragment does not posit that this resolution can be carried out, but only that it is necessary if the "life" of spirit is to be preserved. Furthermore, Schlegel's fragment does not determine whether this combination would occur in the name of systematicity (identity) or of nonsystematicity (difference), whereas, in a dialectical *Aufhebung* of the Hegelian variety, the relation between identity and difference is ultimately determined as identity. *Verbindung*, which carries the connotation of an external connection or linkage, is not yet *Aufhebung*, and we therefore have reason—a reason to which Hegel's well-known execration of Schlegel lends support—to suspect that both spirit and writing here are being determined as neither the identity nor the difference between identity and difference.[4]

Now, to associate system and nonsystem through their common deadliness to spirit, and further to associate both with writing through the same common deadliness, might strike one as precipitate. Consideration of two more fragments may suffice to put one's mind as it were to rest.[5] "In the ancients one sees the completed letter of all poetry: in the moderns one senses [or divines—*ahnet*] its developing spirit [*den werdenden Geist*]" (*Critical Fragments*, 93; 11, 158). Here the system or structural paradigm of ancient poetry is opposed to the nonsystem or becoming of modern poetry; system is letter, becoming is spirit. But this opposition is implicitly overturned and displaced when Schlegel writes in another fragment: "Up to now everyone has managed to find in the Ancients what he needed or desired, above all himself," (*Athenaeum Fragments*, 151; 37, 189). When modernity as spirit finds antiquity to be letter, it is finding *itself* as what it lacks, spirit as letter, as the literal disruption of the opposition between spirit and letter.[6]

But *when* does modernity discover itself in the ancients as what it lacks? It is of some importance to determine the temporal structure of this discovery in order to clarify that Schlegel's remarks on the ancients and moderns exceed the status of "merely" philologico-poetical polemics specific to his historical context, and to determine more precisely the double life and double death of the literal spirit. For Schlegel, the temporality of all historical reading (of any supposedly simple past) is the temporality of the future anterior: "The historian is a prophet facing backwards" (*Athenaeum Fragments*, 80; 27, 176). This will have applied to any reading not only of the past but of the present as well. For in the following, Schlegel declares that knowledge of the present is as miraculous as knowledge of the future: "One always gets a strange, rather suspicious feeling when one thinks one knows that such and such is going to be the case [*wird so sein*].

And yet it is every bit as strange that we should be able to know that such and such is as it is [ist so]—which no one ever notices because it happens all the time [weil es immer geschicht]" (Athenaeum Fragments, 218; 47, 199). What Schlegel thereby will have implied is that it so happens that knowledge as presencing or presentation is necessarily and ceaselessly also performative. What unites the phrases "will be" and "is" into their "will have been" is the "is" of the "it is the case that . . . ," which accompanies each like an Ich. This "is" is an "is" that is essentially a precipitate happening, a Geschehen, and that "is" thus delayed in its reflexive recuperation as knowledge, as knowledge of what then and there "will have been." The duplicity, or Verwirrung, of constatation and performance, knowledge and its occurrence, ensures that the present will always have been the delaying of its past, will always have been too present and therefore not present enough to coincide with itself. No one, Schlegel says, notices that knowledge of the present is as unlikely as prophecy because knowledge of the present occurs, but the fact that knowledge is occurrence is precisely what makes it only prophecy. Moreover, because knowledge is occurrence, because knowledge is such an incredibly happening thing, it becomes precisely *impossible* to notice, to know, here and now, just how happening and promising knowledge is. Finally, since this impossibility applies also to Schlegel's knowledge of its necessity, his knowledge too promises never to have ceased coming and coming our way.[7]

Having "clarified" thus far the structure of the becoming, the letter of the spirit of the encounter between spirit and letter, we still don't know what it might mean that the letter should kill the spirit. What, indeed, is "life"? In the Kantian context of Schlegel's writings, it is "organization" as the self-purposiveness of a supersensuous will posited by reflexive judgment in its objective, that is, teleological, mode.[8] In Schlegel, however, we've seen that the life of spirit is the death of spirit (as the other of writing). Consequently, for Schlegel, organization will no longer constitute the exclusively privileged mode of spirituality, the only "life" of spirit. Death, disorganization, and the letter will have to play some role in spirit as well. Hence, in another one of Schlegel's fragments, spirit takes three essential forms, which one can think of as the disorganized (or "dead"), the anorganic (or "living-dying"), and the organized (or "living"): "The understanding is mechanical spirit, wit is chemical spirit, genius is organic spirit" (Athenaeum Fragments, 366; 75, 322). In other words, the equation of spirit with life—and with the organic body—has given way here to the distribution of spirit across life, death, and whatever might be found between the two, the witticism of their mediation, the joke (on us) that yokes them together. *Wit* would then be the space of a spiritual inscription or an inscribed spirituality that is no longer Pauline or simply logocentric.[9] The model of wit is not the organic body, in which parts and whole create each other simultaneously (as the metaphorical totalization of synecdoche), nor is it pure disembodiment or mechanical inanimation (as radical metonymy), but the organic body supplemented by its disintegration, marked by the law of its nontotality, something very much like the body of the letter in the Lacanian sense[10] as dispersion of erogenous zones, lacking, as Freud put it, any comprehension, any teleological and totalizing *Zusammenfassung*.[11] The body of this writing would be perverse in the sense of polymorphous perversity as reread by Lacan in terms of the *corps morcelé*, the fragmented body, and not in the sense of a particular fixation that would function as a stable replacement of the genital telos that Freud, in contrast to Lacan, still ambivalently posits as the norm.[12] This writing body is the "model" of wit, then, only as the "model" of a dimension of experience that it is the function of "modeling" in all senses (perversely) to deny.

II

How does this thought of the letter—if we can still call it a "thought" of the letter—enter into the texture of Schlegel's fantastic and, in its day, scandalous[13] erotic novel, *Lucinde*? First of all, the novel, whose subtitle is *Confessions of a Clumsy One*,[14] comprises thirteen short chapters, narrated from various perspectives, the seventh and central of which is called "Apprenticeship of Masculinity." Schlegel has turned Goethe's *Wilhelm Meister's Apprenticeship*, the central chapter of which was entitled "Confessions of a Beautiful Soul," inside out, denying (and thereby also confirming) its law while perverting its sense. In so doing, he also ironically positions *becoming*—apprenticeship—at the center, and as an interruption, of *structure*—since the chapters surrounding Chapter 7 concern the narrator's *present* love. In other words, he places spirit at the center of its (dis)articulating letter, places masculinity at the center of the femininity that one can regard the entire novel as attempting (i.e., hoping against hope) to (re)present, since its title, *Lucinde*, names the narrator's beloved. However, because the subtitle, which refers to the narrator's (masculine-spiritual) subjectivity through the notion of confession, is a double of the title, which refers to the (feminine-lettered) object of the narrator's love, the difference between letter and spirit, feminine and masculine, is inscribed here into the border of the feminine letter itself. The difference *between* the central and the peripheral is a difference *within* the peripheral;

the relation between identity (spirit) and difference (letter) is "mastered" or "contained" in the differentiality of writing.

I shall now turn to three passages out of many in which writing is thematized as such in the novel. These passages will not, however, have provided "examples" of the writing of the perverse as a concretion illustrates an abstraction, for the wit they will have "illustrated" is neither a concretion nor an abstraction but the in-operation of illustration: each passage will have fixed the polymorphous as recalcitrant to fixation.

At the outset of the novel, in his letter to Lucinde, Julius first posits an idyllic, quasi-onanistic vision, a vision of overcoming the feeling that people are "ashen-gray figures devoid of movement"[15] and then reflects[16] upon this vision, admitting that it was only a dream. This reflexion takes the reader from an external scene to an internal space, from the image of Julius outside in a meadow to the knowledge that he is standing inside by the window, from fantasy to reality. "It was an illusion, my dear friend, all an illusion, except that I was standing at the window doing nothing and that now I am sitting here and doing something, which is itself little more or indeed even somewhat less than doing nothing" (p. 8). Writing to Lucinde, Julius confesses or boasts that he is doing either just more or just less than nothing. In the medium of reflexion, perceptual, imaginative positing is distinguished from writing in terms of a distinction between nothing and almost nothing, between zero action and infinitesimal, in particular *negatively* infinitesimal, action. The nonpurposiveness and passivity of which Schlegel's novel elsewhere sings the post-Enlightenment praises here receives a peculiar twist. Assuming that doing nothing is pure auto-affection—self-positing and self-negation in mutually canceling balance (Fichte)—doing *less* than nothing would be exceeding this balance in the direction of self-negation, self-mutilation perhaps; and writing is figured here as this *less* than nothing. The self-supporting, self-surrounding phallus of idly sovereign fantasy is here dispersed into the letters Julius is writing as into the other *jouissance* that can neither ground nor be grounded by the signifier of doing nothing or nothing doing.

III

After a brief series of rather complicated mediating steps, Julius replaces the indeterminate interruption of this quasi-autoerotic interruption with a text in which he describes for Lucinde a game they play in order to cool the heat of their mutual presence. In this game, the not-quite-one of the scene we have just considered will be transformed into not-quite-two. The lovers' mutual presence, Julius writes, is "as it were too present," so present in fact that no separation could ever separate them more thoroughly than it evidently manages to do. "How could distance distance us [*uns die Entfernung entfernen*], since presence is for us as it were too present [*da uns die Gegenwart selbst gleichsam zu gegenwärtig ist*]?" (p. 12). If the mutual presence of these lovers is intolerably extreme, the reason why is given in the German word for presence, *Gegen-wart*, which means literally "waiting across from" or "waiting against." If presence is waiting across from, then presence is shot through with the distance of an absence. When brought into association with the fragments we have thus far considered, this can mean that the systematic synchronicity of the (feminine) letter is permeated by the asystematic diachronicity of the (masculine) spirit: the presence of death is filled with the absence of life. In other words, the excessive presence Julius refers to here is an excessive absence: presence is too much presence because it is not presence enough to exclude the presence of the absence of the sexual relation.

In order to deny this absence, the lovers play the "most witty and most beautiful" game of competing to see who can imitate the gender identity, and thus the sex, of the other more successfully. But there will be no *Aufhebung* here, no installation of a symbolic third stabilizing the play of imaginary doubling. Schlegel's description of this mimetic contest concludes: "I see here a wondrous allegory—rich in sense and full of meaning—of the completion of the masculine and feminine to full, whole humanity. There lies much therein, and what lies therein will certainly not stand up as quickly as I when I lie beneath you (in defeat) [*Es liegt viel darin, und was darin liegt, steht gewiß nicht so schnell auf wie ich, wenn ich dir unterliege*]" (p. 13). The play of substitutive representation becomes itself a substitution—an allegorical form—for a present spirit or meaning, the meaning of the unity of masculine and feminine, which does not disengage itself punctually from this substitute. What does separate itself—and separates itself from itself—is the phallus of Julius that stands up out of his relatively failed impersonation of the feminine in response to Lucinde's more successful impersonation of the masculine. Phallic sexuality, as the linear ascent toward the feminine, is here figured as the—hysterical—flight of the phallus or the phallus-identified male from the feminine-masculine figure (Lucinde) toward which and from which it flees.[17] The tale of the erection of the organ of phallic writing doubles as the tale of the turning-tail of the supposed possessor of that supposed organ. The turning-tail and the doubling itself entail in turn a feminization of the male post or the post-male, which in a sense confirms the denial of sexual difference, but in an ironic mode. For it is as if what Schlegel is implying were: yes, there is a sexual relation—only not for us, since (a) the doubled standing-up is always *either* desire *or* terror, is undecidable rather than the (Hegelian) experience of the synthesis of their difference; and (b) the phallicized feminine principle here conquers only to fail to be recognized (or to enter into the symbolic order) in its nonphallic specificity.

IV

This allegory of the "mastery" of feminine *jouissance* by the phallic signifier as the flight, de-position, or strewing of the phallic signifier into its own inscriptive character is repeated in any number of ways throughout Schlegel's novel. I shall provide one further example here. In the chapter entitled "Allegory of Insolence" ("Allegorie der Frechheit"), there is an inversion similar to those we've seen thus far. Although it would lead me too far afield to summarize the plot of this allegory here, suffice it to say that personified *Frechheit*, or insolence, attacks the face (or prosopopoeia) of "die schöne Seele" and says: "That is just a mask. . . . You're not the beautiful soul [*die schöne Seele*], but at most false modesty, often even coquetry" (p. 18). The Schillerian organic ideal of a harmonious agreement between inclination and duty is thus defaced and revealed to hide a fundamental incompatibility.[18]

The scene on which I want to focus, however, repeats this gesture specifically in terms of the spirit and the letter. It occurs when Wit has first appeared personified outside of the narrator, then appeared inside his mind as a Dionysian vision, and then disappeared altogether. At this juncture, which is the juncture as *différance* of the border between inside and outside, Wit is replaced by the hallucination of a voice telling the narrator, "Time is there [or it is time], the inner essence of the divinity can be revealed and presented" (p. 20). This voice demands that the narrator announce the revelation of absolute spirit as the being-there of time. But the narrator finds himself suddenly incapable of speech or song and proceeds to attribute this incapacity to the absence of the prejudices (*Vorurteile*) that would evidently condition any possible voicing of temporality. In response to the insight this attribution constitutes, he hears a voice that tells him *to write* instead of speaking or singing, and that insists that the only knowledge of the absolute is relative, that the only knowledge of the immediate is mediate:

You must not wish to communicate the immortal fire in its pure raw state. . . . Cultivate, invent, alter, and maintain the world and its eternal forms in the continuous alteration of new divisions and marriages. Conceal and bind the spirit in the letter. The genuine letter is all-powerful, the authentic magic wand. The irresistible arbitrariness [*die unwiderstehliche Willkür*] of the high magician ["the magician" is feminine—*Zauberin*], fantasy, touches with the letter alone the sublime chaos of nature in its fullness, and calls into the light the infinite word, which is the image and mirror of divine spirit, and which mortals name the universe. (p. 20)

This passage will have been much less deludedly idealistic than it might seem. Fantasy, Schlegel writes, in its irresistible arbitrariness, touches nature by means of the letter and thus indeed "calls" the logos, the universe, into the light. The "call" is here, however, evidently pre-verbal, since it calls the instance of voice and logic to join with the instance of light, opens the possibility of the sound light of logic while closing off the possibility of its punctual presentation. The call anticipates the call; it is, originally, the recall of the letter. To translate the functioning of the letter here into Kantian terms, the a priori imagination touches the sensuous manifold by means of the letter and thus makes possible a world of experience. The letter is, it seems, a kind of schema, but here not half image, half concept, as in Kant, but rather half image, half disintegration of the image. (Perhaps the Kantian concept too has to be understood as a disintegration of the image—but this is another story.) Like the schema, it (dis)figures time.

Not only is the (calling of the) letter here accompanied by its delay, but it is—despite its characterization as "magic wand"—not some sort of absolute phallus, not the simultaneous instrument and telos of a neurotic faith. For it is not an instrument or tool with which one could identify in the process of its manipulation. Being all-powerful, it must exceed any practical mastery. Nor, being omnipotent, can it be mastered through knowledge. It is no more susceptible of epistemological than of practical mastery by a finite subject.

If the letter does not allow us to "know" the spirit (i.e., itself as other) through practical-theoretical copulation, as the "authentic magic wand" it nonetheless evidently does have the power to conjure something like promising appearances. Preceding as it does the logos, then, the letter constitutes a kind of pre-phallic, pre-logical phallogocenter, the phallus of the mother perhaps, a fetish, but as always also a-systematic, a fetish somewhere *between* feminine or *l'autre jouissance* and the phallicization of "*la Femme*." Magic here is a magic beyond and not prior to enlightenment, the order it conjures that of a non-understanding that proceeds upon and retroactively prevents understanding. The letter is the medium of the signifier, the magic wound by means of which the law imposes itself, but a wound that precedes and prevents the appearance of the law it instantiates.[19] Like an erogenous zone, it perversely and incessantly denies the law it supplements,[20] for example the law that would situate the position of such a zone in a determinate place on the body, or the law that would situate the position of the body within a determinate spatiotemporal zone.

With this inscription of the voice of writing, Schlegel's allegory of the internalization of the externalization of wit breaks off and then resumes with further gestures of argumentative entailment that I shall not consider here. The chapter concludes with Julius's attempt to excuse his excesses by claiming that he is merely concerned to confirm the objectivity, or the tendency toward objectivity, of his love, a confirmation that he says can be accomplished only by "die Magie der Schrift" (p. 24), the magic of writing.[21] The magic of writing, of its silent traces ("stillen Zügen," p. 25), is not so much what would realize as a unified subject-object either the overcoming of the sexual difference or any other ideal, but what would contain precisely the uncontainability of either subject or object, what would retain nonretention, forgetfulness, and loss as the figures of a subjectless and insubstantial desire. Writing sends thus only the unsent (*das Ungeschickte*). If anything sent arrives, what is actually sent, the unsent, fails to arrive. The one for whom this unsent can arrive is consequently only one who is not yet or no longer there. Accordingly, Julius clarifies at this point that he is writing neither for his contemporaries nor for posterity, but for "die Vorwelt" (p. 25), for the former world, pre-world, or not-yet world of the dead. The reader is addressed then by this text as the dead reader, but also as the one who, preceding the text, must read (as a spirit) its not yet and write down (as a letter) its already no longer. "Wit is an explosion of bound spirit" (*Critical Fragments*, 90; 11, 158). Before this text, one reads the graceless beginnings of an endlessly exploded romance.

American Indian Lives and Others' Selves:

The Invention of Indian Selves in Autobiography

Greg Sarris

*O*ne day a little over a year ago I found myself sitting in Mabel
McKay's kitchen, again trying to record the stories of her life so
that I might have them fixed on tape and later be able to organize them
into a meaningful narrative, that is, a narrative accessible to both Indian
and non-Indian audiences.[1] So many people wanted to know about this
famous Pomo basketweaver and medicine woman. What was becoming
increasingly clear that day was that my idea of Mabel's life as she understood it and wanted it understood was very different from her idea. Not
only did she undermine the chronological imperative and other conventions associated with autobiography, but she implicated me as a listener in
whatever she was saying. She did not present her life as a relic, as an independent text, and did not want me to write it as such. Having known
her most of my life, I should have figured this much. Still, I tried to make
sense of her, to find a theme, a center to organize a life story around.

It so happened that on this day my two aunts, Violet and Anita, were
visiting Mabel also. They were busy preparing a meal as I sat asking Mabel
questions at the kitchen table.

"Here, Greg," Violet said. She plunked three potatoes on the table and
handed me a small, sharp knife. "Make yourself useful."

Mabel was talking about a man she had known. I needed to listen carefully. I felt the man played a significant role in the early part of Mabel's life,
a role I had to know more about if I was ever going to get her autobiography—her book—off the ground. But to appease Violet I set down my
pen and paper and began peeling one of the potatoes. Violet sat across from

me with three potatoes of her own. I felt self-conscious; usually I did not help prepare food. I volunteered with the dishes afterwards, and the women could count on me for yardwork and trips to the grocery store. Alone, in my own home, I cooked, but here with Mabel and with relatives I did not. Violet upset routine. She was a tease of course, and I suspected some antic.

Her first potato looked smooth as an egg. The objective, I thought: get the potatoes smooth, perfectly rounded. I could tell she was watching me.

Anita came to the table and began to work on potatoes also. The conversation turned to gossip, centering on a local man's wife who was white. In these conversations I am always reminded of my mother, who was white. I didn't want to hear this talk; I wanted to hear Mabel talk again, but I said nothing.

Anita's potatoes were smooth and egglike also. She held the potato and knife in front of her as she might a basket and awl, as if she were weaving. I hardly had her grace, but to my satisfaction my potatoes were smooth; I'd even gone back and planed any rough edges. And I was finished before Violet.

I set my knife down and leaned back in my chair, just for a moment, just so Violet could see I was finished. But she was not moving: her face was tight, swollen, blushed with color, her eyes set on her pile of peelings where she held her knife, pointing. The peelings, something I hadn't thought of. . . . Her peelings were paper thin, shards of skin, thinner than carrot peelings, almost transparent. I felt the thick, coarse lumps under my hand. I lifted my eyes just in time to catch Violet hiss. "Just like a white man," she managed to say, exploding with laughter. "So wasteful!"

"See," Mabel said, leaning into the tape recorder, which I forgot to shut off, "it ain't always what you think. My life is like that."

It is no secret that American Indian autobiographies are collaborative endeavors. Here I am distinguishing Indian autobiographies from autobiographies by Indians. In the former, which I will discuss in this paper, an editor, usually non-Indian, records and transcribes what was given orally by the Indian subject. Autobiographies by Indians, on the other hand, are written by the Indian subjects themselves. (Most critics would argue that autobiographies by Indians are bicultural texts in that the Indian writers use in varying degrees non-Indian modes of presentation.) Arnold Krupat states, "the principle constituting the Indian autobiography as a genre [is] that of *original bicultural composition*."[2] This principle not only provides the key to the Indian autobiography's discursive type, but "provides as well the key to its discursive function, its purposive dimension as an act of power and will. [It is the] ground on which two cultures meet . . . the textual equivalent of the frontier" (*For Those*, p. 31). Yet seldom is the story of that meeting apparent or revealed in the text; seldom is the kind of interaction I experience with Mabel and my family in my attempts to write Mabel's story exposed for the reader.

Eighty-three percent of the more than six hundred published Indian texts that are autobiographical are Indian autobiographies; 43 percent of these were collected and edited by anthropologists, the other 40 percent by Anglos from many other walks of life.[3] While there is a wide spectrum of editorial strategies for dealing with point of view, the Absent Editor strategy "is both the most venerable and the most widespread editorial strategy," according to David Brumble (*Autobiography*, p. 75). The Absent Editor, as opposed to the more self-conscious editor at the other end of the spectrum, may edit and present the narrative "in such a way as to create the fiction that the narrative is all the Indian's own" (p. 75). As Brumble observes, "Often these editors provide introductions to the autobiographies which describe, sometimes in detail, just how they went to work. But once the autobiographies are underway, the fiction is that the Indians speak to us without mediation" (p. 76).

John G. Neihardt effectively positions himself as an Absent Editor in *Black Elk Speaks*, certainly the most widely known American Indian autobiography.[4] Students are often surprised to learn that the passage at the end of *Black Elk Speaks* about the death of a people's dream and Black Elk's conception of himself as "a pitiful old man who has done nothing" (p. 230) is not Black Elk's but recorder-editor John Neihardt's. They must then consider how the passage has lent the book its tragic sense and how the book might have been different without Neihardt's meddling. Nothing can be discerned from Neihardt's preface or from anything in the narrative that suggests what Neihardt added to or deleted from Black Elk's spoken words. Neihardt says in his preface only that it was his "function to translate the old man's story, not only in the factual sense—for it was not the facts that mattered most—but rather to re-create in English the mood and manner of the old man's narrative" (p. xii). Neihardt says nothing about the questions he posed or the ways Black Elk accommodated or resisted the questions; nothing about the nature of the many oral performances that constitute the text of Black Elk's words; nothing about the Indian translator and his role in the production of the text. Luckily the work of Sally McClusky, Michael Castro, and Raymond J. DeMallie helps illuminate the ways Neihardt shaped Black Elk's spoken words.[5] Black Elk's act of speaking renewed the spirit of Indian revitalization seen in the Ghost Dance Movement in the late nineteenth century. Black Elk's act of speaking renewed the struggle. Yet what Niehardt, a mystic poet, presents is a defeated hero and a transcendent vision independent of its historical and cultural context. The reader can "transcend the ordinary," just as Neihardt had intended, and like Neihardt, "lose himself in the consciousness of those essentially primitive men."[6]

The historical circumstances and interests of the dominant society and its relationship to the American Indian have determined how the Indian is to be seen and accepted into the canons of both academic and popular literatures, as Krupat and others have pointed out. These circumstances and interests certainly influence editors, for, of course, editors seldom act independently of them. The dominant picture of the American Indian in Indian biographies and autobiographies during the nineteenth century was that of the fallen culture hero. We could pity the brave and exotic Indian once he was no longer a threat. In the early part of this century, with the influence of Boasian anthropology, the Indian became a representative, a spokesperson for a fallen, pre-contact culture. More recently, interests in alternative lifestyles, native healing and religion, medicinal plants, and ecology have garnered special attention for American Indian lives. No wonder *Black Elk Speaks*, originally published in 1932 and nearly remaindered that same year, became a classic during the late 1960's and early 1970's.

And then certain popular and critically acceptable representatives of Indian selves created by non-Indian editors often establish a standard and become models for future textual representations of Indians' lives. *Black Elk Speaks* has set the mode for a store of books about Indians' lives, if not in form then certainly in subject matter and language. Even in critical works regarding Indian spirituality and literature, reference is made to "the sacred hoop" and "the tree of life." Carlos Castaneda's *Teachings of Don Juan: A Yaqui Way of Knowledge*,[7] originally a Ph.D. dissertation, not only laid the foundation for a series of succeeding books by Castaneda, but provided a model for countless other writers, most notably Lynn Andrews, who lends a feminist slant to her texts about Indians' lives and the non-Indians' quest for "Indian spiritual powers." Guy Mount's *Not for Innocent Ears* is, among other things, purportedly the autobiography of Ruby Modesto, a Desert Cahuilla medicine woman.[8] Ruby not only expounds the same beliefs as Castaneda's subject, Don Juan, a Yaqui from Mexico, but uses Don Juan's language. Both Don Juan and Ruby Modesto warn their editor/apprentice that to become a shaman a person must be "impeccable with power." I would argue that, at least textually, these editors are there.

The notion of autobiography as fiction, or interpretation, is nothing new. Roy Pascal sees autobiography as what "creates the autobiographer."[9] And Louis Renza observes: "Autobiography . . . transforms empirical facts into artifacts [and] is definable as a form of 'prose fiction.'"[10] John Paul Eakin suggests that autobiography is a reenactment in language of the development of the self. Eakin notes: "In this perspective the writing of autobiography emerges as a symbolic analogue of the initial coming together of the individual and language that marks the origin of self-awareness; both are attempts, as it were, to pronounce the name of the self."[11] In the case of most Indian autobiographies "the name of the self" is hardly the Indian's own.[12] What we have is a reenactment in writing in one language of another's oral reenactment in another language. It is an account of an account such that the Indian's self is transformed, made intelligible to a non-Indian audience. The Indian self has been invented, to some degree, not only by another self, but, of necessity, in terms of the language and culture of that other self.

Critics of American Indian autobiography continue to obscure the Indian self by either generalizing about or ignoring the Indian in the text. The Indian may be discussed in terms of popular interests, such as his or her connections to nature. More recently Indian women have fallen prey to the feminist essentialism of Paula Gunn-Allen, Gretchen Bataille, and Kathleen Sands. Bataille and Sands look at several women's autobiographies "in terms of what [the autobiographies] tell us about the reality of American Indian women's lives," without fully considering the nature of the text's production.[13] Yet such consideration might reveal whose representations of Indian women are "tell[ing] us about the reality of American Indian women's lives."[14]

Scholars who do acknowledge the bicultural nature of the text's production and attempt to explore the Indian's role and what differentiates the Indian perspective from that of the Indian non-Indian tend to identify anything unrecognizable, such as the presentation of seemingly disconnected deeds or actions, as authentic, as Indian, say, as opposed to Euro-American. Just like the scholars who do not give adequate attention to the nature of the collaborative endeavor involved in Indian autobiography, these latter scholars generalize the Indian. From what is at first unrecognizable and subsequently identified as "Indian," these scholars deduce such things as a tribal (Indian, nonliterate, unacculturated, ahistorical) sense of self, distinguishable from an individual (Euro-American, literate, cultural, historical) sense of self.

Brumble identifies "six fairly distinct kinds of preliterate autobiographical narratives"—the coup tales, the less formal and usually more detailed tales of warfare and hunting, the self-examinations, the self-vindications, the educational narratives, and the tales of the acquisition of powers (*Autobiography*, pp. 22–23)—which he claims can be seen at work in various degrees in the autobiographies. What is unfamiliar becomes characteristic of an authentic, ahistorical Other, and is used as a framing device in any encounter (reading or otherwise) with that Other. Difference is now named. The reality of the situation, what Brumble inadvertently obscures despite his stated purposes to the contrary, is that the "self" that is identifiable as Indian, and that has come to signify Indian, is Indian in contact with non-Indian.

Brumble, for instance, concludes that in *Gregorio, the Hand Trembler*, Gregorio's sense of self "was essentially tribal" (*Autobiography*, p. 101). Brumble points to the preliterate conditions at work in the text and concludes: "[in the case of Red Crow, as in the case of Gregorio,] we search in vain for any examination of his self, any self-definition, any sense that he might have been other than what he was. . . . Because the Leightons chose to work with Gregorio and his narrative as they did, we are allowed to see clearly here just how a preliterate, unacculturated, tribal man conceives of his life and what it means to tell the story of a life" (p. 111). Before Gregorio told his story to two social scientists, Alexander and Dorothea Leighton, in 1940, when he was 38 years old, he had listened while the Leightons interviewed other Navahos in his neighborhood.[15] Undoubtedly, Gregorio ordered and presented an account of his life in a way he thought appropriate given the circumstances. Seemingly disconnected deeds or actions are likely to indicate Gregorio's unease with the given genre rather than his inability to examine and define his life.

Arnold Krupat, in *For Those Who Come After*, suggests that the concept of the mode of production "forces us to go beyond any given editor's account of (or silence in regard to) how a text was made in the direction of historical reconstruction" (p. 7). He provides a list of questions that helps readers explore just how the text was made, including the question "How many workers were involved in the production of the final text, and what did each contribute to it?" (pp. 7–8). But Krupat, despite his questions that "help us go beyond any given editor's account," never considers an Indian's perspective in his historicization of the texts he examines except on the third to the last page of his essay, where he excoriates Vine Deloria, Jr., for "opting for ignorance . . . like those who prefer not to inquire" (p. 134). The Indian and any Indian perspective regarding the texts under consideration is ignored. Subsequently, Krupat, who opens his study with a quotation from Edward Said, falls prey to George Marcus and Michael M. J. Fischer's criticism of Said, "[Said, in *Orientalism*,] acknowledges no political or cultural divisions among the subject peoples he is allegedly defending. These [people] have no independent voice" (p. 2).

If non-Indian editors often invent an Indian self in terms of the editor's self and interests, then critics of these inventions continue the pattern by discussing the Indian subject in terms of the critics' interests and ideas of an Indian or simply not at all. Discourse about Indian autobiography becomes more and more about itself and less and less about the Indian who might inform the discourse. The Indian is pushed by the editor, inadvertently or not, from the ground on which two cultures meet and never brought back from the remote, invisible corners of the territory.

Of course there are nonnative editors working with native subjects who do in fact make a conscious effort to expose the joint production of a written text regarding the subjects' lives. Marjorie Shostak's *Nisa: The Life and Words of a !Kung Woman*, while not about an American Indian woman, is exemplary in that the text is presented, as James Clifford has noted, as a braided narrative moving between three registers—that of cultural science, Nisa's narrative, and Shostak's agenda as a woman concerned with women's experience.[16] Clifford observes: "the discordant allegorical registers—the book's three, never quite manageable, 'voices'—reflect a troubled, inventive moment in the history of cross-cultural representation."[17] Privileging none of its three registers, the text highlights the manner in which Shostak's purposes meet with those of Nisa and what Nisa tells as her life story. Closer to home, readers might look at *Piman Shamanism and Staying Sickness*, an ethnographic text created in various ways by everyone involved—Donald Bahr, J. Gregorio, D. I. Lopez, and A. Alvarez.[18]

Clifford reminds us not to forget "that while ethnographies [like Indian autobiographies can] cast encounters between two individuals and successfully dramatize the intersubjective, give-and-take of fieldwork and introduce a counterpoint of authoritative voices, they remain representative of dialogue" ("Allegory," p. 135). But these texts can resist the pull toward authoritative representations of others. Clifford says such resistance "depends on [the text's] ability fictionally to maintain the strangeness of the other voice and to hold in view the specific contingencies of the exchange" (p. 135).

Mabel McKay keeps things strange for me; she certainly reminds me of the specific contingencies of our exchange. She reminds me of what separates us in terms of my gender, my generation, my mixed-blood heritage, and my Ph.D. in modern thought and literature from Stanford University. As mentioned at the start of this paper, she implicates me in whatever she is saying so that *the story* is finally the story of my hearing the stories of her life. Day in and day out I am reminded of what she said to me in her kitchen that day: "It ain't always what you think."

How to Reinvent Your Body in Cameroonian Women's Writing

Frieda Ekotto

*C*ameroonian women suffer a dual colonization. To begin with, pre-colonial forms of male domination persist through economic re-lations, where Cameroonian women have always been seen as objects of exchange between males. A woman's "traditional" identity is defined by her dowry, which values her as a commodity. Simultaneously, under cap-italism, she becomes a different sort of object: commodified labor power, vulnerable to exploitation by the opportunity structures built upon wage labor. This dual struggle moves on the margins of traditional and imperi-alist economies.

For a Cameroonian woman, writing may open up a space of power within such dichotomies as tradition versus modernity, West versus non-West, theories of women versus "other" women. Although deconstruction of dichotomies is a familiar textual strategy, many of us, especially those who experience racial, class, or gender dichotomies on the side of the op-pressed are still within the power of dichotomization as an epistemological and practical weapon. For a Cameroonian woman, the practice of writing may be similarly enforced and structured by the way her possibilities in politics, theory, and literature are constituted for her by dominant dis-courses: in other words, she is told, "This is your body; this is your liter-ature," in the same way that Jean Genet was told "you are a thief" before he even knew "who he was." This ascription immediately excluded him from the language of the just, of the honest people who communicate among themselves and express the "social us" that holds them together as

NOTE: This essay was originally presented at a conference titled "Bodies Apart," held at the International Association in Philosophy and Literature at the University of California, Irvine, April 12–14, 1990.

a body. Then Genet, guilty, could only keep quiet. But at the same time, plunging into the imaginary, he constantly sought "the real" and turned against the other this language that possessed him and of which he takes possession. By escaping into the imaginary, he was able by means of the original rupture to reverse the relationship of dominator and dominated. This mechanism of reversal may "deceive" us, fascinate us, and stir us to an enjoyment by magnifying language, by magnifying its failure. For Genet it is one and the same thing: to seek failure and to be a poet.

Such an "original" construction of the body of literature is performed upon Cameroonian women in a range of acts that are "material and symbolic." The Cameroonian woman's power, like Genet's, is the power to take this construction and transform it for herself and for other women. A Cameroonian woman writer proceeds by mapping into her writing the refigurations of elements from this construction. These elements include her position as a commodity in capitalism and an object of exchange between men ("the market of women") and her exclusion from literary canons and institutions. In *Orphée d'Afric*, Werewere Liking questions the decentering of wisdom by colonial hegemony's book knowledge.

The civilizer came one day, took pity on the barbarians, he came to found a school for them. A kind of school where people learned to trace signs and to say things they did not understand. But what does it matter? These were the same signs traced in his own country, the same things that were said there. . . . Over there, one learned to think in school. Here, it was enough to recite: someone has already done the thinking for us. From the first grade, we needed a bag to carry the load of thoughts; the language notebook. . . . Everything depended on that. It was impossible to learn anything empty-handed.[1]

La brise du jour (Break of day), by Lydie Dooh-Bunya, is the first published novel by a Cameroonian woman in which a subtle analysis of devastation is offered. A victim of unshared, objectless love, the heroine, Zinnia, feels her heart break into a thousand pieces owing to acts of perfidy and the loss of those she loves. Dooh-Bunya set out to convey an everyday experience to Cameroonian men: "Zinnia suffers because of her love, but don't we all suffer because of something, especially our proud men?"[2] A dominant feature of Dooh-Bunya's text is authorial "engagement" (the text itself was enacted in what she called "théâtre rituel"). Whether she is examining the past or the present, talking about the misery and anguish of slavery, the humiliation and frustration of colonization, the shame and poverty of underdevelopment, or the utopia and deception of the "north-south division," the author always places herself on the people's side. Both Dooh-Bunya and Liking condemn all forms of domination and subservience. Both authors present social problems in their novels, not only in a global historical perspective, but also in their actuality (topicality and locality). Hence these writers are able to be stern and critical in regard to contemporary African societies by denouncing all forms of exploitation, including that of women by men.

Cameroonian women writers, such as Beyala, Dooh-Bunya, Kuoh-Moukoury, and Liking (these are among the most significant women writers from the French-speaking part of the Cameroons), are concerned with the construction or reinvention of a body of literature that will displace the reproduction of Western discourse, not only in texture and attitude but also in language and structure. As a voice for women's desires and demands, their writings read like a long list of charges and pleas, which serve as an escape from the tyranny of dominant mentalities and values. By gaining access to writing, the Cameroonian woman is to prove once again, to reformulate, represent her desire for liberation, with the awareness that in this field her direct intervention is crucial.

An aspect of domination that has been seized upon (as an "issue") is Cameroonian women's postcolonial legal status, that of being party to monogamous marriage. This legal status offers only a semblance of protection from persistent precolonial forms of male domination: the sale of women in a patriarchal network of male trading agents, who exchange women among themselves as different sorts of commodities. This new women's literary corpus has therefore denounced both the marriage of girls before the age of puberty and clitoris amputation as serious breaches of the integrity and physical fulfillment of women. Cameroonian women's writings dismantle the historical construction of their literature. Hence these new Cameroonian voices have produced a body of writings that has not yet penetrated the masses. The masses have remained numb and silent because they have served a literary purpose and repository for Western intellectuals and African elites. Against these elites, Cameroonian women writers along with other minor literary groups from Africa and elsewhere form a political community concerned to intervene in traditional culture.

Beyala's novel *C'est le soleil qui m'a brûlée* (It is the sun that burned me) is the story of Ateba. She is nineteen and lives in the Quartier Général, the most miserable neighborhood in the town of Awu, somewhere in Africa. Abandoned by her mother, a prostitute, and raised by a despotic aunt, she wonders why women accept the law, the yoke of the man, why they look for him obstinately, lending, selling, giving their bodies, their wombs, as if life could not be conceived of without a man at home.

Ateba herself will be attracted by one of these men. She will "experience" a man. And in order to discover herself, she will discover and be scorched by the suns of desire, of custom, of traditions hardened in their most oppressive aspects, the suns that dry out the desert rather than life. These experiences will make her aware that what she desires is gentleness, femininity, tenderness. And she will accomplish her entry into this new world by committing a murder as "sacred" victim à la René Girard. For it is necessary to crush violence in order for love to emerge, to kill the man in order that a new female body be born. Here the term "body" will have a different sense: the body is a power, a place, a site invested with the power of production, as in Genet's work. For Genet, to tattoo or sculpt one's body is to project oneself as an aesthetic form. A human body is a space of construction for other social and political signs. If your body is "all you have," as it is for Genet's prisoners or Beyala's women wage-laborers, then you work with it, present it, intensify its productive power. Beyala is concerned with signs as they are produced in writing and on the body, scarifications carried by texts as well as flesh. Scarifications are present in Beyala's writing in its division and spacing, particularly in the ways in which the content is divided according to the distinction between oral and written narrative.

The narrator in Beyala's work does not join the character Ateba on her daily journey, nor does she place herself at center stage. On the contrary, she stays on the border, her only function being that of making people speak, act, and react. The book's focus is not on the personal quest of a main character, but neither is it the dispassionate, cold, neutral report of relationship between the narrator and the community:

As for me the one who is recounting this story, I feel my heart penetrated with fear and my blood coagulating like curdled milk. I see the woman spreading out her hands, spitting sperm at his feet, throwing a heavy copper ashtray at his head. I can see him reeling several times in the face of the woman's repeated attacks, then crashing to the ground. I close my eyes, block my ears, I feel the apocalypse coming for all of us.[3]

The narrator is part of the community she describes, yet she is removed from it; her distance is marked by her "awareness" and also by her being a cultural reminder—a recaller of important cultural information. In this sense, the character Ateba is a vatic source: an utterer, an exclusive font of knowledge for the community.

In the struggle for the articulation of critical intervention, Beyala succeeds in using the European category of minority (which includes the marginal artist, the handicapped, the prostitute, etc.) as a smoke screen to distract those who would censor "subversive" messages in her text. Interspersed within these homages to sociological discourse, we find jewels of hope and subversion, not in cryptic or allegorical form, but rather in a flow of Eurocentric gestures that tend to disguise their harshness. By "paying" her (colonial) "dues," Beyala manages to open a space for radical thought. Her concern with social reality is accompanied by a close attention to how language functions, not so much in the creation of formal beauty as in the concealment of ideology. (This form of vigilance is particularly crucial for a Cameroonian woman writer using the language of her oppressors.)

The people's reservoir of images, stories, rhymes, and songs provides the material of Beyala's narrative as well as the forms to organize it. But at the same time that the isolated, self-conscious artist transposes the act of storytelling into the act of writing, she questions the possibility of survival of those very forms. Transferring oral speech into the conventions of writing (the "violence of the letter," as a Derridean would say) amounts in a way, to betraying it: the process might lead, in the long run, to concomitant modification of these traditional forms. Well concealed under the elegiac surface of the last page of the novel lies the violent subtext of the death of a community, a culture, a meaning. The horizon of the meaning, the dream of a transcendence, has become a solution for Ateba as a self-protective gesture, "hidden in the complex waters of women to come. I understand that there isn't anything to take anymore."[4] If the time of adventures is over, then the novelist is bound to question the silence inscribed in the gestures, considering that people in the community cannot participate directly in the act of writing.

Writing, for Beyala, may also be read in Barthes's playful spirit. Barthes asserts that literature is a liberating practice; it is a space of language, a playground of proliferating signifiers. Writing is happiness and seduction, a process permitting one to love words for their own sake, thereby producing what he calls *le plaisir du texte*. Barthes's ultimate aim is to deflate the myth of representation of reality, of nature, human or not, taken as referent, and to show that literature goes beyond mere representation. Literature is a privileged field owing to its ambiguity: it gives the appearance of having a unique meaning when in fact it has at least two levels of signification (denotative and connotative) and a multiplicity of interpretations. Literary signs refer to other signs and not to a referent. From that standpoint, literature is the domain of a certain freedom, where there is *jeu*, a play with powerful and equivocal words. Barthes calls this *jeu* "the trembling meaning," that is, a meaning that is always polyvalent. Accepting this play, stepping inside the metaphorical space of that supreme game that is language, implies the acceptance of the cleavage between the individual and his or her community. In the case of Beyala and the other Cameroonian women writers, this cleavage can be compensated for only by word, pure voice—*nommo* in Bantu and *sauti* in Swahili, meaning "voice," both indicate creative potential. This possibility is still open to a Cameroonian woman writer. Identifying with the generative power of language and returning to her community as a voice, she is bound to lose herself in this act. Only in this way, death—*writing*—can become a vital resource.

Julia Kristeva writes in *The Powers of Horror: An Essay on Abjection* that it is not "lack of cleanliness or health that causes abjection, but what disturbs identity, system, or order. What does not respect borders, positions, rules. The in-between, the ambiguous, the composite."[5] "Nausea makes me balk"[6] at the object that simply resists categorization. Therefore, "bodies apart" emerges as a category as the result of what Cameroonian women writers might consider their being marginalized, excluded, or even "minoritized" in an abusive way. Within African studies, the spaces allocated to Cameroonian women are limited to their representation as social-scientific "case studies." This space is figured in an absolute "other" time— the time of classical history and literature—which renders them speechless even as they offer innumerable enticements to scholarly study. Once Cameroonian women are confined to the well-guarded "culture garden,"[7] everything that is said about them can be labeled "different" in an absolute sense: they are African, Cameroonian (or, for that matter, Douala, Bamiléké, Basaa, etc.), and thus cannot and should not be touched by Western methodologies. Hence their resistance to classification may be inscribed as a sign that passes imperceptibly between the cracks, the lines, the margins of their writings, as the abject in Kristeva's sense.

By reinventing a new body in writing, Cameroonian women will have freed themselves from the dominant representation of women, a representation "suggested" to them by men through nostalgic praise for the traditional woman in her natural role of mother; or a poem (or a song) about this black woman's physical sensuousness, softness, and bewitching power. But it was their own male desire that men describe in such images: their desire for the eternal Eve, for the mythical woman far removed from the everyday reality of the woman's condition and of human "imperfection"— the abject. When the male writer, African or foreign, does not subscribe to these visions, he proposes the superficial image of the black female dancer (such as Josephine Baker) about whom people remember only the bare breasts, the piercing voice, steps, and movements resembling those of puppets worked by men dressed in white shirts or *boubous* for their prestigious guests in African capitals. But in these puppetlike bodies beat hearts that were profoundly human, serious, and mature and that were seeking to express themselves more each day.

If Cameroonian women's writing expresses faith and hope in the future, it also expresses suffering and bitterness. There is a difference between the aspirations of the Cameroonian woman writer and the condition that society designs for her, between the tasks she assigns herself and the means she has available to her. To use Rey Chow's words, "she experiences daily exclusions of various kinds, many of which are performed at territorial borders. It is the clear demarcation of such borders which allow us comfort and security in which to theorize the notion of 'exclusion' itself."[8]

Her emancipation is still overly controlled by her oppressors. As a case in point, this conference on "Bodies Apart" emphasizes the gap between postcolonial theories of appropriation and the reinvention of writing by Calixthe Beyala, Lydie Dooh-Bunya, and Werewere Liking, to mention only a few significant Cameroonian women. Hence, the conference's objectives are far removed from those of the Cameroonian women producing these so-called "emergent" literary texts.

Corporal Politics:

Diderot's Body of Representation

Mira Kamdar

*O*ne tendency of recent scholarship in Western literary studies has been to seek precedents for postmodern narrative figurations in textual production prior to the nineteenth century. The work of French Enlightenment philosopher Denis Diderot has garnered considerable attention over the past several years as a body of narrative that explicitly deconstructs the author's mastery over his own textual production. Most of the attention lavished on Diderot has been limited to the relatively circumspect area of eighteenth-century French literary studies, and may not be known to a wider audience. Nonetheless, these critical attempts to use analyses of rhetorical and narrative strategies in Diderot as examples of a postmodern will to subvert monolithic categories of phallic mastery and authority are inscribed both in a traditional reading of the liberal intentions of French Enlightenment ideology and in the larger context of post-structuralist literary theory and analysis. Books published on Diderot within the past decade or so by Elisabeth de Fontenay, Pierre Saint-Amand, James Creech, Jay Caplan, and Rosalina de la Carrera have helped define the canon of Diderot studies along these lines.[1]

Diderot is typically portrayed in these readings as an author who engineered the dissemination of his own textual authority in order to give readers and narrators (the latter often women, eccentrics, exotics, and differently abled people such as deaf-mutes and the blind) a rhetorical space provided by the author's generous pen. Diderot's willfully apocryphal narratives are seen as liberating his texts from attempts by the author, by narrators, or even by prospective readers to master them, thereby opening them up to a polyvalent free play of voices, perspectives, and ideas.

Many critical readings focus on Diderot's use of dialogue to engage narrators, author, and readers in complex rhetorical moves whose aim, ultimately, is to elicit a pathetic—that is, a physical—response to the text in the reader. They also cite Diderot's extensive writings on the body (and/or the uses to which these writings put the bodies of narrators and readers) as further evidence of a dialogic strategy of rhetorically induced pathos. Indeed, the current critical canon celebrates the philosopher as one of a very few European male authors to have successfully subverted the oppressive side effects of phallocentric discourse, in part through his textual use of the body.

These interpretations fail to see that Diderot, one of the most influential figures of the French Enlightenment, shares in the political paradoxes of the period's liberal ideology. The most flagrant of these is the paradox of liberality itself: Only he who has power can offer it up to others, and by the very act of giving power away such a person underlines his possession of it. The representational uses to which Diderot's texts subject the bodies of readers and narrators make full use of the complexities of such paradoxes even as they attempt, as one of the primary tasks of the materialist philosophy of the period, to think the thinking body.

Rosalina de la Carrera's book, *Success in Circuit Lies: Diderot's Communicational Practice,* is the most recent contribution to the critical canon I have described here. De la Carrera suggests that Diderot himself is the first victim of the rhetorical *cum* physical strategies to which his texts seek to subject their readers. Citing the famous scene from eighteenth-century French literary history where the actor d'Alainville discovers Diderot crying over a passage he has penned for *The Nun,* de la Carrera argues that here "Diderot is no longer in a position of mastery, able to keep his distance and maintain his objectivity on a fiction he himself has authored."[2] She concludes that, ultimately, the author Diderot becomes "the victim of his own plot" (pp. 19–20). For de la Carrera, the goal of Diderotian rhetoric is the textual seduction of the reader "in its most literal sense: . . . an attempt to put the body of the reader in a position that allows him to touch the 'body' of the text" (p. 170). She further argues that, for Diderot, touching, as it were, the reader's body is "a way of indirectly affecting his mind" (p. 171). However, if Diderot seduces the reader, she concludes, it is not to master him but to "encourage the reader to become active in the production of new ideas" (p. 166).

Although de la Carrera offers a frequently insightful analysis of what she terms Diderot's "communicational practice," she, like others, falls into the trap of too readily assimilating Diderot's complex pathetic rhetoric to an idealized rhetorical regime where textual authority is abdicated in favor of empowering its usual victims. De la Carrera understands mastery as "distance" from and "objectivity" toward the text. I would argue that, as a reader of Diderot, de la Carrera has herself been seduced: for the genius of Diderot's rhetoric lies in the paradox that it conserves mastery over the text even as it apparently undoes it. I submit that in the scene where d'Alainville surprises Diderot in tears, the philosopher is assuming the role of affected reader with masterful craft.

Gayatri Spivak has pointed out the suspect nature of Western theory's attempt to abdicate control of the master's discourse in favor of disenfranchised or subaltern subjects.[3] I have tried to show elsewhere that Diderot's rhetorical strategies are no less suspect on this account.[4] I wish to draw attention here to the particular way these strategies make use of the body. At stake, above all, is mastery over the textual parameters within which Diderot's text frames the interaction between interlocutors, the most important of whom are author and reader. In support of my analysis, I will draw upon the work of Philippe Lacoue-Labarthe, perhaps the one reader of Diderot not seduced by the philosopher's apparent liberality. Lacoue-Labarthe reads Diderot's narrative prestidigitations as moves designed to reinforce, not subvert, the authority of the text. Francis Barker's work on the textual subjection of bodies in bourgeois discursivity will also be helpful to my argument.

Diderot is best known to a general readership for his co-editorship, with d'Alembert, of the *Encyclopedia*. Readers of Goethe will be familiar with Diderot's *Rameau's Nephew*. Some will have heard of his novel *The Nun*, which gained notoriety in this century when French cinematographer Jacques Rivette made a film version of the book in 1965 starring Anna Karina in the title role.

Both thematically and formally, much of Diderot's work constitutively locates itself in the body. Putative works of fiction, such as *The Nun* or *Rameau's Nephew*—which feature hysterical lesbians and a frenetic schizophrenic respectively—thematize the idosyncrasy of bodies in serious departure from the corporal norm. Diderot's more scientific *Eléments de physiologie* explores the body as a topos for epistemological exposure and deployment, while various texts of political inflection, such as those collected in his *Oeuvres politiques*, chart the workings of the body politic as communal organism.

The discursive parameters of Diderot's texts formally link corporal thematics with the dialogical incorporation of the text's interlocutors. Jay Caplan, in *Framed Narratives*, situates the dialogic interaction of Diderot's text in the not quite empirical yet not wholly decorporealized bodies of the interlocutors of author, narrators, and readers. He convincingly attributes the meeting place of body and language to an "elliptical rhetoric," "a figure that summarizes and elides the pathetic movement" (p. 70) of a text that shuttles back and forth between pathetic anarchy and virile authority, between individual variant and ideal type (p. 74). The aim of this rhetorical ellipsis is to move the reader through a solicitation of pathos.

I find Caplan's reading of Diderot to be most sensitive and provocative. Yet, like other canonical critics of Diderot, Caplan ultimately finds the shuttling movement of the Diderotian text to be indecisive, and undecidable. I suggest that there is, paradoxically, a fundamental decisiveness to any elliptical movement of a rhetoric that seeks to return pathetic anarchy to virile sovereignty: the pathetically effected dialogism of the reader's implication in Diderot's texts aims not at undecidability but at conserving ethical authority for a master-narrator, and ultimately the author.

The rhetorical figure that operates the paradoxical move to ethos through pathos in Diderot is hyperbology. Hyperbology names the most extreme rhetorical paradox; the paradox that enables the great actor to play all roles equally well by being identifiable with none. According to Lacoue-Labarthe's analysis of hyperbology as the figure of authorial apocryphy in Diderot, the general subject of enunciation of Diderotian dialogue evinces, in a way analogous to that of the great actor, a metaleptic slippage in his identifiability by occupying both the enunciative position of the author "Diderot" and that of one of the specific interlocutors in the dialogue.[5] Lacoue-Labarthe emphasizes the political decision of Diderot's mimetic paradox wherein pathetic uncontrollability is returned to ethical sovereignty. He observes that this decision "proceeds, under the threat of madness, from an ethics: wisdom. In other words, sovereignty" ("Diderot," p. 34).

As de la Carrera and Caplan find, the mode of Diderot's rhetoric of pathos is fundamentally persuasive, and as such, incorporative. Yet the persuaded reader can only be incorporated by rhetorical ellipsis as an alien body. In Diderot's rhetoric, the elliptical movement between opposing poles of pathos and ethos is always a departure from and a return to the side of ethos, whose difference from pathos must be preserved even as it converts it. Alluding to the peculiar economy of dialogue, Diderot writes that through dialogue, "one gives passion its change."[6] The impersonal "one" (*on* in French) identifies the rhetorical condition of ethical authority with an unidentifiable enunciative position. The impersonality of "one" signals a subject of enunciation who would maintain his sovereignty by being no one in particular—by being unidentifiable.

Diderot writes: "Dialogue is the true way to instruct; since what do the master and the disciple do? They never stop engaging in dialogue" (*Apologie*, p. 112). In its persuasive rhetoric of pathetic solicitation, the Diderotian text is always subject to and the subject of a master's discourse, which Diderot identifies with the sovereign figures of the wise man ("le sage"), the great actor, and the great courtisan. The paradoxical role of these sovereign figures is the primary project of Diderot's *Paradoxe sur le comédien* and the *Essai sur les règnes de Claude et de Néron*. In the master/ disciple configuration of dialogue, the reader is "disciplined" by Diderot's text. Etymologically, "disciple" comes from *discere* (both "to learn" and "to follow"), and is semantically related to *docere* (both "to teach" and "to lead"). If the master and the disciple "never stop engaging in dialogue," as Diderot writes, it is because the disciple is interminably *assimilated* to a position whose mastery depends upon *dissimulation*.

In crucial opposition to the Platonic model of ethical sovereignty, where virility and virtue (*vir*) arise from the identification of body with utterance and the subjugation of passion by reason, Diderot defines the master's discourse as fundamentally mimetic, that is, as an utterance never idiosyncratically the utterer's "own" but always typically other. The famous argument of Diderot's *Paradoxe sur le comédien* is that the great actor is not the one who so identifies with the role he is playing that he loses himself in it, but the one who is equally suited to play all roles because he is identifiable with none. Likewise, Diderot argues in the *Essai sur les règnes de Claude et de Néron* that the great courtisan, like the true sovereign, never speaks on his own behalf but always on behalf of the nation whose interests he represents.

The master finds his mastery in the formal parameters of dialogue itself. In his mimetic incorporation of various interlocutors, the master, as general subject of enunciation, articulates all the positions of utterance in the dialogue, turns hesitation into persuasion, and returns pathos to ethos. To speak in another's place of enunciation or to make another speak in one's own place is not only to give slip to the connection between authority and language, to introduce an inadequation between utterer and utterance, but also to incorporate the alien words of another. Diderot embraces mimetic identification as a rhetorical device capable of both alienating the reader from his pathos—"give passion its change"—and of assimilating him to the masterful ethos of the author/general narrator. It is precisely when he is most moved, most pathetic, that the reader recognizes the immovability of sovereignty.

The staging of this operation in the *Rêve de d'Alembert* makes explicit the operation's dependence on elliptical rhetoric, or that dialogically inflected space where bodies and language are compromised. In the *Rêve*, the dreaming d'Alembert figures a physiological state of corporal and discursive anarchy that his mistress, Mademoiselle de l'Espinasse, transcribes and their friend, Doctor Bordeu, explains. Mademoiselle de l'Espinasse is completely perplexed by the apparently delirious ramblings of her sleeping lover, d'Alembert. Led toward understanding by Bordeu, she comes to see the body's operation and organization in political terms, saying: "The animal is subject to despotism or anarchy."[7] At this point Bordeu, *doctor* that he is, picks up the dialogue, clarifies Mademoiselle de l'Espinasse's remark, and lets her follow the political analogy through in a perfect example of the master/disciple dialogue:

[Bordeu:] Subject to despotism, very well said. The origin of the bundle commands, and everything else obeys. The animal is master of himself, *mentis compos.*

[Mademoiselle de l'Espinasse:] Subject to anarchy, where all the threads of the network are in revolt against their leader, and where there is no longer any supreme authority.

[Bordeu:] Marvelous.   (*Rêve*, p. 346)

Bordeu clearly plays the role of master here, substituting scientific and philosophical explanation for delirious dream talk and leading (*docere*) Mademoiselle de l'Espinasse from utter confusion before the dreamer's discourse to an understanding, albeit figurative, of physiology. But there is another, sovereign level of mastery going on, and no moment in the text is more exemplary of it than that of d'Alembert's sleepy ejaculation.

Curiously, neither the dreaming d'Alembert nor his mistress faithfully attending at his bedside are aware of what Bordeu and the reader immediately grasp: that d'Alembert's dream is a wet one and that Mademoiselle de l'Espinasse's response to it is sexual. As Mademoiselle de l'Espinasse tells it: "Then his face colored. I wanted to take his pulse, but I don't know where he had hidden his hand. He seemed to experience a convulsion. His mouth was open, his breathing was rapid. . . . I looked at him attentively, and I felt moved without knowing why, my heart was pounding, and it was not from fear" (p. 300). Later, when Bordeu explains the anarchic state of the sleeping body and the physiological basis of dreams, d'Alembert professes his ignorance of the result of his own sexual dream. This ignorance is explained by Bordeu, who answers that sleep

is a state experienced by the animal where there is no longer any coherence; all harmony, all subordination ceases. The master is abandoned to the discretion of his vassals and to the frenetic energy of his own activity. . . . If the action starts with the voluptuous sprig nature has destined for the pleasure of love and the prop-

agation of the species, the image awakened of the object of love will be the effect
of the reaction on the origin of the bundle. If this image, on the contrary, first arises
at the origin of the bundle, the tensing of the voluptuous sprig, the effervescence
and the effusion of seminal fluid will be the consequences of the reaction. (p. 360)

In the state of sleep, despotism falls to anarchy. Anarchy is defined as the
reversibility of the chain of command between a passive master-brain and
active vassal-organs. With consciousness shut down, the imagination provides a representational field of endopsychic projection upon which random memories or the desires of individual organs play. The dreamer is pas-
sively subjected to the representational whims of body parts in mutiny, over
whose actions he has no conscious control, as d'Alembert's reply to Bordeu
illustrates: "Thus there is the rising dream and the descending dream. I had
one of them last night; as to the route it took, I don't know" (pp. 360–61).

Of course the reader is well aware of the route d'Alembert's dream
took—that it was a "descending" dream—just as earlier the reader recognized what Mademoiselle de l'Espinasse did not: where d'Alembert's
hand was, what it was up to, and why his mistress's heart was pounding.
In both instances, the reader's recognition is uncoaxed by Bordeu. If the
reader knows what d'Alembert and Mademoiselle de l'Espinasse ignore
about themselves and what Bordeu never explicitly states, it is because he
is complicitous at that point with the position of the master's discourse,
with the sovereign position of the general subject of enunciation who, ever
unmoved, always knows each interlocutor's motivations.

Bordeu supplements a scientific explanation of physiological disarray
to d'Alembert's unconscious dream talk and Mademoiselle de l'Espinasse's
naively figurative feminine understanding (her metaphor of a spider in the
center of its web to explain the relationship of consciousness to reports
from far-flung regions of the sensory empire is famous in eighteenth-
century French literary studies). At the same time, the reader supplements
the formal dialogue with a recognition of the representational scene on
which this dialogue takes place, the level of utterance of the general subject
of enunciation, while he, as reading subject, completes the rhetorical field
of that enunciation. However, the dialogue thus instituted between the
general subject of enunciation and the reader is no more reversible than
that between the master and the disciple. For in that moment when the
reader recognizes that he knows something about d'Alembert and Mademoiselle de l'Espinasse that they themselves do not, he also recognizes that
the general subject of enunciation has known it all along.

In this respect, the subjection of the reader in Diderotian dialogue be-
trays a debt to a Cartesian rhetoric of reading. Francis Barker has analyzed

the relation of body by text inaugurated by Descartes, among others, to show how a textually instigated decorporealization of the body and its concurrent relocation in bourgeois discursivity generated a reading subject responsible only to the internal regulations of the text's own rhetorical field. Barker shows how the "self-regulation" thus engendered in the reader by the text emerges in the seventeenth century "as a feature of the legibility of the text as such."[8]

In the context of Barker's observations, Diderot's dreaming d'Alembert and the textual uses to which his body and his discourse are put bear a startling resemblance to Freud's case histories in which, "because the neurotic subject's inner controls have failed, the authority of a master-narrator, legitimated by science, must be invoked in order to objectify the subject in such a way that it can assume its subjectivity again" (*Private Body*, p. 57). In its representation, d'Alembert's textualized body serves a profoundly incorporeal subjectivity, whose limits become those of textuality itself in a complicated mimetic play legitimized by reflection on the body. D'Alembert's regret over his spilled sperm and his idea of "saving" it for scientific observation illustrate just this point. He mumbles dreamily: "I would have fewer regrets. . . . Nothing must be wasted of what can be useful. Mademoiselle, if it could be collected, put in a flask and sent to Needham early in the morning" (*Rêve*, p. 301). Like his dreaming body, d'Alembert's sperm will afford the material upon which science will cast its discursive reflection. According to Barker, in the emerging bourgeois discourse of the seventeenth century, "the flesh is made to contribute, as a material, to the science which is to dominate it" (*Private Body*, pp. 96–97).

Speaking of Diderot, Lacoue-Labarthe maintains that mimesis, "precisely to the extent that it assumes a subject, a pure *person* [*personne* in French, meaning also *no one*], is by definition *active*. Possession, on the contrary, supposes—the underling himself or the support, the matrix or the malleable matter on which to strike the imprint" ("Diderot," p. 33). D'Alembert's emission is not wasted in the text of the *Rêve de d'Alembert* for it is the seminal culmination of a complex mimetic practice that assimilates the body to language. This practice is a powerful rhetorical operation that seeks to produce the ultimately sovereign subject: he who is master of the body as of death. The doctor Bordeu explains:

The great man . . . will reign over himself and over everything around him. He is not afraid of death, a fear . . . that is a crutch the robust seizes to lead the weak wherever he wants; he will have broken the crutch and will have freed himself at the same time from all the tyrannies of this world. Sensitive or mad people are on stage, he is in the audience; it is he who is the wise man. (*Rêve*, p. 357)

The central philosophical debate of Diderot's *Entretien entre d'Alembert et Diderot* concerns the passage from inert or insensate matter to living or sensate matter, and then to what Diderot calls "an active sensitivity," or living matter organized under the governance of some kind of consciousness.[9] This, of course, is the debate in which materialist philosophers of the eighteenth century, such as Diderot, had the greatest stake. I would propose that the *Rêve de d'Alembert*, which immediately follows the *Entretien*, answers the question of "active sensitivity" rhetorically in a way the first text's explicit discussion of the question cannot. Diderot, as formal interlocutor in the *Entretien*, states: "The philosophical instrument is sensitive; it is at the same time the musician and the instrument" (p. 273). In the *Rêve de d'Alembert*, Diderot is explicitly absent from the dialogue. Instead, an unidentifiable general subject of enunciation provides the stage of the text's rhetorical play even while remaining offstage. The incorporeality of the *doctor*—he who leads, or the master in dialogue's master/disciple duo—seeks to defeat death, that fate of the body-bound, by subjecting the reader's body, with its sensitivity and its pathos, to the sovereign mastery of hyperbological rhetoric. The passionate body of the reader as it is assimilated through Diderotian rhetoric becomes the instrument of a materialist philosopher whose conquest of the body, and therefore of death itself, is attempted by playing the role of consummate musician. In his dialogues, Diderot shows that he is a *virtuoso* of pathetic rhetoric, a concert master of the textual body.

Bodies in the Light:

Relaxing the Imaginary in Video

Dorothea Olkowski

*I*n his essay "From Work to Text," Roland Barthes writes that the reader of the text is a kind of idle subjectivity, that is, she is a subjectivity who has relaxed her imaginary.[1] This comment comes in the context of the question of the text's irreducible plurality, a plurality that is not just a question of a variety of interpretations and ambiguous contents, but a matter of the text as an explosive and disseminative "woven" or clothlike phenomenon. Says Barthes:

> The reader of the Text could be compared to an idle subject (a subject having relaxed his "imaginary"): this fairly empty subject strolls along the side of a valley at the bottom of which runs a wadi. . . . What he sees is multiple and irreducible; it emerges from substances and levels that are heterogeneous and disconnected. . . . All these *occurrences* are partially identifiable; they proceed from known codes, but their combination is unique, founding the stroll in difference that can be repeated only as difference. (pp. 76–77)

Barthes, of course, is using the term "imaginary" in a Lacanian sense to mean "the register, the dimension of all images, conscious or unconscious, perceived or imagined" (p. 76). For my purposes in this essay, Jane Gallop provides an especially insightful explanation of the imaginary; it is, she writes in *Reading Lacan*, made up of imagoes: "An imago is an unconscious image or cliche which preferentially orients the way in which the subject apprehends other people. In the imaginary mode, one's understanding of other people is shaped by one's own imagoes. The perceived other is actually, at least in part, a projection."[2]

Gallop's is an especially useful explanation insofar as it conceives of the imaginary as socially and culturally determined through the mechanism of the imago. Beyond this, the point, for Gallop, is that the imaginary always blocks our apprehension of the *real*, of the originary text, and that perhaps the most we can do is to try to "catch the functioning distortions of translation as translation (not the *real*, but the *symbolic*)" (p. 67).

Indeed, this seems to be the point of a great deal of contemporary film analysis centered on the experience of looking. But is it possible to conceive of film spectatorship differently? When I look at the terms Barthes uses to describe such an imaginary—an explosive cloth, a disseminative weaving, a fairly empty subject, a relaxed imaginary—each adjective seems to stand in a structure of disjunction with regard to the noun it modifies, but Barthes *affirms both* terms of the disjunction. I cannot let this operation go by unnoticed. That is, even if Barthes's wanderings along the wadi remain somewhat coded, do his comments and the form in which he makes them imply that it may be possible to do something other than merely "catch" the functioning distortions of translation? Is it possible to do other than break through the imaginary for the sake of the symbolic, that is, the linguistically organized social realm? Is it possible to relax the identifications that constitute the imaginary? Or more radically, to encounter the so-called inaccessible real? What's more, can an examination of video images play a role in clarifying the "relaxation" of the imaginary—insofar as they are not subject to socially and culturally coded narrativization to the same degree as film?

Feminist film theory, in its approach to these questions, finds itself facing the mirror image of patriarchal culture on the screen. Although some recent theories have suggested that the subject-spectator may be, if not multiple, then at least split,[3] it is my hope to show that even this concession is inadequate when questioning the moving image: for it is, I believe, the movement of the screen image that is at stake here. And if the moving image is in question, perhaps its most intimate form, video, will unravel secrets of the subject more easily than the big screen.

When I first began thinking about video I was inclined to agree completely with Judith E. Stein and Ann-Sargent Wooster, authors of the essay "Making Their Mark," which appears in the book bearing the same title and which serves as the catalogue for an exhibition of women's art that toured the United States in 1989. Stein and Wooster claim that video art is "an expanded version of kinetic painting and sculpture; a tool for political activism and communication . . . [and] a subset of broadcast television."[4] The authors add: "In the early years [of video] (1968–74) many people saw video as a radical political tool for enfranchising the previously disenfranchised by giving them access to television. Others, during this time, including many artists and critics, also saw it as expanded painting or sculpture" (p. 67). In any case, there was a general sense of agreement that video is the art of the future, an outgrowth of the visual arts, shown largely in art galleries, museums, and alternative viewing spaces.

I am still inclined to see video in this light (even, to a certain extent, the home video unit), and it seems to me that Stein and Wooster are also correct when they point to video as a spin-off of the sculptural arts of the 1960's involving *kinetic, electronic, industrial, and technological* artistic forms; that is, they emphasize its technological and electronic aspect. Yet I find it interesting to see how quickly and how widely video artists utilized the new medium "to construct private performances, using the television screen as a *mirror*," according to Stein and Wooster, and how such use is related to the problem in film of the specularization of the female (pp. 67–68). Perhaps, however, video did not so much provide a *mirror* for women as it gave them access to a line of expression, a line of productivity. As Stein and Wooster write, "[w]omen artists working in the early 1970's often emphasized masking and unmasking, trying on new or lost personae, male alter egos, and the physical and psychological masks of race . . . this work aimed at identifying previous concepts of gender and liberating women from them, especially those that diminished women and reinforced their sense of otherness" (p. 88). Even more, the authors state that since women have historically been represented in the media as the object of men's desire, a critique of this *representation* of women is central to video produced by women (p. 145). Feminist video, they claim, makes women the *subject* of their work, asserts the validity of women's existence and experiences, challenges accepted ideas about women's experiences, redefines and empowers women in relationship to media and the culture (p. 145). In other words, video, as a productive process, does not so much mirror the patriarchically coded world within which women live as it relaxes or aims at relaxing the imaginary, which, insofar as it is determined by the dominant phallocentric and capitalist culture, takes women as objects, defines their experience, and leaves them powerless.

In film theory, it appears that the unrelaxed imaginary has engaged spectator-theorists for a long time. Prior to feminist film criticism, spectators, at least spectators of the classic Hollywood film, did not "catch" the functioning distortions of translation as translation. In order for this to happen, the entire mechanism of Freudian and Lacanian analysis was called upon to account for two phenomena: first, the cinematic pleasure in scopophilia, that is, "surreptitious observation of an unknowing and unwilling victim," and second, the narcissistic pleasures of cinema. This, of course is Laura Mulvey's famous thesis, from "Visual Pleasure and Narrative Cinema."[5] Mulvey laments that these two pleasures are subject to "a world ordered by sexual imbalance . . . [in which] pleasure has been split between active/male and passive/female," so that, invariably, the "determining male gaze projects its phantasy onto the female figure which is styled accordingly. In their traditional exhibitionist role women are simultaneously looked at and displayed" (pp. 808–9). This is because, for Mulvey as for most if not all feminist film theorists, the imaginary is coded as masculine, coded by an oedipal society in which woman is defined only as not-phallic, thus not-male, and it is this failure that, in Western society, becomes the prototype of every other kind of loss. I might like to push this thesis even further to ask if the conception of the "imaginary" is not itself a product of dominant social and cultural forces that characterize the unconscious as what can only symbolize, imagine, or represent *jouissance*, an absent *jouissance* that is *real*, thus impossible?

But Mulvey's thesis rests on still other presuppositions. Let us look for a moment at a feminist film theoretician's formulation of these suppositions. Many theorists connect the work of avant-garde filmmakers to video, because, presumably, they are concerned with similar visual problems. In "The Avant-Garde and Its Imaginary," Constance Penley is skeptical about the success of "structuralist/materialist" avant-garde cinema directors (notably Malcolm Le Grice and Peter Gidal) in producing a politics of perception through the disavowal of narrative and fiction, as well as through the elimination of symbolic and associative representations.[6] She bases this skepticism on Christian Metz's formulation of the desire to look:

[I]n "The Imaginary Signifier" Metz emphasizes that what is "characteristic of the cinema is not the imaginary that it may happen to represent, it is the imaginary that it is from the start. Basic to the constitution of the cinematic signifier is that it is *absent*: unlike in the theater where real persons share the time and space of the spectator, the cinema screen is always the "other scene"; it is a recording and what it records is not there at the moment of its projection. (p. 11)

More fundamental than the absence of the cinematic signifier, for Penley, is how the cinematic signifier combines presence and absence in a manner that corresponds to the functioning of ego, image, and body in the Lacanian imaginary. Thus she claims of the cinematic signifier:

[I]t is more "there" than almost any other medium (because of its density of perceptual registers) and less "there" at the same time (because it is always only a *rep-*

lica of what is no longer there). This structure of absence and presence exactly describes the characteristic functioning of the imaginary according to Lacan: the ego is constituted by an image, that is, something that is a reflection (which is there) of the body (which is not there in the mirror). (p. 11; emphasis added)

The claim that the cinema screen records, replicates, or represents what is not there at the moment also leads Metz, as quoted by Penley, to conclude that every film (and it seems to me, then, every video as well) is necessarily a fiction simply because whatever we see on the screen takes place in an imaginary space and time; it represents what is not there when the viewer is there (p. 14).

Penley tries to show that the increased materiality of the avant-garde film does not solve the problem of relaxing the imaginary as Metz describes it, since avant-garde techniques such as showing an empty white screen or an actual piece of film come only at the cost of losing the film as film, in its instance as film. And more critically, she claims, this "loss" of the film as film simply increases the strength of the imaginary by repeating the infantile and narcissistic drama of possession and loss, thus increasing the desire to look (p. 12). If this is the case, I am forced to agree, at this point, with Metz, Penley, and others, that any relation to an image must be imaginary; that is, if, as I noted at the beginning of this paper, the ego itself is constituted by images (the first of which, according to Lacan, is the image of the subject in the mirror) and all the rest of the images are doubles of this double, then it is impossible to separate images from this fundamental imaginary operation.[7] What this would mean is that the primary identification in film is not with the screen but with the subject's own activity of looking; since the moving image cannot exist without the look of the spectator, it is the camera that the spectator actually identifies with, something that neither avant-garde film nor video can do without.

Accordingly, it is in this more determined sense that the film spectator is scopophilic and voyeuristic. Sitting in a darkened theater, cut off, really *prohibited* from speaking with those around us, actively engaged in sanctioned scopophilia, "desire within the limits of the law" says Penley. Certainly, a difference in the circumstances of viewing is one respect in which video does not conform to film: video is often viewed in a lighted room, and the video screen is small, lit from within, its images electronically constituted. But despite the difference in video's viewing space, and despite the potentially more sociable situation of video viewing, we cannot yet claim that video is *not* subject to the same law, for it still involves spectators and the act of looking.

In "The Apparatus," Jean-Louis Baudry claims that narcissism is involved in the spectator's relation to the screen, but in a way that seems to me to be even more totalizing with respect to the imaginary. Penley explains that "apparatus," for Baudry, means not only the camera, lens, and projector but also the "subject of the unconscious without which the cinematic institution could not (would have no reason to) function" ("Avant-Garde," p. 15). Baudry sees the cinema as the final and most perfected material realization of what he takes to be a crucial but unconscious aim of the human mind: to return to the scene of the unconscious (pp. 15–16). Baudry seems to think this aim is carried out by all the arts, but especially cinema, whose special function is to satisfy narcissism by providing the subject with dreamlike perceptions that satisfy desire through the "fantasmatization of the subject," the unconscious representing itself (p. 16). Baudry writes: "Would it be too risky to propose that painting, like theatre, for lack of suitable technological and economic conditions, were dry-runs in the approximation not only of the world of representation, but of what might result from a certain aspect of its functioning which only cinema is in a position to implement?"[8] According to Baudry, the dry runs are always already operating, yet he specifically traces them back to Plato's cave, a prehistoric cinema that produced the first simulated and slightly displaced dream-state, a cinematic "impression-of-reality," an underground site where the unconscious can represent itself ("Apparatus," p. 113).

The basis for the analogy between the spectatorship of moving images and the experience of dreams lies, for Baudry, in Bertram Lewin's hypothesis that the film screen (with only a slight displacement) corresponds to the dream scene, which itself corresponds to the hallucinatory representation of the mother's breast on which the child used to fall asleep after nursing. As such, Baudry says, the film screen "expresses a state of complete satisfaction" (p. 117). The film content corresponds (again with only a slight displacement) to the dreamer's "primal scene" (as well as to other mnemic traces), repeating the child's early impression of being awake (p. 117). Such "archaic" forms of hallucination supposedly structure *any* desire. Baudry continues: "It is the desire . . . to return to this phase, an early state of development with its own forms of satisfaction which may play a determining role in his [the spectator's] desire for cinema and the pleasure he finds in it" (p. 118). Baudry claims importance for the "[r]eturn towards a relative narcissism, and even more, towards a mode of relating to reality which could be defined as enveloping and in which the separation between one's own body and the external world is not well defined" (p. 119). He locates the imaginary for the spectator of the moving image at an ideal point prior to separation. Metz locates it at the moment of separation. But for both authors, the imaginary moves inexorably back to the mother and to the Law that must code desire. Baudry adds that the desire to return to primary narcissism is, in turn, motivated by an original "hallucinatory ca-thexis of the memory of satisfaction," the mother's breast again (p. 121).

Many hesitations arise for me at this point—but since I want to try to initiate a new approach to these theses, even if it is only provisional, I will discuss three hesitations, addressing one of them in detail. The first is this: if the desire for moving images on a screen is motivated by satisfaction tied to the mother's breast, what motivates this first desire? If desire needs to be motivated by a first satisfaction, then either there is no such thing as desire or the question of desire is not answered by Baudry. The latter would seem to be the case since if desire is always a question of regaining some original site (whether phallus or breast), desire is really loss, lack, not de-sire. This exposition of desire goes back to Plato's *Symposium*, where de-sire is formulated precisely in these terms: "[E]veryone who desires, desires that which he has not already . . . and of which he is in want";[9] that is, a desire is always *for* something that one lacks. In the same dialogue, Aris-tophanes' humorous story about the once *complete* globular humans who were cut in half by the gods for their arrogance and now run around in despair looking for their other halves in order to be complete again pro-vides a mythological base for the belief that the negative nature of human desire is directly related to our loss of a complete self. It also indicates that any reading of desire as lack and incompleteness remains a function of our dependency upon all-powerful gods (who in the Freudian reading are par-ents). Are we condemned to a Platonic reading of desire or is it possible, even necessary, to think desire in a positive and productive sense?

Gilles Deleuze and Félix Guattari have suggested a non-Platonic, non-Freudian reformulation of desire. They claim that far from being directed toward some object, desire is creative: where there is desire, "something is produced."[10] They fortify this position by agreeing with Marx that the pre-sumably separate spheres of "production, distribution, and consumption [presuppose] . . . not only the existence of capital and the division of labor, but also the false consciousness that the capitalist being necessarily ac-quires, both of itself and of the supposedly fixed elements within an over-all process" (*Anti-Oedipus*, p. 4). This means that all distinctions between production, distribution, consumption, and recording, as well as all dis-tinctions within those categories (specifically, actions and passions, distri-butions and their coordinates, sensual pleasures, as well as anxieties and pains) are part of one and the same process of production: "the recording processes are immediately consumed, immediately consummated, and

these consumptions directly reproduced. This is the first meaning of process . . . incorporating recording and consumption within production itself, thus making them the productions of one and the same process" (p.
4). This approach further invalidates the distinction between humans and
nature (or humans and gods). Instead, Deleuze and Guattari postulate only
a producer-product, for production as a process "overtakes all *idealistic*
categories and constitutes a cycle whose relationship to desire is that of an
immanent principle" (p. 5, emphasis added). With this postulate, psychiatry (following avant-garde film) becomes materialist, and *desiring production* is the concern of materialist psychiatry. Such an approach to the
notion of desire can only be tentatively outlined here, yet it will have re-
verberations in the discussion that follows, particularly insofar as Deleuze
and Guattari warn that desiring-production proceeds along a variety of
wandering routes (rhizomes) until and unless it is "subjected to the re-
quirements of representation," in accordance with which it yields to a despotic signifier, where production is *"no longer production of the Real, but
production of something imaginary"* (pp. 54, 55, emphasis added).

   In feminist film theory, an oedipal coding operates as Deleuze and
Guattari note, as a despotic signifier that, by means of representation, "re-
casts the history of partial objects into that of castration (lack)" (p. 73).
While there are Lacanian theorists, such as Joan Copjec, who admirably
avoid the "stable subject" of feminist film theory, this avoidance does not,
it seems to me, go far enough. Even though, for Copjec, "[t]he speaking
subject *cannot* ever be totally trapped in the imaginary" ("Orthopsychic
Subject," p. 67), she goes on to argue that this is because all picture-
making, all graphic arts, consist of material, therefore opaque, signifiers
that only refer to one another and so never reach their supposed or intended signified (p. 68). We are still trapped in the imaginary insofar as we
desire what appears to be missing from representation even though it is
not. My objection (following Deleuze and Guattari) is to this theorizing of
representation and the visual field.

   This leads me to my second hesitation. Penley notes that the claim that
film is the "natural" culmination of centuries of developments in painting
follows a reductive logic, a logic that "offers a formalist and idealist description of inevitable aesthetic progress in the resolution of a series of formal problems posed by the medium [of painting]" ("Avant-Garde," p. 17).
Such a logic would reduce the entire history of painting, and perhaps visual
arts in general, to a single tradition and a single set of visual problems—
those of visual idealization—while reducing all spectatorship to idealism
with regard to the subject. Svetlana Alpers and other contemporary art his-

torians have begun to address the overvaluation of theoretical and spec-
tatorial idealization in art history, specifically that of the Italian Renaissance conception of perspectivism, which Baudry connects to the camera's
eye. In the Renaissance, idealization was accomplished by relating the
viewer's eye (which is prior and external to the picture) to a central vanishing point within the picture so as to produce, as Alpers observes, "a
framed surface or plane situated at a certain distance from a viewer who
looks through it at a second or substitute world." In the Renaissance this
world was a stage on which human figures performed significant actions
as chronicled in the texts of the poets. Significantly, Renaissance painting
"is a narrative art,"[11] and certainly it is an idealization with regard to visibility. There is some evidence that it is precisely this idealizing perspective
that nullifies difference and establishes the power of the scopophilic and
narcissistic perspective in the arts. This approach seems to be what Stein
and Wooster reject when they write that video is not only a spin-off of contemporary artistic forms but also a part of the attempt to identify previous
concepts of gender that diminish women. Additionally, if film is the culmination of a centuries-old search for the perfect form of expression, what
is video? Should we call it the postimaginary, or, following an implication
I will address shortly, the "un-imaginary"?

In fact, there is considerable dissent over this claim of a single line of
development of the visual apparatus. One recent opponent is Friedrich Kittler, who in his text *Discourse Networks 1800/1900* proposes another
model for discourse networks and visual networks of the century beginning with 1900, a model determined largely by psychophysics, which supposes another sort of "apparatus." Kittler writes: "Experimental subjects
[of Wilhelm Wundt's tachistoscope] . . . sat, chained so as to hinder or even
prohibit movement, facing black viewing boxes out of which, for the duration of a flash . . . single letters shone out. *This is modernity's allegory
of the cave.*"[12] Thus the modern Plato's cave exists for the sake of measur-
able test results—that's why the subject is and must be helpless. So for Kittler psychophysics is what makes film possible, for it investigates only the
movements of material, with the result that "[m]an in his unity decom-
poses into illusions dangled in front of him" (p. 224).

Along with technological development came a reevaluation of pleasure.
Why, after all, can the eye not find its pleasure in something like the printed
type or even the actual sound of a poem? "Psychophysics," concludes Kittler, "discovered the rules of literary automatic writing long before the sur-
realists" (p. 227). Thus he claims that the *real* sounds of the phonograph
and the *real* marks made by a typewriter mean that "psychophysics and

media subvert the imaginary body-image that individuals have of themselves and substitute a forthright positivity" (p. 237). In film, movement
is recorded, and so must be recognized, as "technologically real, no longer
only in the imaginary" (p. 244). There is, Kittler remarks, nothing between
technology and the body. This, I believe, is the sense of desire and the sense
of the unconscious that I am attempting to articulate here; the unconscious
of production, desire as process of production, connection, linkage, "partial objects, and flows," as Deleuze and Guattari write (*Anti-Oedipus*, p.
54). It's not even a question of unstable subjects, but of what Deleuze and
Guattari call *assemblages*; not the imaginary but the real. The link between the unconscious and film is psychophysiological; it is media, not the
imaginary. Unfortunately, Kittler goes on to claim that the "seamless
unity" generated by the film projector raises this real to the imaginary, as
if the real were not fantastic in itself (think, for example, of surrealism), as
if it must be intercepted by the interpretive function of representational
thinking predicated on lack. Paradoxically, Kittler himself addresses the
question of lack in a separate essay that I will discuss shortly, and it is the
notion of lack and its relation to representation to which I will finally turn.

  The third and final hesitation that I will address here is as follows. If,
as Metz claims, we are tied to the lighted screen on which moving images
appear by the irrepressible draw of possession and loss, regardless of how
these images manifest themselves, and if, as Baudry says, infantile satisfaction produces desire, how can film theorists like Gertrude Koch claim
that women are absent from the movies in increasing numbers? "The female images in films by men draw only on the repressive demystification
of woman. Her riddle, her bisexuality becomes no more than a superficial
stimulus in soft-core pornography."[13] In other words, what needs did the
(much criticized) classic Hollywood films "satisfy" that contemporary
films no longer meet? Or, to put the matter without the presumption of a
negative constitution of lack or need in desire, what desiring production(s)
operated in these early films that is (are) no longer operating? No one can
argue that classic American films do not tend to trap women between alternative false images. Women are represented either as weak, good, and
family oriented or as strong, evil, and phallic. Yet, somehow, Koch seems
to imply, classic moving pictures produced, for women, new connections,
new associations, new linkages. Strangely, the melodrama of even completely stereotypical films like "Stella Dallas" (Henry King, 1926) as well
as of their more radical counterparts, for example, "Queen Christina," in
which Garbo played a bisexual role, still attracted female spectators. Unfortunately, Koch seems to say, the image of the vamp has disappeared

from the screen, and the "autonomous, narcissistic woman has made way for that diffuse female image which only distinguishes between friend and sex object" ("Why," p. 53). Empty TV stereotypes, she concludes, are much more satisfying than today's American movie heroines, because anything can be projected onto the televised images of women. What is this strange movement by which the seemingly captive spectator evades the site of her capture and definition, and sinks instead into the electronic TV monitor (video)?

According to Koch's account, melodrama, as a form, provided women with a clear enactment of desirable female differences—differences, however, that soon became colonized and sanitized into sterile sexual objectivity and/or dramaless friendship, that is, the imaginary of contemporary film. Paradoxically it is Kittler who addresses this question of the sterilization of desire and the colonization of difference, in his essay "Dracula's Legacy," a reading of Bram Stoker's late-nineteenth-century novel *Dracula*. Kittler reframes the whole tale of Dracula (the little monster) with another tale, that of the Transylvanian Count Vlad Tsepes—Vlad the Impaler, so named for his habit of impaling his enemies on stakes. Kittler places the Count amidst "whole forests of stakes on which corpses rotted." No undead, Vlad "desired blood, but within the economy of waste rather than of need . . . he sat in the midst of the dying, giving a feast in pure excess."[14] Thus, the modern retelling of Dracula transforms the tale, equating the wasteful impaler with the undead who need blood in order to continue their post-life existence, making it a story of *loss* rather than excess. Ignorance or deletion of this frame allows Stoker to write the colonization of desire, of the Other, of the Stranger, of the desires of the Stranger, and of the "heart of darkness" (p. 153).

In Stoker's tale, Jonathan Harker records terrible hallucinations during his visit to the Count's castle: wolves block his escape, female shades both threaten and seek to seduce him. All transparent coverings for Harker's own desires, says Kittler. On Kittler's account, Harker keeps his desires (thus his own recognition of loss and lack) at bay by staying awake at night writing, writing everything in his journal in stenographer's shorthand (a reflection of modern concessions to the male's classical training in handwriting) till the cock crows (p. 153). Saddled with a nonproductive conception of desire, Kittler cannot conceive of the hallucinations, shades, and wolves as a series of linkages by which Harker connects to phenomena outside the limits of his domestic situation—a series of becomings. But if Harker's experiences are construed in this positive way, stenographic writing may be seen as less a technique of avoidance than a means of accommodating these linkages by making little marks on a page, productive data like those the tachistoscope generates. But the process of becoming other overwhelms Harker: although he initially undertook the strange voyage beyond the borders of known lands with anticipation, even pleasure, in the end he flees the Count. Having escaped, Harker returns to the restrictive domestic situation he had once sought to flee and forbids himself even a glance at his markings; he turns his diary over to Mina, his fiancée/typist—the prototype of the modern scientific producer—for whom the diary is a mass of data to be transcribed and who becomes, as Kittler says, "the central relay station of an immense information network" (*Networks*, p. 354).

Harker gets off easily. When Mina's friend, Lucy Westenra, is seduced nightly by the Count, she too retains dream memories: something black and tall, red eyes, a feeling of sinking into deep green water, the sound of singing. Unfortunately, Kittler identifies this as the Oceanic feeling, the imaginary, a feeling whose validity—on Kittler's account—has been questioned by science. Thus, for him, this is why Lucy's desire "disappears from the files" ("Legacy," pp. 157–58). Kittler complains that the scientific discourse of the young (and lovesick) Dr. Seward can only record the obvious scientific markings: the sign of the bites and the loss of blood. Even so, he notices that another scientist, old Dr. Van Helsing, pays attention to Lucy's symptoms, taking even the most fantastical of them seriously, including the nightly seduction by the prince of evil ("Legacy," p. 158). That is, he takes them to be not the imaginary, the Oceanic, as both Kittler and the "scientific" but classically trained Dr. Seward maintain, but real, as real as the projections of the tachistoscope on the screen, as real as Harker's markings in his journal. And so Helsing takes Lucy's *becoming-vampire* seriously as well.

Of course, when Lucy in turn attempts seduction, there is no question but that her fate is sealed. Her own fiancé drives the stake through her heart, thereby reestablishing his privilege. Kittler concludes from this: "According to the discourse technological conditions of 1890 women have two options: typewriter or vampire" ("Legacy," p. 160). But this conclusion seems to conflict with the facts of the novel. "As the novel ends Mina Harker holds a child on the lap [the mother's breast and the phallus return] that for 300 pages held a typewriter. Lucy, while she was alive, killed her mother and after her own death, or apparent death, sucked the blood out of children. . . . Let the femme fatales lust after the radical Other, for every Lucy Westenra, there is a Mina Harker" (pp. 161–62).

In fact, in Western culture, in order to avoid Lucy's fate, the fate of the "femme fatale" (whose image women embraced in classic Hollywood film), women have armed themselves either with the Western techno-scientific apparatus of the real embodied by the typewriter or (as feminist film theorists have done) with the psychoanalyst. The typist, Mina, is hypnotized; though she inhabits a border of the heart of darkness, it is not the imaginary. Rather, she serves as the radio sensor and transmitter between the Count in his coffin in the dark ship's hold and the scientific colonialists who listen to her as to a telephone receiver.[15] She is connected to a network of linkages that include the vampire, the typewriter, her transmitting activity, and the scientists who receive it. But, with Kittler, Mina places her typewriter in the service of the privileged imaginary (what I have called the idealized specularization of perspectivism), and in doing so she accomplishes the final colonization of Dracula, of the Other, of becoming, reducing his discourse to psychopathology. Productive desire, connection, linkage, Lucy's *becoming-vampire*, no longer have a place of refuge among the colonials. The Count's coffins are sterilized so no more messages can be sent from or received there. Another reading of Dracula (not Stoker's and not Kittler's) might take the blood-sucking activity as a kind of transmission and not as a loss. The privileging of the imaginary may also explain why there are so few women at the movies. In many contemporary films, desiring-production no longer has a place of reception and connection. Dematerialized, capitalized, and pathologized, it has been replaced by the negative conception of the lack, but lack is not productive desire, and the female viewer knows it. To go to a certain kind of movie or to see certain kinds of idealized images is to join the "undead." Not excess and connection, but lack and loss.

Has the video, especially the feminist video, been any more successful than narrativized, idealized film in making room for productive desire instead of lack? Is contemporary feminist video also the realm of the undead, the imaginary, the psychopathological, the site of sterilization and colonization? The same question could be asked of feminist and avant-garde film. These are not questions that can be answered easily. I have tried to show that some contemporary psychoanalytic assumptions about the nature of specularization and spectatorship are highly problematic. But are there any alternative theories in sight? Stein and Wooster want to tie such a theory in with a "new, nonhierarchical theory of culture that identif[ies] high art, photography, and electronic and print media as equivalent subjects of art" ("Mark," p. 145). This they propose in order to overcome the distinctions between original/copy, authentic/inauthentic, function/ornament. Such a theory would not simply "leave the functioning of discursive and signifying systems—the domain of phallocentrism—unquestioned."[16] Without such a theory "sex roles and their social values cannot be seen as ideological/political effects, consequences of the reproduction of power relations."[17] Perhaps Deleuze and Guattari's insistence that desire is social production, not lack, and that such production has a plurality of forms of organization is closely related to this approach. This would also seem to correspond to Barthes's call for pluralism and multiplicity. If so, then the task is to examine the effects of the social production of desire and the various processes of production, as well as our various cultural attempts to repress productive desire ("Oedipus," say Deleuze and Guattari, "presupposes a fantastic repression of desiring machines"; *Anti-Oedipus*, p. 3).

What process of production operates, then, in the work of contemporary feminist video artists? Let me conclude with a brief look at a single video. Here again is the problem I began with, the question of video as a "radical political tool," "an outgrowth of visual arts," a spin-off of sculptural art forms, a new medium in which "to construct private performances, using the television (video) screen as a mirror." How is video clearly *not* a *representation*, and thus not an idealized specularization of the female? (I cannot here address the video specifically as a moving image. While such an address is, in many respects, key to any theorization of film or video, it is in itself an enormous project and must for the moment remain tangential to this essay.)

The piece I will discuss here is not well known except among video artists and those who view such works. It is *Split*, by video artist Ardele Lister.[18] *Split* consists primarily of an interview with a seventeen-year-old female runaway intercut with images of the same young woman seated in a coffee shop, writing an angry letter to her mother, and with another set of images of her carrying a kind of doll near some railroad tracks. In the video, most of which takes place outdoors, the young woman holds the microphone. Lister, the presumed interviewer, remains offscreen, her voice generally inaudible. As she speaks, the runaway (whose name we never hear) grimaces, snorts, turns her head side to side, makes gratuitous comments, and refuses to take the interview or her hopeless predicament seriously. Visually, she is tightly framed by tall hedges on either side, and by her own account, she is also framed by a social situation that provides her with no apparent alternatives.

But here, in Lister's video, in spite of the camera and interview situation, she remains the uncolonized Other. Perhaps this is partly because Lister shows the young woman as excessive; behaviorially, she is all affect. She articulates her story amidst an economy of waste, an excess of affect and an excess of life itself: thrown out by her parents, discarded by the colonizers. Filmed against no particular background (not even the boy-friend's car, which would have begun to provide clues for a particular spec-tatorial recolonization), the young woman takes her time, takes up the viewer's time, in answering her interviewer's questions. She tries my spec-tatorial patience; I watch and grow bored. I want her to cut out the snort-ing and grimacing and to get on with her story, have it over. She does not, nor does the video force her to do this. Certainly, in this regard the video is not a representation in the sense addressed in my second hesitation above; the image is not "a framed surface or plane situated at a certain distance from a viewer who looks through it at a second or substitute world."[19] There is no narrative continuity, no syntagm, no paradigm, no presence given through absence as I described earlier in the discussion of desire as positive and productive. The rules of usage for the language sys-tem—syntagmatics—are not operating here.

This is not to say that the video image is nothing but chaos. If it is not a representation it may yet make sense as a sign. Following Deleuze, I would say that when *signs are eliminated from semiology*, it is always for the sake of the *signifier*.[20] In this case, the signifier is Platonic-oedipal lack under the patronage of a patriarchally coded privilege that seeks to main-tain the power of the static imaginary at the expense of real becoming (just as Mina abandons the typewriter-transmission for the role of wife and mother in order to ward off the becoming-vampire that Lucy has under-gone to her utter detriment). The real apparatus of scientific-technological media and its productions is eclipsed by the power of the signifying regime that interprets all images not as signs but as idealized representations, rep-resentations subject to patriarchal domination and oedipalization.

The video image in Lister's *Split* is itself like the young woman: over-produced. Given the norms of idealized specularization, there is too much light, too much shadow; the image is too grainy and there is not enough resolution in the image. Also in spite of the expectation (created by the location) that the set will be relatively closed, many elements contribute to an open set: the off-camera presence of the video artist, the out-of-field noise of cars whizzing by—unseen but heard—as well as the young wom-an's own gaze, which, rather than being directed straight at her interviewer or at the viewer, continually follows these sounds as well as (seemingly) her own whims (I continually expected to see someone enter the scene from the direction of the young woman's backward glances). The steady driving rhythm and grainy moaning voice of the out-of-field music tend to hold the viewer's attention. But the words "Fuck off, leave me alone," sung by a male voice, simply offer another connection, another linkage in this chain that demands decolonization—not only the female is threatened by the imaginary. If a narrative emerges at all, it is only as a *consequence of the type of visibility the video images have.*[21] Certainly, this is the advantage of video. As an offshoot of kinetic, electronic, technological, and sculptural art (and perhaps even like certain casual home-movies before it), we spectators do not necessarily expect to find any overarching narrative theme, only a sense in which something hangs together and makes sense, something produced by the organization and visibility of the images themselves, and not something determined in advance by a patriarchically coded structure, linguistic or otherwise.

In the video, the young woman appears to have handled her rejection by both of her (divorced) parents as an inconvenience, or at worst, a big pain. But the interview location adjacent to a busy road, "somewhere" outside, near some hedges, seems to indicate that having left each of the parents, she has nowhere to go. At the time of the interview in Lister's video, the young woman lives out of her boyfriend's car. The question that *Split* poses but does not answer (yet) is, how long before this Lucy Westenra either becomes another Mina Harker or has the stake of Western social and political forces driven through her heart? The video seems to imply: not long. It seems to me, however, that when and if such a thing occurs, it is not Lister's video camera that will produce that effect; that is, even though the video presents a certain image of the young woman, it does not *represent* her. Yet the video, as an artistic event, does not have the power to keep away the phallocentric or capitalist, or idealist and representational discourse governing the young woman's life that will most likely force her to break off her transmissions with the uncolonized or decolonized others.

Electronic Bodies/Real Bodies:

Reading the Evening News

Peter Brunette

A growing body of work undertaken in the last few years has attempted to move beyond the debates concerning objectivity that
occupied the earliest studies of television network news. More recent theorists now recognize the futility of trying to determine whether a particular
news item conforms to reality or is "distorted," given the fact that "reality"
is itself always a construct and unavailable as a measuring stick of reliability. Increasingly, television news has instead been described as an attempt to contain and domesticate the disruptive, contradictory forces of
the real within a set of coherent conventions provided us by the dominant
ideology. According to this model, already-written narratives, with barely
concealed plots replete with heroes, villains, and victims, are placed like
grids over the real and served up to us in two-minute reports that implicitly
claim to exhaust their subjects.[1] This process is never a smooth one, however, for the recalcitrant real, which television news must obviously turn
to for the material, particular signifiers of its prefabricated ideological signifieds, often has a rough-edged quirkiness that the discourse of television
has difficulty mastering.

This is a model that is, for the most part, convincing and productive.
Nevertheless, it is also the case that these ideological signifieds are themselves more rough-edged and unstable than cultural critics sometimes want
to believe. In other words, the conventions provided by the dominant ideology, itself riven by contradiction, often seem, finally, more incoherent
than coherent. Furthermore, the inherently disseminative nature of the
televisual text (like all texts) also always allows for "unauthorized" read-

ings, as it were, to occur, readings that are themselves sometimes self-contradictory.[2] Whatever ideology may "intend" (and such an intention, if it can be said to exist, will itself always be divided) is defeated in advance by the materiality of the message's signifiers, which may always be organized (in other words, given meaning), simultaneously or subsequently, in many different and competing ways.

In any case, the continual conflict between "reality" and the unstable conventions of the television news—which theorists have often described as "masculine TV" because of its claims to "seriousness" and its putative relation to truth and reality (vs. the "silliness" of its feminine opposite, the blatantly unreal and stylized soap opera)—results in making the news not all that much different from the rest of television. John Fiske has usefully summarized the situation in his book, *Television Culture*:

> For all its attempts to impose a masculine closure and sense of achievement, the news shares many characteristics with such drama as soap opera—lack of final closure, multiplicity of plots and characters, repetition, and familiarity. The apparent formlessness of soap opera approximates to the multifacetedness of the real, so the struggle within the news to control the disruptive forces of reality is reflected in its formal dimension by the struggle of a masculine narrative form to impose its shape upon the feminine.[3]

Most of the work that has been done on this masculine soap opera, the evening news, either has employed an empiricist content analysis or, more recently, has attempted to analyze narrative form and the relation of that form to a certain ideological or mythic content, in the Barthesian sense, that is received by the viewer. My intention here is to offer a modest contribution slightly to the side of the second category of analysis by focusing on the narrators (and, by implication, the narratees) of the news, rather than on the narratives themselves. I want especially to clarify the epistemological and phenomenological relations between, on the one hand, the authoritative *virtual bodies* that television news creates for us out of electrons on the charged surface of the cathode ray tube and, on the other, what we might call, by analogy with film theory, the pro-televisual or *real bodies* upon which these representations are based. (Of course, such a construct as a "real body" is in a sense always a representation itself, never able to be taken as pure origin, that is, outside of, or before, the play of signification. Hence, the opposition I have just posed, though useful to the present argument I hope, is itself ultimately untenable and deconstructs itself at every turn.)

We might begin by considering the matter of the televisual gaze. As film theory has amply demonstrated, every fictional film elaborates a complicated exchange of glances and looks that involves the characters diegetically with one another, covers over the gaps and discontinuities produced by the apparatus that might otherwise inhibit the efficiency of the work of representation, and, at the same time, neatly sutures the viewer psychologically into the spectacle.[4] We voyeuristically follow characters around and through actions and a space that are, by their very nature, both real and virtual (represented electronically) at the same time. The terms of the unspoken contract are that these characters pretend not to know that we are watching them, and we pretend not to know that they are pretending. In the process, we are created and create ourselves as subjects who dutifully occupy the productive slots intended for us (again, not without contradiction), and who are, in fact, at least partially defined and constructed as sentient individuals by our very ability to make sense of what we are watching.

One of the things that distinguishes television news (and other so-called "informational" shows) is that unlike drama, the news never attempts to disguise *our* presence, our looking. We are always acknowledged by being directly, openly addressed; when we look at television anchors, they look directly back at *us*, in a kind of staring contest that one might have with one's cat. In this contest, though, it is always we who blink or look away, out of boredom or, more likely, because any television presentation, even the news, is little more than part of an ongoing electronic and informational/entertainment "flow" (an important concept in television studies) in the American living room or den that is only intermittently heeded.[5] We look away, but the anchors never do, for this is the focus of their day, of their existence. We think we watch them, but they watch us, or a virtual us, even harder. Try moving around the room: while your eyes must rotate to continue looking at them, their eyes always follow you without even having to move—a well-known optical effect that signals their oneness with the apparatus. It might be objected that what they are practicing, or simulating, is not the "gaze" as it has come to be defined in film theory, but rather a simple form of eye contact, in everyday life a guarantor of sincerity that would, by extension, enhance the believability of the news. This effect is surely present to some degree, but eye contact in real life is never so intense and unremitting. Something else must be going on here.

This "gaze" then, for want of a better term, this gaze directed toward us, seems powerfully coded as authoritative, strong, and masterful—and thus "male" in the socially produced construction of gender—even when the anchors are biologically female.[6] It pins us, again in the terms of classical feminist film theory, turning us as it were into its female objects—

though now the operation moves in the reverse direction from the cine-matic one, through the camera/projection system that makes up the ap-paratus. But unlike the cinematic female objects of the male gaze, we have the freedom to look back, indeed the obligation; we become subjects and objects of the gaze at the same time, and, through this confusion of gender reversals, perhaps come to inhabit a curious electronic bisexuality. Or, given that we know in some way that the anchor's gaze, though powerful, is always a virtual one, in actuality directed at a camera, not at us, perhaps it merely gives us the subconscious *frisson* of a harmless electronic cross-dressing. On one level, we seem to be interpellated directly, forcefully, ap-parently without mediation. On another level, however, a level I want to explore further in a moment, the mediation is always there and is itself often so clearly foregrounded that the constructedness of the delivery of the news paradoxically becomes both naturalized and obvious (or natu-ralized because obvious) at the same time. In a sense, it turns into a site of natural artifice.

This gaze that comes from the anchorperson is operationally crucial to the effect of mastery over reality that the institution called "the network news" wants to establish, but it is only part of a larger system. More gen-erally, the news cannot pretend to an authoritative rationalism that is not contingent (contingent, that is, upon the fact that human beings make mis-takes and are usually not authoritative, no matter how powerful the insti-tutions they are a part of) as long as its "producers" (in the widest sense) are perceived as human—or, better perhaps, as completely or only human. Thus, the news for the most part conceals its real "producers" (those that actually have that title) and attempts to turn anchorpersons and reporters into decorporealized, electronic bodies that seem to revel in their insub-stantiality and flatness and that apparently allow them to transcend the limitations of the merely human.[7] These infinitely malleable electronic bod-ies can be metaphorically thrown around the world by satellite, summoned and dismissed in a microsecond. The advent of computer graphics has mul-tiplied these effects: images come spinning toward us, diamond-shaped, square, oddly twisted, or in freeze-frame, for it is now possible to present the image in virtually any way desired. The intended message, of course, is that we are getting the news no longer from fallible people but from elec-tronic simulacra who have been freed from human contingency. Electrons do not make mistakes, nor can they have biased personal opinions that would affect the "objectivity" of the news.

At the same time, however, the curious side effect of this electronic bombardment is to foreground the artificiality of the enterprise. As is well known, classical realist drama always presents itself as natural rather than constructed. What is unique about the television news is that it presents itself as both constructed and natural at the same time. It makes it clear to the viewer that it is explicitly involved in the production of knowledge— that is what the "producer" does, after all—and one is meant, on one level at least, to be impressed by the great amount of time and resources that the network expends in this production.[8] (This aspect is often touted in advertisements in large newspapers, still the arbiter in the inner world of journalism itself.) But while the fact that the news is produced, and produced through some effort (and is therefore not natural), is continually foregrounded, still the (apparent) ease with which the production is actually mounted and realized, daily—and on CNN's Headline News, every 30 minutes, around the clock—signals a natural inevitability and mastery of and in the final product that metonymically causes the viewer to accept that product as a transcription of the real that is more or less beyond question. Assisting in the production of this effect is television's increasing emphasis on *im-mediacy*, that is, both speed and the absence of mediation (through the use of satellites and so on), which implies that there has been no time for editorial reworking of the "raw" reality that is placed before us.[9]

This dual effect has become greatly enhanced with the development of computer graphics, mentioned above, that have become a staple on all the networks, in sports, news, and entertainment. When these ostentatious displays first appeared, they served as signifiers of a kind of a "gee-whiz" validation of the network's mastery. The built-in Brechtian *Verfremdungs-effekt* basically told us "We are so powerful that we can do anything we want with reality!" yet simultaneously implied that this (manipulated) reality would nevertheless remain unaltered and that such a display of mastery in effect *guaranteed* a privileged access to the real. Since the novelty has begun to wear off (the graphic effects are now seen much less frequently than they were even a year or two ago), and the excessively exuberant has been tamed, we can see such visual play more clearly, I think, as a further instance of the ambivalent electronicization of the body. The humans contained in the story we are about to see can be fragmented, flipped around, spun, thrown at us, because they are only electrons after all. But once we have begun to watch a story, once, in other words, the various human roles have developed into a narrative schema and a primitive form of identification has been established, the tricks stop, for once introduced, the "human" (often specifically foregrounded as such, as if opposed to the ambivalent anchors) is never tampered with. At that point, we are encouraged to react with all the "proper" human emotions to all the proper reinforcements of the various mythologies that television provides us.[10]

In all its formulations, such an opposition between real and electronic (with the attendant confusion of these opposites) is clearly a classic repetition of the well-known Derridean distinction between *speech* (in terms of the present essay, the real body) and *writing* (the electronic, or technological, body). We know that the electronic body is secondary, by definition insubstantial, technological, and therefore associated with death,[11] a mere effect; yet at the same time it is also primary, for we watch the news not for the real bodies, of course, but for the electronic bodies and what they can do for us (and, after all, the electronic bodies are by definition all that we ever normally see).

Nevertheless, these dead electrons, though they stand in principle opposed to the natural, real, living body, are also meant to be read as sharing in the mysterious inevitability of nature, a simple "thereness" that is beyond questioning. Electrons are natural too, after all. This nature, in a sense, thus encloses technology within itself (and vice versa—for it is this technology that purports to give us the real, that is, nature) and in the process deconstructs the opposition between *physis* and *technē*, a distinction crucial to ancient philosophy and the long history of Western metaphysics ever since.

A related issue is television news's manner of address. Briefly, in terms of the description of the "postal principle" developed by Derrida in *The Post Card*, the evening news represents a form and content that is curiously open about being addressed to everyone and no one.[12] Actually, the news is more generally and more anonymously "sent" than specifically addressed, for though it pretends and appears to be directed toward an individual addressee (the anchor's gaze is paramount in this regard), it obviously does not depend upon our reception of it for its existence. (With cable, we are always already wired to accept the transmission, thus always in the process of accepting it, but we need not turn on the television set.) The related death-sense of the anonymous technological, tied with mindless, sexless, yet unstoppable reproducibility, comes across most strongly perhaps when we enter a showroom of an electronics store and see 50 or more copies of the same anchor facing us from the wall, all of them addressing all of us individually. In theory at least, it is not inconceivable that if exposed frequently to this multiplicity, the always makeshift basis of subjectivity itself could be threatened. But persons—on any show, of course, not just the news—quickly become patterns, massive electronic mutations of flickering colors and shapes, and die as individual selves. Our subjectivity is maintained by treating the wall of TVs as decoration, thus totally denying the address, or more commonly perhaps, by focusing on one television set at a time.[13]

As part of the "postal," the system of television, like any other system of communication, consists as much in relays and stopping places, where all manner of things can happen to the network signal (local station censorship, local commercials, weather warnings, or program information running in a strip along the bottom of the screen) as it does in the supposed directness of its destination. As such, it manifests the spacing that necessarily accompanies all forms of technology and the *technē* and that, in fact, as Derrida shows in *The Post Card*, constitutes the very idea of the event itself. This idea of inherent spacing, of course, runs counter to the immediateness that is thought to be especially characteristic of television. This putative im-mediateness, in turn seeks to make such spacing disappear, in effect, to reduce it to a nothingness, a thing of no thickness, no space (but such a "thing" would already be a contradiction in terms).

Despite the many effects of the decorporealizing process we have been discussing, it is curious to what extent each anchor and reporter always painstakingly strives to project her or his own uniqueness—one is a real down-home boy with a twinkle in his eye and a Southern accent, and another is tall and literary and a bit condescending.[14] On a practical level, these "personalities," through their very familiarity, can be used to "hook" the viewer at the beginning of the broadcast and, more generally, to promote viewer allegiance. Yet their individuality also at times seems emphasized in order to mitigate the very depersonalization, presumably alienating at some psychological level, that is needed to enhance the authority of the news.[15] Guests on their newscasts nearly always address them by their first names—"Dan" or "Connie" or "Peter" (to do otherwise would be to appear hopelessly stuffy and out of touch)—but the guests themselves, no matter how much less well-known in actuality than the anchors, are always respectfully addressed by their last names or titles.[16]

The effect of this naming dynamic is twofold, and contradictory: the personality of the anchor is emphasized, but at the same time he or she is seen as someone with a service (or even "technical") role to play in a larger structure that transcends the self and the individual personality, a structure involved in the production of knowledge.[17] (Most employees in service roles in America today identify themselves—especially the young, with whose youth the anchors seem to want to identify—by their first names alone.) To complicate things further, even though, as Fiske has pointed out, the anchor "does not appear to be author of his/her own discourse, but . . . speaks the objective discourse of 'the truth,'" nevertheless, "the news reader's [anchor's] personal traits, such as reliability or credibility, are often used to underwrite the objectivity of the discourse."[18] (For this viewer, at least, the truth of Fiske's observation is confirmed by the fact that the news on CNN, despite its own panoply of technological tricks, carries much less authority than the news of the three principal networks, presumably because of the lesser degree of familiarity of its personnel, who are much less heavily promoted outside their own network.) The impersonal mastery effect, in other words, cannot be simply or uniformly opposed to what might be called the "personalization" effect.

In the ambivalent and contradictory translation of the real body into the electronic body on the evening news, invariably part of the body gets left out. While a real body is always in some sense a "full" phenomenal event, electronic bodies are by definition always only partial, their remainders something that can only be imagined, and this too can aid in producing the requisite effect of mastery. What is left of the body, both male and female, on the television news is almost invariably the upper body in the case of the on-location reporters, and, in the case of the anchor, only the head, shoulders and, at most, upper chest. (Except of course when the anchor is "on location," thus specifically using his or her body in order to authenticate the news through spatial position—a problematic that will be discussed later.) Now, it is clear that such cutting off of the body is conceived by the producers of the news as simply being more visually efficient or emphatic, but it can also be regarded in a Bakhtinian light, as another manifestation of the dynamics of the carnivalesque, in which the head is the source of Reason, whereas the lower body represents all that threatens the supremacy of Reason and so must be kept out of sight. This economy seems to correlate well with the depersonalizing project of the television news: electronic genitalia or anuses, in other words, are a contradiction in terms.

The relation of the anchor's body to that of the "on-location" reporter is also interesting in this respect. The fact that we usually see more of the body of the latter can be easily explained, in terms that are visual as well as ideological, by the necessity of incorporating the local landmarks (the particular choice of which would also deserve close study) as part of the authentication process. Seeing a full, or a fuller, body in a particular place obviously ensures, or seems to, that that body is actually where it claims to be. Yet there is more to it than that, as Fiske observes:

[P]artially positioned further away and discursively subordinated is the reporter, who signs off as both an individual and an institutional voice. Her/his function is to mediate between "raw reality" and the final truth spoken by the news reader. Different reporters can make different contributions to the same "truth"; they need individual signatures so that their "truths" appear subjective, "nominated" [in the Barthesian sense developed in *Mythologies*] and therefore lower in the discursive hierarchy than the "truth" of the news reader. (*Television Culture*, p. 288)

In other words, it should come as no surprise that as the voice of the final truth, the anchor (as opposed to the reporter) is, except in special circumstances, always represented by the upper body alone. To strengthen Fiske's particular point here I would add that, on American network television at least, the reporter is virtually *always* introduced by the anchor by name. The anchor delegates his own personal authority, as it were, and that of the institution, to allow the reporter to speak; yet, as Fiske remarks, the utterance of the reporter is always kept within a very tight frame. The anchor takes on a kind of metaphorical role as the master at a huge epistemological switch, even if the actual electronic switching is in fact done elsewhere.

It should be noted in this connection that the so-called "experts" who are invited onto the news show (and who occupy the same phenomenal space as the anchor) *never* look directly into the camera, for they are seen, complexly, as themselves part of the "reality" (despite their own obvious personal effect of authority) that the anchor must mediate and guarantee. The institution has not had the opportunity to validate their discourse, nor do they have any commitment to the institution, thus they have not earned the right to address us directly. Nevertheless, they *do* of course look into the camera when they are to be read as directly addressing the *anchor* from a different studio, say, in a different city. Here the effect is more complicated, since an electronic dialogue is created by having the anchor in turn address the expert by looking into the camera, in effect splitting his or her gaze between the virtual spectator and his real interlocutor, whose body resides uneasily somewhere between the real and the electronic. In order to orient the viewer, often such a conversation begins with the anchor and the expert on the screen, side by side, looking at their respective cameras, at the same time; the feeling that results here is that both are addressing themselves to some vague electronic space (the Apparatus?) where their electronic bodies can meet.

This electronic space is also evoked in a few gestures commonly found on the network news. One example is the way the anchorperson looks down or to the side or off (while uttering the meaningless verbal formulas that smooth the movement) in order to indicate the transition to the taped report, a gesture conjuring a kind of virtual electronic space "out there," in the middle of which the report and reporter seem to be created instantly by the power of the network. (Both the anchor's verbal and visual gestures, by the way, like the "sign-off" at the end of the news, are always purposely idiosyncratic and thus constitute additional signifiers for the paradoxical creation of individual personality discussed above.) Another example is the gesture in which the anchor occasionally glances downward, as though reading from written notes. Clearly this tic is a vestigial remnant of the legitimizing link to the written of the print media, but it has now largely disappeared from the mise-en-scène of the news performance.

The coveted effect of mastery that we have been describing, always precarious, is further threatened by the messiness of the real—both the "reality" represented in its reports and the reality of its own staging—and its refusal to be quietly tamed by the "masculine" narrative of the news. Television news, as we have seen, fosters a kind of ambivalent Brechtian effect that underlines the fact of its own production in order, paradoxically, to heighten our sense of its mastery. But this self-reflexivity always threatens to go too far, of course—as for example when a technical problem occurs—and thus to end up by dismantling the mastery effect. When Dan Rather looks at the wrong camera, thus suddenly and forcibly removing us from the power of his virtual but penetrating, Panopticon-like gaze, the elaborately constructed fiction of a direct encounter between subjectivities—united through a mutual interest in the objective and authoritative conveyance of reality—is rudely shattered and revealed, if only momentarily, as the fiction it always is. Or when the tape of the reporter on location doesn't roll properly, and human duration reasserts itself over the artificial instantaneity of electronic time, as when Bob Schieffer has to ad-lib to cover a technical foul-up: he stutters and looks confused, and the mastery effect instantly dissolves. When mistakes like these occur, television people conceive of it as a gap in "professionalism," for it is this very professionalism, like the aesthetic of "invisible editing" that ruled Hollywood during its heyday, that has become the putative guarantor of truth and authority on the evening news.

The discordant reality of the news's staging can also be revealed in moments that are not, strictly speaking, moments of technical difficulty. Thus, for example, reporters and anchors can occasionally find themselves torn between their real bodies and their televisual bodies, especially when the report is live. In recent reporting on the changes in the former Soviet Union and the rest of Eastern Europe, for example, a great emphasis has been placed—in advertisement and articles in elite newspapers like the *Washington Post* and the *New York Times*—on actually having the anchor on the spot, "where the action is." Of course, since all the news is produced electronically, one of the purposes such presence actually serves is artificially to enhance the network in the eyes of those "decision makers" and "trend setters" whose background and education continue to make them judge television news according to criteria connected with the print media. Once upon a time, after all, the person informing us of events actually had to be where the news was occurring. In terms of television discourse, however, all that is usually accomplished by this expense is to create a conjunction of photogenic electronic background and star anchor that also allows us to get the "personal responses" of the anchor, as part of the campaign to market him or her simultaneously as a real person.

Normally in these situations, the anchor addresses the television audience in the usual fashion, with the ultimately (and quickly) unimportant addition of the photogenic background. The complication arises when another reporter is included—in order usually to enhance the feeling of importance or ongoingness of the event and the sense of teamwork—for this completely changes the phenomenal structure of the news event. Thus, when Charles Kuralt appears in Red Square with Dan Rather, Rather must actually speak to him, engage him, meet his eyes, as his human interlocutor. If he does this, however, then he cannot at the same time also meet (or produce) the gaze of the camera in the manner described above,[19] and the scene is turned into a drama that we watch rather than one that watches us. Furthermore, the shot is from the side, showing their faces in profile, which, in terms of the conventions of television news, is awkward and unengaging. We look on, feeling left out, mere spectators, interpellated only indirectly by the apparatus, as in fiction films, but here there seems to be even less space (because there is so little time and so slight a narrative to produce an identification) for us to find ourselves within. Even more problems arise with the dialogue, for since we are now supposedly watching an actual, unrehearsed encounter, the lines cannot be read off (for one thing, without resorting to old-fashioned cue cards held off-camera in the wings, this would be physically impossible, since the TelePrompter is attached to the camera). Yet the reporters and anchors—and by implication, of course, the whole institution of the television news—seem torn between the desire to have things scripted and the desire to rely on ad-lib remarks. Scripting would in principle preserve the effect of mastery, yet would seem simply *too* artificial and thus would ultimately reduce the effect of mastery.

Ad-libbing would seem more "natural," but by its very nature threatens to spin out of control and make the reporters and anchors look like bumblers, in other words, humanly contingent.

Further complicating things, the two-shot, while perhaps momentarily useful for conveying visual information, especially concerning the background and the reporter's or anchor's relation to it, is not nearly dramatic or emphatic enough for an audience used to getting its news through the tight close-up. In addition, the effect of mastery, vulnerable perhaps in these special circumstances, must be reinstated, and this is more easily achieved through the direct-address system that has already been described. At some point in these encounters, then, the camera will zoom in tightly on the anchor or the reporter who is to deliver the main part of the story, and this person will turn to us directly to reproduce the situation in the news room or in a normal report from the field. In this operation, the other is erased visually and to some extent phenomenally. But not completely, because for the first few moments at any rate, the spectator seems to retain a lingering memory of the previous situation. The memory of this "real" situation can for a second at least make us acutely aware that the reporter has turned away from his or her human interlocutor, in a rude act of denial, in order to address us. Despite the awkwardness and alienation this gesture may provoke, however, the pro-televisual, real-space phenomenal situation is quickly forgotten as we are sutured back into our "normal" relationship with the reporter or anchor, and the authority of the news is preserved.[20]

On the usual news set, the achievement of the electronic authority we have been discussing is made easier by the fact that the anchor is indeed anchored. He or she has a vast electronic network to call upon, but remains behind a desk, spatially and thus visually compact. This situation is completely unlike that of programs, such as *Wall Street Week* or Alistair Cooke's introductions on *Masterpiece Theatre*, whose reports are staged in a kind of real space. The problem for these programs is that the only formal codes available for representing this real space (as opposed to the electronic space of the anchor's desk),[21] for accommodating the movement that is considered important for visual variety and a "comfortable" feeling, are cinematic codes. These codes insist that any cut be justified by a sufficiently large change of angle; otherwise the cut will be read by the spectator as a "jump cut" because it calls attention to itself in a disturbing manner. In theatrical films the shift of camera angle can be virtually any size because "the talent," as the industry calls its performers, are *not* looking at the camera. On non-news television information shows, however, be-

cause the talent are delivering information to viewers in the television manner, that is, "directly," television codes insist that they continue to look
straight into the camera. The result is that negotiating the shift of eye contact from one camera to the other over the gap of the cut is almost impossible to pull off smoothly and thus inevitably appears unprofessional and
sloppy.[22] (Interestingly, it is the accommodation of this non-space and non-
place, the cut, that causes the difficulty in the system.) Since the authority
of these shows, however, is much less than that of the news and since the
"information" they convey is foregrounded as subjective opinion, this does
not cause a crisis in the system.

This problem is avoided in the news broadcast first of all by capitalizing
on the incredible narrowness of the real space of the news set to transform
it easily into an electronic, flat space. Even more important, because the
shots are so tight, the shifts of camera angle, while actually quite large, are
perceived as small because the actual physical movement required of the
anchor is tiny, usually no more than a slight turn of the head. In addition,
these shifts of camera during the news program are coded much differently
than are shifts elsewhere on television; on the news they serve primarily as
relatively heavy, even stylized, punctuation marks that indicate the succeeding paragraphs of the advancing narrative of the broadcast.

It may be useful, finally, to consider a bit more closely the nature of this
flat space created by the news. An offhand remark made by Jean-Luc Godard in his video *The Making of "Passion"* is telling in this regard. In the
video, he complains facetiously that the poor newscasters do not get to see
the pretty pictures on the screen as we do, because the pictures are *behind*
them. Actually, I think viewers register these devices, these little eruptions
of the graphic—which must be read, a commonplace activity that nonetheless contaminates the putative givenness of the figural—as being located
on the same plane as the anchorperson's head. Yet he or she clearly cannot
see them. Then where are they? Again, the space created is electronic, and
the foregrounded electronic (and always clearly "thought-up," or constructed) nature of these graphics seems, as it were, to bleed electrons into
the rest of the frame, thereby assisting in the process of turning the anchor's
real body into an electronic body with no thickness at all, just like electrons. This sense of electronic flatness is in principle contradicted by the
other bodies we sometimes see in the out-of-focus background—along
with the globes, large maps, television monitors, teletype machines, and
innumerable other "knowledge props" of the television news set—which
serve to provide a kind of a thickness to the set that can ostensibly be read
according to the protocols of Renaissance perspective. Paradoxically, how-

ever, they do not add a sense of reality, because even these human bodies, whatever their real function, have, at least for the 30 minutes we see them, been turned into television studio props; thus their human phenomenality is once again denied, and they become flattened. In any case, whatever sense of thickness that survives works to signify the vast pool of personnel and expertise the network can draw upon to provide such authoritative news production, and thus both possible views of the set—read either as thick or as flat—would serve the same end.

In this essay, I have been less concerned to advance a specific thesis than to explore certain contradictions that are produced nightly on the network news. My formulation of these contradictions would obviously benefit from expansion, refinement, even, perhaps, refutation, and is, undoubtedly, riven by its own contradictions. Throughout, my goal has been to show that the texts of popular/media culture are seldom univocal, as theorists, to my mind, all too often have believed. The growing and vital field of cultural studies has since its birth occasionally erred, I think, by offering certain ideological readings—in the process, sometimes ascribing to the text an "unconscious," but an unconscious that is often remarkably free of internal contradiction—that do not fully recognize the massive heterogeneity and instability of all (these) texts and the crucial and volatile work of individual spectators in making meaning. The notion of an overpowering, self-consistent "ideology machine," whether at work on the television news or elsewhere, may have served a purpose at one time, but its usefulness is clearly at an end.

Transcendental Narcissism
Meets the Multiplicity (Lacan: Deleuze)

Peter Canning

*M*etaphysical narcissism is called transcendence, but when God
died "I" became transcendental, "unity of apperception" withdrawn from the vicissitudes of space and time. Quite a trope! In our day
this transcendental supposition is breaking down, and the shapes of time
must be integrated directly into the conditions of experience. While de-
manding a fundamental restructuring of the theory of knowledge, the narcissistic crisis calls for an even more basic reconstruction of the subject in
desire, in its basic attitudes toward life and death.

Imagine time has sides, somewhat as space is symmetrically oriented
to the posture of the subject. However, time is asymmetrical. The subject
faces from this side of time into a not yet materialized future forming on
the other side of the "living present." But the invisible side of this moment
has an absolute sense, which is death. We are always alive on this side here
as we speak, but there is an Other side of this lifetime, which accompanies
us everywhere in our comings and goings, a kind of absolute Then in relation—or nonrelation—to this here-now.

Now our death affair is not a pretty picture, and to be aware of it takes
a toll. It is something we need desperately to convert into the "labor of the
negative" (Hegel) in order to stay in balance and remain oriented to the
proper side with positive goals. In fact, consciousness—of death, that is,
which is its primary sense and the primal event of becoming *human* being
(becoming aware of the fact that we are going to die, that "all men are
mortal")—is the originary human trauma.

If there is no Where to *be alive* on the other side of time, then how do
we wind up? Perhaps as "I"—conscious of ending nowhere on the other
side of the limit I anticipate, this famous finitude I *am*—as I release myself

and lose it, one finds oneself returning now and again as someone or something somewhere else. Being born is, after all, like a return, but of what, of whom? Death might be the true Link from ego to ego (Ego who is without a link or a clue, who is the very *form of denial* of this transition). How do we approach that Other side while keeping our bearings on the plane of this one, without denial or the endless, obsessional labor of negativity?

With Lacan

The event of coming to consciousness is the primal human emergency, for it marks nature with the emergence of its self-awareness as another, as man—but man is the technical animal, an "unnatural" animal, that "dangerous supplement." Life became aware of itself as such in man (who is the name of this event), but it could do so only from a point outside itself—even if the outside must thereby be included within. Death is the outside-in-life that man imported into life's self-consciousness as consciousness of death.

Truth is defined traditionally as the "adequation of the intellect with the thing." However, in the case of dying, what can we possibly know, given that death is over the limit of time and therefore of the empirical conditions of experience? This impossibility must be counted into the "knowledge" (or consciousness) that humans carry in their "spirit which bears death and maintains itself in death" (Hegel). It is as though a kind of spiritual "black hole" were included within the space-time of living consciousness, an "event horizon" that the conscious ego cannot cross without losing itself, that is, losing consciousness. From beyond the horizon one does not return, unless as another being born.

The Other side of time has written itself into this side as "death"; to know and to *say* that we are going to die ("all men . . .") changes the meaning and the truth of death, which truth receives the continual re-marking of its being counted into the conscious life of its subjects. This is what Lacan indicates by the "subject of the signifier": the primal signifier is the *sema* (Greek "sign, tomb"), which inscribes itself into the ego as *memento mori*, both anticipation of an inevitability (as Heidegger says, "unüberholbar") and remembrance of the dead, keeping the loss in mind. The very structure of subjectivity is that of a protracted anxiety and mourning. What has been lost is unconscious life instinct, what we may call *primary libido*.

The emergence of the theory of narcissism coincides with a fundamental rethinking of what Freud calls "the most sensitive point in the narcissistic system," that is, "the immortality of the ego."[1] Now since the ego never was immortal (except in retroactive and compensatory fantasy), this touchiest point "so hard pressed by reality" can only refer to the innocence or ignorance of death (as "necessity," *Ananke*), which got lost when the ego found itself coming to consciousness. Before exposing itself to this experience of impossibility or impossibility of experience, the living being was unaffected by death except as danger, harm, accident or incident, arriving from outside. The trauma begins with the mutation of physical pain (or its anticipation) into psychosymbolic "death," which migrates to the interior. It is an event inaccessible to conscious memory as such, which on the contrary it brings into being—along with the "symbolic order" of an unconscious affected by the crisis. In this sense we may speak of a primary unconsciousness of death or instinct of immortality—which is the meaning of "libido" according to Lacan, or Freud's "primary narcissism." A second or secondary unconscious (unconscious proper) emerges here at the threshold of disappearance of the first, which it aims to recover. The Lacanian *objet a*, "cause of desire," is the "representative" of this primary libido-instinct that the ego, forced into consciousness or "subjectivity," refuses to abandon.[2]

Now the primal object is the imaginary ego itself, which in its emergency tries to restore its *Unsterblichkeit* in the substitutive form of an ideal self shielded from the depredations of time and death. This is the "ideal ego" onto which "self-love" becomes "displaced."[3] The structure of this displacement (*Verschiebung*) manifests the *décalage* of self-consciousness. Ego can never catch up to itself or measure up to its ideal ersatz, which has effectively hijacked its libido. Whence the syndrome of rivalry and aggression inherent to the phenomenon of love, whereby we hand over our libido to the other. Love, says Lacan, is "always reciprocal"—mutual narcissism, with each yielding to the other his or her invulnerability, filling the other's gap. But love is thereby charged with a burden it cannot bear, as each is required to restore the other's narcissism, when in fact the beloved has appropriated the lover's libido by becoming his or her ideal. Whence the paradox, hardly noticed since it is only the norm, of a love that can turn instantaneously to hate when the lover withdraws libido from the other's self-image, which it invested with lovability.[4]

God or Language, the Other begins as the quasi-"symbolic" agency, which Freud names ego ideal, that mediates this libidinal transfer. Love, says Lacan, is the "desire to be One,"[5] to restore the imaginary wholeness lost through the marking of the subject with the signifier, the *sema* or tomb representing it for all the other tombs. Each lover must have the power to confer desirability or compensatory ideality on the other. This eroto-morphic power derives from the ideal Other and hooks the subject into the symbolic network. The power locates itself in the gaze and voice (*objets a*) permeating the field of audiovisibility. The ideal arises like ectoplasm, like the psyche from a body falling in battle, out of the trauma in the primary ego (or pre-egoic innocence), in the aspect of an image in which I see myself but under the aspect of the Other I cannot see as gaze, because it is (dis)located within self-perception, somewhat as death within life. The ideal arrives in a triple instantiation: as self-image ("imaginary" ideal ego already alienated from primary unconsciousness), as the symbolic ideal *of* the ego, and finally as superego or conscience measuring the ego against its self-idealization and determining the mood of the subject in self-relation. The superego voices the imperative of *jouissance* directing the subject both to identify with the power of erotic judgment and to receive the sentence as ego from the Other. Or, in Freud's language, the superego mediates and represents the id to the ego.[6]

In his repetition and retrieval of Kant, Heidegger defines the subject by the temporality of self-affection.[7] This means, as we now see, that "I is an Other" who affects me with self-consciousness, self-observation and the voice of conscience. This "I" is the "transcendental ego" or ideal unity gathered and synthesized from the dispersal of empirical consciousness. It can only be experienced as Other, because consciousness consists in this spatiotemporal *décalage* and self-displacement of libido alienated and re-stored by the grace of love—the internalized Other that I am for myself grants me self-unity as the "satisfaction [obtainable] through the fulfill-ment of this ideal."[8] Kant formulates this procedure of recovery as the "cat-egorical imperative," by which I affect myself with the image of an ideal action whose principle can "serve as a universal legislation."

"The essence of truth is freedom."[9] In this declaration Heidegger con-solidates the results of the first two Kantian Critiques, the possibility of freedom defined through self-affection, which we are now repositioning in the Freudian field. Truth is the process of self-inscription that determines the subject in its knowledge and in its actions. In the first Critique we learn of the conditions of experience, that they are the same as the conditions of its phenomenal object: space and time as forms of intuition; the categories as determinations of unity; the schemata as procedures of unification, rules for conversion of the categories into "determinations of time." Substance, for example, must appear as "permanence of the real in time"; causal nexus as "regular succession," according to the Leibnizian principle of sufficient reason: no change without reason, everything has a cause.

Psychoanalysis is concerned with the nature of "truth as cause" (Lacan), cause of desire. The truth is marked and altered by its own inscription whereby knowledge and consciousness become counted into truth. The truth of instinct under the influence or the ban of consciousness is *drive*. Drive is instinct affected with consciousness, with the "truth of death" (phylogenetic trauma) becoming known (as the unknowable) and causing the desire of the subject, desire as subjective essence.

The emergence of the ideal provides the "condition for repression,"[10] that is, for the division of the ego and formation of a (secondary) "unconscious" on the Other side of consciousness. The drive must aim to push death out of consciousness, that is, to protect consciousness from itself. Death was included within consciousness as its immanent Other side, the anticipation of coming to an end at any moment. It is the object of repression through which we save our libido by displacing it onto the image of a seamless (timeless) unity—the ego as substantial self-identity enduring through all change. This is the meaning (and the drive) of "transcendental narcissism."

Kant denounced the metaphysical Narcissus as a "transcendental illusion"; but the transcendental ego as "unity of apperception" itself imposes a factitious condition that prevents the ego from apprehending the manifold *as multiplicity*—that is, as a many-fold and, in truth, non-unitary reality. In its metaphysical drive, the ego suppresses the multiplicity of itself and of its transcendental object-variable. Otherwise it would have to include the space-time differential within its transcendental self and object, which would begin to fluctuate and modulate their formal essence. The hidden objective of the "universal legislation" of the second Critique is to legislate the ego itself into transcendental unity by excluding the "pathological object"—the "empirical" space-time of dispersal—from consciousness, which otherwise fears to fly apart like human tribes at the fall of Babel. The "desire to be One" thus dominates the entire project of transcendental idealism, whose imperative drives the ego to unify itself with its object of theoretical and practical experience. On the other hand, to affirm and grasp the manifold as multiplicity . . . including a plurality of lives. . . . It is a question not of abandoning the *synthesis* of experience but only of giving up the transcendental illusion of unity and affirming difference as immanent differentiation and variation. Why is this so difficult?

What is at issue is something in the nature of language; what is at stake is the shaping of the concept, and eventually, of the ego itself. By way of a conceptual language we are able to impose a "nominal" unity on the dispersed multiplicity of the real, to gather and select discernible (nameable) traits, phenomenal elements of perception, and synthesize them into images capable of serving as referents to discursive concepts. This is the nature of understanding, the "discursive intellect"—to impose an order on experience. How do we decide what to select and how to combine, in what arrangement or (Deleuze) "assemblage," *agencement*? The answer is given by the nature of the relation among the orders or "powers" of experience, which Kant divides into "faculties" of intuition, sensibility, understanding, reason, and imagination, which Heidegger brings forth as the unacknowledged hidden "root" or ground, or *Abgrund* (abyss), of the others. Imagination as the force of the multiple also grounds Deleuzian "disjunctive synthesis." It is the transfusion of desire into knowledge. The crucial distinction is between desire for compensatory satisfaction in the service of a narcissistically determined Other and desire that recognizes, affirms, and synthesizes multiplicity as such and introduces us to another order of time and event.

What guarantees the reality of this world? Consider Descartes before the piece of wax: since I am the same throughout the transformations of the wax, I can verify its identify—it is the same "substance"—through all change of shape. But who guarantees my own identity—who bears witness for the witness? It is God (for which Kant substitutes transcendental conditioning) who assures the identity of the witness to identity—the continuity of time-substance—and who serves as the ultimate principle of reality. Freud saw fit to invoke a "reality principle" that determines action in its effect of truth (reproductive success) by the experience and memory of pleasure and pain associated with distinct traits of perception in specific combinations. The "truth" of an action is in the reproduction of the act and of the actor. But beyond this "modified pleasure principle" of instinctual satisfaction it is the narcissistic crisis, it is consciousness, that determines the subject in its desire and its drive.

What is the "satisfaction" demanded by desire and researched in the drive? Here is Freud's argument in *Beyond the Pleasure Principle*, apprehended at its "most sensitive point:"

The attributes of life were at some time awakened in inanimate matter by the action of a force of whose nature we can form no conception. Perhaps it was a process similar in type to that which later caused the emergence of consciousness in a particular stratum of living matter. The tension which then arose in what had hitherto been an inanimate substance endeavored to cancel itself out. In this way the first drive came into being: the drive to return to the inanimate state.[11]

But why does Freud not preserve and renew the results of his own previous investigations? It is not "the awakening of life" that is the trauma—how could "inanimate matter" determine the drive or desire of a life that on the contrary appears determined to preserve itself and to increase its power? If the aim has become to return to the inanimate, it is because life could not support its own self-consciousness (the dialogue with death), which Freud names analogically in the second place. So we must revise the statement thus: "The tension which then arose in what had hitherto been an *unconscious* substance endeavored to cancel itself out." Consciousness reacts upon a life that it affects with knowledge of the truth of its finitude—this is what "causes" the death drive to emerge. The concept of the drive must be adjusted to the implication of narcissism in the basic instincts of sex-reproduction and hunger (aggression), which it resynthesizes and turns into the *drive for unconsciousness*. This is the meaning of *jouissance*: the primary *jouissance* of un-self-conscious libido ("instinct of immortality") was lost or blocked by the emergence of "death" into consciousness. Life is a struggle to be sure, but when you know it is all for "nothing"—this is when the whole affair becomes a problem.

Or consider Nietzsche's presentation of the emergence of "bad conscience" in reactive man: every living being suffers and dies, but the human has redoubled his suffering with the demand to give a *meaning* to existence and to suffering itself. So he has invented a God who enjoys the spectacle of our misery. Now either this god who gets *jouissance* from our pain is a sadist, or we have offended him in some way and our life in suffering is a punishment, our existence answers for an original sin, the Prime Crime.

The book of Genesis tells the story of how man committed the malefaction of getting to know good and evil. He ate the poison fruit, now he suffers psychic indigestion for the eon. What did he find out by crossing the line in fatal disobedience? He had been living happily and eternally in his little kindergarten Paradise where life and knowledge were mutually exclusive. The Father's only prohibition was against knowing. Again this must be reconstructed: it is the event of coming to consciousness that was naively (or cynically) interdicted retroactively, as the Garden story was devised to account for our "fallen" state. The primal parents realized they were mortal when they ate the signifier, passion fruit. They had been innocent, like children, like animals. They did not then lose their immortality, they lost their unconsciousness, they became human. They became "mortal" by redoubling natural death with self-awareness and the mark of finitude. After they came to know and speak, they longed for simple innocence.

This is how the truth became effective and spoiled primary *jouissance*. When we turn our aggression inward against ourselves in moral conscience, guilt, and self-subjection, as well as outward against whoever gives the lie to our strategies of denial, we act as agents of the superego, itself serving the *jouissance* of the Other. The internal command to *jouir* is telling us to go *unconscious*, and to contrive a semblance of unconsciousness we interpret suffering as retribution in the name of the outraged Ideal Other. Techniques of transcendence—religion, love, drugs, orgasm, racial and political *Schwärmerei* of unity and nationhood, family morality, technology—all promise to take us back to *jouissance*, whereas "the difference between the pleasure of satisfaction demanded and what is obtained provides the driving momentum" of the industry of culture, the culture of the death drive.[12] For it is true after all that death is the surest way to drive out consciousness, to end all suffering absolutely.

Freud opposes the death drive with "the efforts of Eros to combine organic substances into ever larger unities."[13] But he also emphasizes the element of hatred implicated within the ideal of unity and erotic self-fusion, the egomorphic transcendental form of social bond or lovers' link. "It is always possible to bind together a considerable mass of people in love, as long as there are others left over on whom they can take out their aggressions."[14] This "leftover" required to close out the totality of an erotic-ideal state is a function of the Lacanian *objet petit a*, which in its "anal" mode conditions the process of unification *wenn nur, only if* and when it has been obliterated. An embodied symbol-symptom of disharmony must be invented, localized, isolated, and eliminated in order for the group to be established in imaginary harmonious oblivion. The empirical itself is the annoying rem(a)inder of the delusion of transcendence—practical reason has not shown that it can liberate itself from this condition, which is manifested in the transcendental fantasy of eliminating the "pathological object" from desire (the desire not to desire).[15]

Let us examine the logic of anti-Semitism in its virulent, Christian-Nazi form. The function of "the Jews" within Christianity exposes the entire structure of mortified consciousness. Christ is the savior, the bridge between God and man, reimmortalizing humanity, but the Jews are in the way, denying the divinity of Christ with his messianic vocation. In other words, they stand precisely in the place of "consciousness of death" obstructing Christian *jouissance*, denial of death and displacement of libido onto the fetishized ideal man-god. The Jews negate the denial of denial (no, Christ is not the son of God, the savior of mankind; we are all really going to die), even if Jewish religion and nationalism assert their own fantasies and substitutive fetishes. Religion, after all, is the "universal neurosis of mankind," said Freud, the flight from reality. However, to be positioned as the very enemy itself, the murderers of Christ—that is, refusing Christian transcendence, as those who "killed" Christ by negating his divinity and his believers' salvation—this is to become inevitably the object of an intense lethal-erotic aggression.[16]

The social body sews itself up around the incarnation of its own impossibility, having located the obstruction in a phenomenal symptom, and routs it out while denying its a priori structuration in the social webbing— through recurrent failure to recognize the empirical leftover's prior transcendental function, forever reenacting the moment of oblivion and *jouissance* (getting unconscious), extirpation and extermination.[17] (Whence the compulsion to orderliness, the cleaning ritual, constantly searching for filth—which it dutifully produces.) The *objet a* in this sense covers for the time gap through which death enters consciousness, but also through which the transcendental ego ceaselessly reincarnates its lack of incarnation, enacting the fantasy of erotic self-cohesion (a pragmatic-aesthetic "transcendental illusion") by initiating socially embodied action in reaction formation. The *objet a*, of positive or negative value (and always both, as love switches to hate in polar oscillation), functions on the screen of fantasy as a soul-plug for the void; it is the cork of time, the Image.[18]

Within the family, the ego's trauma is renewed in the Oedipus complex, an ambivalent investment in a familial-symbolic substitute (being replaced by one's own kin or double). For "parental love," which manifests "the parents' narcissism born again"[19] and reinvested in His Majesty the Baby, is finally an unhappy affair that ends in the break up of Oedipus (love triangle, with baby—or defeated parent—becoming the sacrificial object).

The narcissistic structure of exclusion and denial of "finitude," which Heidegger diagnosed throughout Western metaphysics and Freud exposed at the heart of consciousness and self-relation, has built itself into the symbolic order of language and the Other, the condition of possibility of social and sexual relation. As hypostasis of human memory and anticipation, the Other can sustain itself only in metaphysical fantasy and myth, with the "pure semblance" of being it finds in the *objets a*.[20] These objects support a maternal Other—the only real Other, which is the mystery of the womb. The signifier is the only real element of the Other; hence the subject, as living mortal body, cannot transpose itself into the monumental signifying order except in fantasy. By the operation of "suture"[21] the subject's body of existence becomes the *objet a*, sacrificed to the Other while becoming *substance jouissante*. Thus the subject finally submits—while transmuting itself in fantasy into an immortal Other Body—to being "represented by a signifier for the other signifiers" (Lacan) in the symbolic chain.

The transcendental subject was a makeshift solution to a perpetual human crisis. Is it not time to take heart and let it go? Heidegger formulates the temporal structure of *Sorge*, the "totality of the structural whole [of Dasein's dis-closure of Being-in-the-world]" as *Sich-vorweg-schon-sein-in (der Welt) als Sein-bei (innerweltlich) begegnendem Seienden*.[22] Time (-image) loops back into perception-consciousness (in the gap between them) as futural scenario, becoming the "thread" (Deleuze) that (under the aegis of the transcendental ectoplasm) stitches the division of the subject it has opened up: "time moves into the subject, in order to distinguish the Ego from the I in it. It is the form under which the I affects the Ego, that is, the way in which the mind affects itself . . . the form of interiority."[23] Any operation to rescue the ego from "time consciousness" has therefore to liberate the ego from itself—that as, from self-subjection to its Other half, under whose aspect it affects itself with the image or the scene of absolute future annihilation (the mirror-cracking stage, which even in Deleuze's text "time" tropes thus: "Death moves into the subject and affects the ego, etc."). The death-image (destruction of self-image) enters life-time by folding into the form of interiority it opens, this feedback loop: *vorweg-schon-in als bei*, which is the temporal shape of the *Sich*'s self-projection ahead of itself into its will-have-been, Self imagining itself (in the future) past. The *image* of time is the stitch of the *Ich*'s departure and return to itself from afar, even beyond life, from the other side of time—which opens the drive for closure.

And so we find the ego sewing itself up in this transcendental primal scene with imaginary material from the very "form" (or Unform) that is said to be the enemy. Consciousness divides the subject from itself—from its *objet petit soi*—withholding and preventing completion of itself as plenitude of being-lacking-nothing, no longer subject to the vicissitudes of time: no more subject, period. Total fusion. But as the romantic object (the complementary double) further dissolves into the allegory of its perdition (Paradise Lost, which is the *temporal form* of the Garden), the subject self-divides into an "ironic" spectrum or series of substitute personae—not even, as de Man says, in a "synchronic structure" of "simultaneity,"[24] but, as Deleuze says, in an "infinite modulation" or "oscillation" and vertigo, which is the subject's unending *décalage* with itself, cutting itself off to speculate infinity, but then looping and stitching back the Other from the absolute (no) future.

The transcendental ego has become the Other's speculative agent and moral-desiring messenger, less a form of interiority than an involuntary and recalcitrant division of itself, a prying open—by whom (since the Super-Ego only represents "the Law as it is *misunderstood*" [Lacan])? Heidegger may answer, to avoid theomorphic misapprehension, that Dasein calls *to itself*, "to afar from afar,"[25] across the *temporal* distance from the origin. Freud derives the voice and panopticon of conscience out of the splitting-doubling of Narcissus on contact with "reality" and upon Ego's reflecting or echoing its Ideal. More precisely, the Other's agent (ego ideal) monitors and criticizes its ward as conscience within consciousness. The transcendental Other (hypostatic Ideal)—operating "between perception and consciousness" (Lacan), thus within the categorical field—becomes the genetic instance of the censor controlling the threshold to consciousness on behalf of internalized moral-cognitive codes setting standards of judgment for determination of value and meaning. This is how the imperative of *jouissance* elaborates itself in the regime of egoic desire-as-lack and the drive to end all drives.

Group or individual, ego is the psychic form of sickness—temporal self-consciousness, or the earth's skin disease. Yet ego will never relax its effort to reinvent its situation, to compose a glorious new body "without need of any organ," with a "simplified and indestructible life."[26]

Can we not invent another, nonlethal, liberation form of self-composure, a new image of time, or a way of living, thinking time without image?

And Deleuze

To transcend means to step across to the other side—there where there is no time, or where time begins in the source of consciousness, where it becomes a *concept*. The Deleuzian synthesis operates a conversion of consciousness, the genesis of a subject-multiplicity.

The classical doctrine of recirculation of souls and indirect transcendence of bodies is well documented—though nonetheless difficult to perform. Dante wants to go to hell, Virgil knows the way—he inhabits the medium he helped create—and is willing to be resuscitated or re-created by Dante to accompany him, being Poets together. They are very close, though they live a thousand years apart. Thus the word and tradition of poetry is the milieu of their transcendence and their meeting place—a pro-visional afterlife, as Proust reminds us somewhat deflatingly and in a crit-ical mood, since after all, one day the sun will go out and the earth grow cold, and all the pages of books will wither and decompose or there will be no one left to read and blow life into them.[27] This is one form of the substance of eternal return: the spirit that is lying dormant, folded into the book and like a genie, can be broken out and liberated. What Pierre Klos-sowski names Roberte or "Nietzsche," *souffle* and intensity, Vernant, cit-ing ancient Orphic-Pythagorean texts, calls the *logoi, discours* that be-come, with practice, psychic links. The soul, transfusing into breath gath-ering suspended in diaphragm, separates and escapes from the body, perhaps to travel in time or to return.[28]

The material of Psyche, then, its substance, are the discourses or spirits, animae in which intensities become enfolded and which, when excited, un-fold and get released to travel into other bodies, animate new lives, or else remain suspended until they find a liaison or take a new lease on life. This is it, no doubt. *Coca-cola c'est ça!* But what about me, little Big-Time, mor-tal, only-go-around-once, all or nothing Me, His Majesty the Baby, what do I get out of this? Am I nothing to be save fluctuation of intensity, vagrant emotion discoursing through amorphous time, perhaps moving somebody somewhere, subsisting but never existing, never self-present but in others returning "my" words in theirs? And where do my own begin? It's all so indirect. To wake up someone else . . . I sense it is—I am everywhere going nowhere, I'm not sure, this can't be what I intended.

The turning point, however, is *Yes there is life after death, only it isn't mine.* It does not belong to my memory of me, my "me-me-more-me" (Joyce), I can't remember a thing from one life to the next (you cannot even grow and *become* while at the same time remembering—who you were an hour ago). But consider this: say death is the other side of time; what is on this side? It is always life, always alive, even if attacked by self-consciousness, transcendentally, existentially vitiated by *dédoublement* with the Other outside-in consciousness seeking unconsciousness and de-nial, in reaction formation, moribund subject of the substance-Life. Life has never been without its other half, not even before it was compelled to anticipate and interiorize and negate its enemy. *But it has also never died.* Whatever is alive in us has remained in force, mutating, wearing out and dying only individually but never in itself, in its power to live and re-create itself, continually recombining elements for a new departure. Life has never ever been dead ever since Natura began physing and futuring itself;

it has merely transferred from one body to another; while Ego, become split and subject, tried to find itself again in fantasy or in ecstasy on the other side of time. When something speaks in me, death speaks, the subject, or *semainei*, it makes a sign (*sema*, tomb-sign). Has there ever been a language of life?

Life has always been here now; this is it. Only *I* have died, over and over, to be reborn continually. I is an Other and another. This is what Nietzsche grasped or felt, on reading Spinoza in the summer of 1881: a wave of emotion came over him, and as it broke (his ego) it formed a sign, of the genus *circulus vitiosus dionysus*—the transcendental *experience*, experiential form of an ego reternally turning into another, home again, back from the interval of oblivion. Whether this be "one" life in which I change forms and exchange souls, intensities, or whether we sense all the lives and times of all souls and egos—even those of animals, plants, and elementary particles, taken in their series, their ensembles, and their lines of flight ("escaping spatiotemporal and even existential coordinates")[29]—as the manifestation of a single life-force or drive. It is true that the concept of drive, like that of desire, has been forced to include its outside—death—within it, and that this inclusion, as self-consciousness, is the source of our previous difficulties.

Deleuze's response to this predicament is neither to exclude death from consciousness nor to retreat into unconsciousness, *jouissance*, transgression, or the *objet a* as form of sacrificial offering, culture of guilt as the price we pay for a modicum of arbitrarily circumscribed social-egoistic cohesion. (The Lacanian school, as evidenced by the final pages of the *Quatre concepts*, does call a halt at this limit, to cross which it considers "untenable.") Death must become an *experience*, which, while it does alter, undo, and remake the ego continually, nevertheless permits something—life—to pass through. This gap no longer signals the end of the ego without its rebeginning as id in someone-something else, because the ego has lost its form of unalienable finitude, its private identity and proper name ("rigid designator") or rather, these begin to divide and multiply. The name of this gap is Body without Organs (BwO). It is a pure space-time interval dividing intense gradient matter (Cosmic Egg)—which changes shape and nature with each division of its "morphic field"[30]—from within a life now distributed "disjunctively" through and across manifold lives that are never strictly mine. What then should I care about these other lives? Why should I care about these others who continue "my" life only by some kind of metaphysical pun or joke? Because "they" are no longer rivals or substitutes for "my" life; "we" is no longer the exclusive imaginary enclave.

Instead, "I" have splintered, fractured, and multiplied through death into the elements spanning across into new lives, born wherever I find I am. *Wo Es war soll Ich werden.*

Nietzsche signals that after the "death of god" there recurs the birth of Dionysos, the splintered god of continual *sparagmos* reincarnating. I am searching here to synthesize the current reunification of this diasynchronic movement of eternal return in a metamorphosed figure of consciousness (Narcissus) as virtual, trans-actual multiplicity or continuous re-creation and renewal of life-form and -time. The Other becomes Body without Organs, between perception and consciousness, when the subject's verbal "passage to its own division in *jouissance*" becomes "determined as disjunction" and the subject "becomes a sign."[31]

Let's try to remember: it is not I nor you who are alive anyway. We settled this, "I" am already dead in anticipatory resolution—in the best case (usually I am in denial and looking for a way out or someone to blame). Some unknowable trauma—of which "death" only provides a nominal definition—has been transferred from parent to child, from unconscious to unconscious, through countless generations of neurotics (normal humans). Why not then rediscover or reinvent oneself *as someone else*?

Now this may seem another twist of a joke, the schizo or hysteric who "identifies" with a series of personalities. But "character formation" is itself the simulacrum of a more rigorous transfer, or rather passage, from ego to and across the Body without Organs, the interval between *phusis* and *thesis* or *nomos*, interstitial tensor between nature and reactive self-consciousness. It points to a mutation in human consciousness or a new medium of intense connection, chaosmic communication, and transmigratory conjunction. When the Ego discovers this morphogenetic field, it (as usual) misapprehends its situation. For the Ego, as imaginary being, is already a BwO in its own "anticipatory resolution." It just does not yet know its destination.[32]

For the individual, death does arrive once and for all ("but for a new departure, since I is another?").[33] But for the transcendental person now decomposed into a spectrum of tonalities, these tones or moods form a new potential. The BwO opens a passage into other lives—not "for" the ego or the *same* person, but *through* the "tragic irony" of consciousness and into the multiplicity of lives being lived on earth simultaneously and successively. But this succession is now condensed (through "connective synthesis" renewed by affirmative disjunction) into a transpositional conjunction, transfinite mode, the polyvocal expression of One Univocal

Being or *Natura naturans*. This being is without beginning or end. A dia-synchronic multiplicity.[34]

For Lacan, Spinoza was the outer limit case, or Kant really ne plus ultra. Kant is restrictive with modal imagination, not clearly distinguishing it from fantasy. But neither Deleuze's BwO nor Spinoza's Natura is imagi-nary anyway, they carry futural dimensions or potential.[35] Under this as-pect (*sub specie cupiditatis*), Deleuze doubtless represents a "regression," to the Body without Organs as substance, with its desiring-machine attri-butes and modes—even divided and separated by a "real distinction." But the BwO is not a pre-egoic entity; it is a post-egoistic construction, a schizophrenic reconstruction to be sure—but can anyone today seriously doubt the potential of a schizomorphic (nomadic) thinking even partially released from the hegemony of the ego, that is, the double-binding impo-sition of Lack in its transcendental apotheosis? The very possibility of com-munication—not only with others, other "finite modes," but with one-self—depends on breaking this barrier through the interval that separates "us" from each other. This is the function of desire, its "real inorganiza-tion":[36] to carry us through and beyond death-consciousness into the becoming-multiplicity where, after all, we have always been.

Can we invent another form of time? of consciousness? The time-form as given in Kant's "first analogy of experience" is the form of "perma-nence," the schematized category of substance, which supports the subject in self-identification and in the transcendental illusion of its substantial to-getherness as one. Time endures the same, as substrate, *hupokeimenon*. Thus it is unitary time that forms or determines the subject. But isn't time that which never ceases to pass, which flees and is never the same time? But it is always the same never the same. Yet relativity physics and even the experience of rush before the approach of sudden death indicate rather a kind of event horizon, a variable threshold that renders time both elastic and constrictive. The beginning or end of the world, or of the self, disap-pearing apparitions, stretch and contract toward their own (im)possibility.

Ego hangs like a drop of liquid being in its elastic lifetime membrane, but from what does it hang? From nothing, but it hangs on to the nothing, in Angst, its native affect. It is equally true that this nothing by which it is determined in its abandonment opens it up to everything and anything, which it can become in the decoded space of freedom.[37] Yet as long as this freedom is determined by the encounter with egoized death (*Vorlaufen*), it is only a set of variations on the theme of finitude (Dasein is still an avatar of the subject). Still, this is a way of multiplicity that opens the Ego out beyond itself, if only for a display of personal identifications, "repetitions," or even a combinatory of bodies and affects. For its part, by way of commodity phantasms, Capital compensates the subject for the "social links" it has stripped or decoded him of. The phantasm sutures him into a scene of enjoyment with an object, where he figures as the person in the empty place held open for him, abstract consumer, a hungry void bound to others by prestige or love or communal Hunger.

Yet even the forms of media take us past the anachronistic phenomenology of time consciousness. We have need of a new phenomenology, not just of mind but of the modalities of mediation. Media, sensorium of Capital; technology, organs of Capital *we are* (Butler). Ego is well wired and plugged into this *dispositif* and vice versa, an integrated circuit. It is difficult to locate oneself in the world closing in even as the subject is multiplying and opening out over long distance (in tele-phony-vision), where "everyone is everywhere at all times" (Whitehead).[38] There is no more past; everything returns to the future presenting itself. But is this human? Is it even alive? Do I care? Who am I fighting for; what am I dying for? It is difficult to situate oneself when a contaminated perturbation in the *Umwelt* over there is here before you know it, across the atmospheric membrane that is everywhere (a cloud of Chernobyl dust, an oceanic tarn of toxic substance). With the multiplication of ego particles and their inmixing with other imaginary beings, who is oneself anymore? With multiple recombinations of chemical particles inmixing with my body—is it paranoia, or is the world coming to an end?

The ego began as an apocalypse. When the individual cut loose from family ties and tribal bonds, it thought the world would melt. And it is as was predicted, with the sun god (nuclear energy) coming down to marry the earth, in solar desire. Is it a conspiracy, do we say it to keep it from happening? The world is not quite over yet Earth already is coming to see itself in an image and be baptized with a name: Gaia. Does this mean it has become an Ego? An apotheosis of Narcissus? The identity of current generations of mortals has already begun to be confused with that of the earth itself in their atmospheric epidermis and synthetic weather patterns; and as the life span of this new crop of humans merges with the "fate of the Earth," something strange is happening. The duration of this generation feels identical with that of nature itself under the assault of post-mammalian technologies. The birth of a divinity is a great event. But will it live?

An emotion is an intensity wave, a fluctuation. "We of the present day are only just beginning to form the chain of a very powerful future feeling, link for link. . . . Anyone who manages to experience the history of humanity as a whole as *his own history* . . . if one could burden one's soul with all of this . . . if one could finally contain this all in one soul and crowd it into a single feeling . . . this godlike feeling would then be called—humaneness [*Menschlichkeit*]."[39] Humanity? We waited all this time to celebrate the apotheosis of . . . humanity? But let's not let the nervous chic tic of antihumanism—which passes for surpassing humanity—that is, human self-hatred, that most fashionable strain of cynical flus, anesthetize us to the rhythm of Nietzsche's transvaluation. First, this "humanity" or humaneness is not a Personalitas or an Ego but an emotion, a *Stimmung* or soul-tone that causes or allows the psyche to resonate with its full potential amplitude. This emotion eventually receives the name of god (Dionysos). It not Gaia an emotion? Dionysos is the discontinuous, disjunctive consciousness of Gaia. These are names of being that we share, this living Topos, our surface membrane. But are we too wired with hardware and programmed with software to feel it—or is the media not the very condition of its emergence in emergency? Transvaluation of narcissism, transfiguration of Narcissus.

There might then be two kinds or even times of eternal return—both of which rip into but also dilate the universal Baby in wireless communication (imagination) with its differential avatars and emotions. On one axis, that of a diasynchrony that Nietzsche introduced onto our conceptual, metaphysical field, egoic desire and subjectivity is overcome on the *plane of temporal consistency*, on which an emotion compresses into a single intensity wave, synthesizing at Eternity Junction diverging paths of all the preindividual and impersonal singularities that have made a difference to the being I am becoming in returning through "my" remembranes. Not even the influences we undergo, says Deleuze, but the insufflations we are. "The dissolved ego opens to series of roles, because it raises an intensity already comprising difference in-itself, which penetrates all the others through and in multiple bodies. Always another breath there is in mine, another thought in my thought. . . . All real thinking is an aggression."[40]

The other axis would be that of a simultaneity of affections of an ego no less dissolved but into a potentially recomposite Narcissus (transvalued as BwO) that is hanging tenaciously on to or strangely recovering its "pure instinct of life, of life without need of any organs."[41] But can Big Baby Earth communicate to itself without "media," in the manner of occult influences, on particle waves of pure thought, of pure emotion? We must distinguish between the organs of mediation, perception, and translation, and the affects or powers these organs are designed or discovered to induce. At the level of the abstract Machine diagramming the BwO there is only informal matter and nonspecific function.[42] The ego there disperses into "a series of singularities in the disjunctive network, or intensive states in the conjunctive tissue, and a transpositional subject over the entire surface, passing through all the states . . . of its avatars."[43]

Together the double-axis distribution of intensities composes the synthesis of repetition as production of a difference or eternal return of the future: the future (life) returns or remains never quite the same as itself. The Ego-Id relay has always been its form of mutation and recombination.

The paradox of eternal return is that it does not make the past recur, it synthesizes the future, *il ne fait revenir que l'avenir*. It is the point of entry into life, into being. But the Body without Organs does not form, the eternal return does not *happen now*, unless you let it take you by surprise. This is what Deleuze calls "metamorphosis of the agent," Narcissus-Dionysos in the instance. Narcissus is the name of the ego in crisis, of whom Freud and Lacan drew the diagnostic chart. Nietzsche and Klossowski assisted with the rebirth of a new god, Dionysos, coming and going with every intensity in the chaosmos. Deleuze, in the finest hour, saw or felt the emergence of Tony Artaud's "body without organs" (which Lacan too evoked) as metamorphic field potential or intense matter of creation.[44] Metamorphosis means ego-I go where id-it goes, between lives. Earth, we're I am with you. *Wo Es wird, werde Ich. Erde Ich.*

Once upon a time, the sun . . . transformation of libido, *turning sunlight into libido*. Now that was something new and different! Libido becoming transductive recording energy of code, transcoding itself some hazard or other, fell back upon the sun becoming it, life!, working and playing and resting and saying (somewhat afterwards): So that's me! Connecting and distributing singularities in semi-aleatory Markov chains (by prior relinkage). The chance of an Aion! Libido and Death are the two faces of time: Libideath. Aion (Greek "lifetime" or "eon") is the lifeline of time, the timeline of life, traversed by the two-sided instance of libideath. Life keeps on coming on, like a mean monster that won't go away. It suddenly appears at the unpredictible moment, far from equilibrium (within the indeterminable "amplification of a fluctuation"),[45] and begins to increase and multiply blessed events in the long Run, the big Event.

So Earth is becoming "libidobject" (J.-A. Miller), something indefinable, alea poised right here in the middle of nowhere except just right to take a cut of biotonic sunlight, to make a world of yum-yum, with genetic-structural love energy. Aion and Gaia: I propose a wedding toast! (Don't whisper a word but She's already pregnant, with gods and goddesses, multiplying like crazy.) My parents are my children. You keep on coming alive even after I'm all over on the other side of time.

The Multiple City

Time is milieu or dimension, the Fold. Multiplicity means many-fold, manifold, but what is a fold or dimension? A line is the dimension of the "thread of time," the time line. As dimension, this means the line is everywhere immanent to the time it lines or threads. Of course, the line is still a spatializing image of time. If we think of it folding back upon itself or looping back into itself, crossing itself, we attain an image of anticipation and recollection, the stitch of time.

We have still not produced a figure of time without image. For this we must think of Dimension not as the line but as the *becoming* of the line, not the fold but its *folding*, the curvature of time, clinamen. This means that immanent to time itself is the interstice between times (the smallest interval), time as productive of difference, the "form" of differentiation of each thing from itself, of each becoming different from itself. But in this interval, within this self-differentiation of form, we must conceive of a pure divergence that, still on the order of the time line, makes the curvature of the line. Of course, the interval, the interstice ("standing-between"), as discontinuation of the line, does not allow it to "consist" ("stand-together") as continuum with itself. What then does make it stay together? The duration of the interval itself, at each of its endpoints, touches the line and holds it together. But what if time consists of open intervals or "irrational cuts" (series of points without beginnings or endpoints)? Now how will it connect itself up?

These questions repeat endlessly. What we must imagine or conceive is that in the interstice something is produced that does endure—until the end of the interval. The human problem or crisis occurs when the end reflects itself or folds back into the interval to become coextensive with the entire span of duration, of life-time. Death then becomes a dimension of all life and medium of all thought, the "other side" of every interval of time (of whatever *durée*).

Now the Deleuzian or Nietzschean revolution (Deleuze as born-again Nietzschean) consists in the following. To convert the apocalyptic Ego, as form or substance of conscience-consciousness of the end, from the regime of death-consciousness (egoism) to the *interregnum* of Id. Everything changes nature as a consequence; in particular, memory and the regime of memory too undergo conversion—into the interregnum of forgetting and mutation (renaissance).

Now this is the most delicate operation, for the ego is not about to give up its prerogatives—consciousness and memory—for the unknown and unimaginable "future life" that signifies everything it rebels against: death, sexual reproduction, and so on. It is true that sexual reproduction is not the answer. On the contrary, it has been used by the ego to attempt replication of itself through childbearing—with all the oedipal, racist, and familialist consequences we know about. What we should imagine is a region of space-time and life-time governed by what Deleuze and Guattari call the Abstract Machine. This Other interval is the Body without Organs, child of the marriage of Aion and Gaia, consisting of a pure interval of living duration (qualitative multiplicity) and an intense matter.

Does this mean that the BwO, Aion-Gaia, or the Gayon is Id? Certainly. But "the Id" must be redetermined as a material Idea. In a restricted sense, it is the abstract Animal of Geoffroy Saint-Hilaire,[46] the genetic combinatory "in person," life-generation machine. In this sense, the Ego's conversion sends it into death as into the abstract where it undergoes dissolution and reshuffling of its memories. But are memories not lost, is memory not the Lost? It is so, which is why the regime of memory too must undergo a new conditioning and submit to forgetting as to a mutation of consciousness.

This double conversion, to Id and to forgetting, or quasi-memory (improvisation) releases the Ego from its abject subjection to death-time and into pure life-time—purified of its bad conscience, metaphysical longing, and sense of guilt. Of course, the Ego does not want to be released, and marshals all its forces of conscience in the name of morality, decency, even life itself, to prevent the change of regime (the opening into the interregnum). For it is true that many atrocities can be committed in the name of liberation from good and evil, whereas the mutation we are calling for confronts the Ego with its death as never before—a kind of transcendental egoicide. The regime of the Ego—of lacking transcendence, of the missing ideal, of the community of One, of the expulsion of the other, the bad object—is itself the holocaustic regime (or Empire of the Hole). Thus the "conversion" of Ego is indeed a kind of abolition, but also a transcendental mutation that transfuses the Ego with its fore and afterlives—not its family of genetic descendents, but the transvolutionary Family that is here right now on earth, playing, struggling, living, and dying (to be born).

God(')s Wink: The Book of Job, the University's Concern for Its Students, and Other Parables

Laura Zakarin

> We learn while sleeping.
> No one notices that he learns, only later,
> that he has learned. When it is too late to prevent it.
> Even when it comes easily, all learning is traumatic.
> —Werner Hamacher

> Make no judgments where you have no compassion.
> —Ann McCaffrey

*S*ome topics are very difficult to talk about. Studenthood is one of them. Unlike other topics to which professional thinkers have devoted years of their life in study, the *crisis* of academic life, which always resides as it were in the essence of things, exhibits itself most painfully in the impassioned decisions we make in our thinking about Studenthood. That may well be because—unlike the studentism that we currently practice—"Studenthood" as such does not exist.

Graspable only so long as it is presented in its metaphysical structure, Studenthood remains as elusive an idea as the basic right to happiness, the promise of charity and love, the joint covenant of brotherhood and sisterhood, the endless pursuit of knowledge, and what we sometimes call *jouissance*.[1] Outside of utopian images, outside of what could only be the reflection of an ultimate metaphysical situation of history, Studenthood altogether transcends direct presentation. Insofar as it can be indicated only indirectly, only from a distance—only, as we say, when the focal point of history, which is the condition of all seeing, allows what is nevertheless invisible to be traced before the eye—it can exist only as a parable. If it becomes somewhat visible through parabolic meaning, it can do so only if the reader is willing to follow in understanding. And here is the trick. As parable, which is quite literally a "thrown beside," Studenthood becomes appreciable only when the one who comes as student, that is, the "I" who comes in the name of "student," is not only looked *at*, but looked *in* the eye.

Studentism, meanwhile, does not require such respectful looking; on the contrary, it avoids and even circumvents this gaze. It is a condition resulting from altogether different principles of behavior, and its practice depends on the habitual sleight of hand through which an infinite number of individual students may be transformed into a single Student Body. In consummate form, studentism allows the business of academic institutions to take place. It sustains institutional agendas precisely because of how it checks the dangerous realization that within every university's student body, individual students walk around in their own unique bodies: bodies that, despite this or that similitude, retain their distinctness from all others and house singular desire. These bodies, however denied or disallowed, live and breathe apart from the university and even outside its realm of authority. They do not coalesce into a neatly packaged student corpus. The virtue of having student bodies exist on campuses is that no somatogenic responses can arise from them. As a consequence of this transforming tale, the body itself at once becomes a strangely forgotten region and a site of disfiguration.[2]

We need only consider how the effect of studentism manifests itself on whole student populations to see how it diminishes the value of student life. Manipulated into desired position by the demands of normal progress, for example, most students shuffle through the system unable to think the possibility that the rules of the game could be questioned. As they feel their way in this kind of blind man's bluff, they maintain their existence by clinging to the hope that, with enough artful maneuvering, the endgame quarter or semester will never come. They pray that their sensed inadequacies, which all students fear belong to themselves uniquely, will never be found out. The lucky ones, those that manage the game successfully, are not found out. Others are not so fortunate, however. Of these, some drop out, some are expelled, some suffer breakdowns, and some even take their own lives. But who among us has the compassion and courage to think of such casualties along the wayside, of the lengths taken and the handsome prices paid so that the terrible promise of "success" can be kept? As a community educated in the Humanities, let us imagine that we do.

Let us agree that studentism justly deserves to be apprehended for what it is: a performative tale whose academic pulpability is palpable—and precisely because it serves up so nicely on a plate. When dispensed in regular amounts, it well satisfies the appetites of huge administrative offices and bureaucrats. When ingested at regular intervals, it gives the illusion of fullness and suppresses the hunger for real and immediate contact among teachers and students. Yet such foodstuff does not nourish like a meal of substance; instead it is the food with which we stuff ourselves to fool ourselves about impending starvation. We accept the rhetoric of "equality," which argues that fairness exists so long as everyone is equally denied due consideration. We vigorously compete against each other for the all too slim pieces of pie. Secure in our knowledge about the perils of rumor and the fragility of reputation, we indulge in gossip about the juicy mishaps of others with an easy conscience. We hardly notice how empty we feel, so politic are the emaciated. In that they expertly pretend to administrate academic need, our studentisms help us to get by.

No wonder, then, that Studenthood catches the pupil's eye. A promise never fulfilled, it remains that through which we chart our progress and of which we long to catch a glimpse. The condition of a student in a university is like the condition of a comet in the universe, which by virtue of its parabolic curve only briefly looms into view, but whose invisible trajectory remains long after the heavenly body has arced its course and disappeared back into infinity.[3] No one knows this fateful condition better than the graduate student, the example among others of being both student and teacher. Returning year after year, attending to the imperatives of the university until at last graduating to the point of no return, he or she knows that the meaning of this progress slips by understanding. Herein lies the paradox of the parable to which the student cannot help but submit: this likeness, which is as well the parable of Studenthood, rests on the incommensurability between what is given and what can never be given directly.

Allow me briefly to point elsewhere and thereby perform exactly what I mean. In recent years, critical inquiry has focused on various texts of disaster that have taught us to learn about uninterrupted catastrophe.[4] This catastrophe is related to what we forget to learn—what we learn to remember to forget—about the profound connections between ourselves, history, and the university. In the eye of the storm of this, our academic progress, it is the pupil who becomes all too familiar with Walter Benjamin's "angel of history," who stares in horror at a single uninterrupted catastrophe "which keeps piling wreckage upon wreckage."[5] In strolling through such grounds, while pursuing academic destinations at which one never arrives, the student suffers what is both impersonal and arbitrary injury with each step taken. As Nietzsche notes in his *Untimely Medita-tions*, it is a journey on which one bleakly regards the terminal symptoms of the thinking man's unhealthiness and how such unhealthiness breeds in the "gruesome houses which the generation of public opinion has built for itself."[6] Such sad constructions, which we, academically speaking, could call our history, unquickened as it is by the exigencies of the present, are the very scaffolding of a terrible will to "knowledge" that wants to know nothing of "life" itself. We engage in philosophical interrogations that al-low us to question the unity of the universitary body and focus on the crises that lead to the decisions through which cowards are overcome and by which the brave become subordinate. But, alas, we have not yet thought how Studenthood works to question the terms of this interrogation.

Situated precisely at the origin of everything that we do (or think that we do), that we think about doing or do about thinking, nothing is ad-vanced by distinguishing problems in the life of the student. The condition of Studenthood cannot be delineated through a pragmatic depiction of particulars (institutions, personal relationships, customs, etc.), which, on the contrary, it evades. In regard to its inner unity, Studenthood cannot be submitted to such questioning if, to the degree that it could be a way of life, it would be a life that lacks the courage to submit itself to anything. Foreign, even hostile to the university at times, however, Studenthood has a place in our academic reflections as a chance event that, in the event of its having a chance, as Jacques Derrida has suggested, would be "the chance of an instant, an *Augenblick*, a 'wink' or a 'blink,'" taking place "in the twinkling of an eye."[7] But how is such a chance to be kept?

We might, for example, wonder, as Benjamin does, about the residual condition of "student life" that is at the outset focused on the contours that guide "life on the inside." In his talk before his fellow students, given in Berlin at a 1914 meeting of a leftist Free Student Organization, the twenty-two-year-old Benjamin suggests, "The distinguishing feature of student-life is, in fact, resistance to submitting itself to a principle, to permeating itself within the Idea."[8] This "deeply settled, domiciled indifference," through which and by the authority of which the conditions of an academic life may be imposed, is perhaps nowhere more glibly hinted at than in the claim we have all heard: that when one leaves the university, he or she fi-nally gets out into the "real" world. A strange claim this, which not only pretends that the university is not in the "real" world but also pretends that the "real" world is not in the university. But whether or not we are to play this uncanny "hide-and-seek" game and agree to the impossible conditions of possibility for having an institution without imposition—or what Samuel Weber calls the "conditions of *imposability*"—we must first agree that academic institutions are imposing in their existence.[9] That is to say, first of all, that universities exist, and that for those whose existence is intertwined with them, the existence of academic institutions is rather imposing. Even if we were to say that universities have nothing to do with life, we would still have to admit that the very Idea of a University entirely shapes the life of the one who follows it.

According to its own essence, Studenthood, whatever it might be, tolerates no resolution. It obligates the researcher to teach, the teacher to research, and the student body to serve as the living apparatus through which such clandestine communities of thinkers assign to themselves their uniform origin in the idea of knowing. This origin, a secret if not a fiction, shows itself most clearly in the honest barbarity of the compromise—between the Idea of Knowing and Knowledge, between the Idea of Academia and The Academies—struck on behalf of the revolutionary greatness of any university's task, namely, to ground its community of knowers. Nietzsche, well aware of the nature of the community to whose serious consideration he wishes to commend his conversation, notes in his lecture *On the Future of Our Educational Institutions*: "I know it to be a community which is striving to educate and enlighten its members on a scale so magnificently out of proportion to its size that it must put all larger cities to shame. This being so, I presume I may take it for granted that in a quarter where so much is *done* for the things of which I wish to speak, people must also *think* a good deal about them."[10]

The university is, in fact, a place, a place in which many remarks are made and which is remarkable, at least, because of the happy indifference with which it prepares the student's soul to celebrate its noisy pastimes. Who would believe that a position such as that of the student could—in these frenetic times of bewildering activity—even so much as exist? As Nietzsche fondly observes while recollecting his own academic experience from youthful memory, "It is necessary to have lived through it in order to believe that such careless self-lulling and comfortable indifference to the moment, or to time in general, are possible" (*On the Future*, p. 17). Even as Studenthood, according to its own essence, tolerates no resolution, the solemn *act* of being a student derives its very significance from this earnest resolution: that students are to do nothing definite except isolate themselves, the better to sit and meditate, and each be inspired with the same thoughts. For Nietzsche, the *act* of being a student is the very resolve "to *be* a silent solemnization, all reminiscence and all future; the present . . . to be as a hyphen between the two" (p. 27). In the course of its lectures and seminars, in the space created by its totality of teachers and students, lies the uniformity of the university and the easy peaceableness of those who abide in its secular kingdom. And yet, those who pass by each other—always straining toward a better view of the situation and perhaps toward the type of clearsighted discoveries that can only reveal themselves to the disinterested eye—are the teachers and students, who push onward and never catch a glimpse of what it might mean to find each other at last in this monstrous game of "hide-and-seek." The student body always remains unofficial here, behind the teaching body; and what Benjamin would call "the upright foundation of the University"—embodied in the "Education czar," that is to say, the secretary of education whom the president, and not the university, names—is "a half-veiled correspondence of the academic administration with the State Organs, over the heads of the students (and in rare and fortunate cases, over the heads of the teachers also)" ("Life of the Students," p. 47). If, as Benjamin claims, "uncritical and unresisting surrender to this condition is an essential feature of student life" (p. 48), then we should not be surprised that the student voice has never made itself decisively audible. Because of its very undecisiveness, the student voice always remains imperceptible.

The massive irony, the inherent falsity that is prerequisite to the trueness of student life and Studenthood therefore lies in the necessity of resisting the temptations while being caught up in the illegitimate, transitory waiting period imposed by studentism. For what is a student tempted by, according to Benjamin and Nietzsche, but his or her own disposition to savor his or her own youth. And what makes the student anxious but the knowledge that he or she cannot always remain Nietzsche's beloved "frivolous spendthrift." Even the students of our time, who spend their allowance of adolescence on a singular purchase—spending it all in one place, keeping the faith during the waiting period of their college studies, and all in the hope of opening their eyes before the light of adulthood, which consistently promises to appear but nonetheless is denied to them from year to year—even these students are aging people. They are not even the youngest generation. And for this reason, if for no other, it is with heroic resolve that they recognize their age at all; in doing so, they recognize, in the blink of an eye, what Benjamin has always known, "that a richer species of adolescents and children already lives, to which they can only dedicate themselves as teachers" ("Life of the Students," p. 53). For such reasons as well, Benjamin argues, students often do not discover themselves in their existence and, not recognizing their age, grow idle. Sometimes, out of a great yearning for youthful contact and the admitted need for someone to submit to vocational training, they even become teachers.

But even Benjamin, who eventually turns his back on the university, has enough of such depictions, which remain ineffectually locked in the domain of future studentisms and the misshapen forms of our present academes. The significance of the condition of Studenthood becomes understandable and possible for him only when grasped in a somewhat different structure, what he calls "its metaphysical structure, like the Messianic Kingdom or the Idea of the French Revolution": "The current historical significance of students and the University, the form of their existence in the present, thus deserves to be described only as a parable, as a reflection of an ultimate metaphysical condition of history" (p. 46). If we are inclined to take Benjamin at his word, then we need to consider the path he proposes we take in the direction of parable. Rather than submit our discussion of Studenthood to the dangerous reductions of vocational training, or the "job," which both Benjamin and Nietzsche long resented, let us seize the opportunity posed by the pun of this "J-O-B" and turn to one of theology's most painful parables. The *Book of Job*, a parable that meditates on the profundity of pain and the profanity through which even the good suffer, may allow us to entertain what is at once our most radiant and grayest of questions: what does it mean to have a hostility toward the university that is neither gratuitous nor conventional? In considering this, we might wonder what it would mean to have a hostility condensed around the university's radical complacency and radical incapacity to recognize the dignity of the language of suffering. Harboring suspicion of such language being the most profound of the universities' activities, we might find that what provokes hostility toward the university is something that has not just personal but also philosophical implications.

Written in an elegant Hebrew that, syntactically, is sometimes nearly impossible to translate, the *Book of Job* at times varies so greatly from translation to translation that it barely seems to be the same text.[11] While such variation has moved certain translators to accuse others of "intentional distortion," it does open our discussion of the book to the possibilities of performing acts of committed interpretation. For example, one of the key verses of the book can be taken to mean either "I will fear God" or "I will not fear God," and there is no way of knowing for sure which of these two not so subtly different statements is the one the author intended. More important for our purposes, however, are the different interpretations of a passage generally considered to be the book's most crucial, a passage whose various translations are not even remotely similar. For the sake of advancing our argument, I will confine our translation selections to the two most popular choices. Although, according to the view that has predominated rabbinical scholarship since 1920, Job affirms his faith with the statement "I know that my Redeemer liveth" (19:25–27), he may as well have said instead "I would rather be redeemed while I am still alive"—which would be a very *different* matter requiring no gloss for the meditator who understands pain.

If this possible difference in translation reveals its value to us, it does so at the end of the parable, when Job's despair is acknowledged by Yahweh: "And Yahweh turned the fortune of Job, [and Yahweh restored everything to Job in double amount]" (42:10–11). In reward for his not so silent rebellion against the unanimous condemnations of his comforters, and his vocal pious endurance, therefore, Job lives the rest of his life with twice the blessings he had before. Job's comforters, on the other hand, are punished for not having spoken what is proper in response to another's pain, and for lacking the courage to speak the truth of their own fears about God, the almighty father and teacher who strikes without warning and for reasons known only to him. In other words, they are punished for trying to secure their own comfort at another's expense.

While unwillingness to confront fear and admit to feelings of vulnerability is by no means uncommon, what is uncanny about the compulsiveness with which these men of learning attempt to forestall self-knowledge is the way in which that compulsiveness repeats itself in the sacrifice of the other. Consider the following anecdote from Werner Hamacher's discussion of a teacher of his who professed his desire to shoot his own students in the lecture hall: "One can now ask oneself what my teacher was afraid of: not to be a teacher but rather a comedian; not to have students but rather spectators; to be a teacher who teaches something which he does not want and does not know; to have students who study something other than he does, namely the teacher himself, and who measure him against something which he is not."[12] Driven by his fear that his students know even better than he that he teaches from an empty chair, the professor imagines mastering the teaching scene by violently emptying the hall. Unable to bear his own anxious affliction, the professor indulges in murderous thoughts and fantasizes about inflicting pain on the bodies of his students. What is so striking about this perforating fantasy, which speaks the desire to inflict pain on another in order to interrupt the pain felt by the self, is that it never calls suffering itself into question. Indeed such an "either/or" logic altogether suspends the possibility of questioning the necessity that *someone* suffer, and as a result ensures that suffering will continue.

As both the anecdote and the *Book of Job* reveal, suffering is what happens when the reaction to pain is to try to push it away. In other words, pain comes with the territory of life, but suffering is extra. Whereas pain runs in cycles and eventually ends, suffering—unless interrupted by compassion—only begets more suffering. In a world where everyone dies, where we witness the death of others and others will witness our own death, pain cannot be avoided; suffering, on the other hand, is avoidance itself. It is an unhealthy act of resistance against pain. It is a reaction to the fear of what might happen if pain were allowed to be felt, and an addiction to the means by which pain is avoided. In this process of trying not to feel what cannot be felt, shrinkage occurs; the being contracts, taking up residence in the smallness of the self. To get at the root level of such compulsion, however, discomfort must be experienced as a natural consequence of being alive.

Job's suffering is indeed compounded by the judgmental comments of his friends, who claim they speak in an effort to offer him comfort, but in fact only seek to comfort themselves. When Job—who does not question his afflictions, but questions the injustice of his afflictions—asks "why do I suffer," the friends take it upon themselves to provide theological explanations. In doing so, they mistake his cry of pain for an invitation to theological discussion, and even convince themselves that they are helping Job by explaining why God has selected him for unmitigated tragedy. They had, after all, "agreed together to come to pity and console him" (2:11), and as Eliphaz says, "You are dejected! But who could refrain from speaking?" (4:2). However, the friends do not speak from a point of sympathy; what they say is instead motivated by the fear that unless an explanation that is specific and localizable can be found for Job's unparalleled suffering, than all is chaos and no one is safe from unjustifiable punishment.

Maintaining the claim of conventional theology that "no ills befall the righteous," the comforters insist that Job's pain is God's way of punishing him for some previously unrecognized wrongdoing. While their insistence might seem reasonable enough—indeed "pain," "punishment," and "penalty" are all etymologically linked, and in Latin, for example, share a common root in the word "poena"—this explanation is specifically disallowed both by the opening prose, which carefully details how before his misfortune Job "was a perfect and upright man, fearing Elohim and turning away from evil" (1:1), and by God himself, whose own words echo those of the opening, when he boasts to Satan after the first round of testing that to

consider his servant Job is to know "There is no one like him on the earth;
he is a perfect and upright man, fearing Elohim and turning away from evil
. . . he still clings to his perfection" (2:3). As Rabbi Harold S. Kushner explains, the reason the comforters heartlessly assign blame for his suffering
to Job himself is that they are struggling with three propositions that all
appear to be true but of which, logically, only two can be true at any one
time. The three propositions are: (1) Job is good; (2) God is omnipotent,
and nothing occurs unless he wills it; and (3) God is just and fair.[13] The
problem of trying to make sense of all three propositions together is clarified by Kushner:

> If God is both just and powerful, then Job must be a sinner who deserves what is
> happening to him. If Job is good but God causes his suffering anyway, then God is
> not just. If Job deserved better and God did not send his suffering, then God is not
> all-powerful. We can see the argument of the Book of Job as an argument over
> which of the three statements we are prepared to sacrifice, so that we can keep on
> believing in the other two. (pp. 37–38)

Able to affirm any two only by denying the third, the comforters choose
to reject the proposition that Job is good. Denying Job's goodness is far
easier than denying God's perfection. Moreover, if Job is somehow responsible for the misfortunes that have been heaped upon him, then the
comforters are in the clear—especially so if they insist on the propositions
that argue on the side of God. If the victim is at fault for his own misfortune, then the evil that befalls him is no longer irrational and arbitrary.
Finding a reason for Job's misfortune brings relief to the comforters, albeit
the sticky relief of *schadenfreude*. Though they do not wish Job's ill fate
upon him, they nevertheless are grateful that the misfortune has befallen
him and not them.

The pleasure that the comforters derive from Job's pain and suffering
reveals itself in what they say to counsel him and how they respond to his
grief. They offer pious platitudes, recommend that he pray for understanding, and advise him to take his lesson to heart by repenting for the sins he
must have committed to deserve so severe a punishment (5:8–18). Their
hollow words are abusive, and only serve to increase Job's torment. The
comforters offend as they sit in judgment of Job's pain. Having never experienced similar losses, they have no sense of his despair and no means of
gauging the depth of the mourner's grief.

What the comforters fail to understand is this: Job is overwhelmed by
his losses not only because they are all-encompassing but also because they
occur simultaneously. The first messenger barely finishes reporting that

"the Sabaeans made an incursion," took the oxen and the donkeys, and slew the attending servants ("I alone am escaped to tell thee!") when a second messenger arrives to tell Job that a fire has fallen from heaven to devour the sheep and all the servants except for him. While the second is yet speaking, a third messenger arrives to report that he alone has escaped the Chaldaeans, who have raided the camels and put the other servants to the sword. Even as Job is learning that his whole wealth has disappeared in a stroke, the final messenger arrives with the most terrible news of all: a great desert wind has destroyed the house in which his sons and daughters were feasting, killing them one and all (1:14–19). Though Job suffers under the impact of his multiple tragedies, the friends remain relentless in their criticisms. They suggest that, for all he knows, Job's children may have brought their own deaths upon themselves: "If your sons have sinned against Him, He has delivered them up to the fruits of their transgression" (8:4).[14] They moreover admonish him for complaining in such plaintive tones, and for crying so loud and long. Having sat Shiva with Job for the week, the comforters are anxious for the mourning period to end. Impatient with his grief, they ask, "For how long will . . . your mouth be a great wind?" (8:2). In other words, having observed the customary seven-day period of formal mourning yet finding no end to Job's suffering, the comforters accuse him of not making "normal progress." Painfully aware of the time to be lost, they have no time to be pained by someone else's losses.

This inability to experience fully the pain that belongs to another is impossible to overcome, a fact that becomes abundantly clear when the pain we are talking about is a bodily one. No one can know what it feels like to be inside another person's body. No one can *really* know what it would be like to crawl inside another's skin. Though we can register our interactions with others in terms of what we feel toward them, only our own flesh hurts us: and a man's "flesh grieves only for himself" (Job 14:22). In that our bodies clearly define the limits of our physical being, they irreparably separate us from one another.

Job, who flesh crawls with maggots and whose skin is cracked and oozing, is utterly isolated in his pain. His "bowels seethe continually with agitation" because of the sorrow which confronts him (30:27). Men mock him and spit in his face; his wife is repulsed by his breath; his servants treat him as a stranger; and even children show scorn for him (19:14–18). Shunned by those who once sought his aid, Job has become "an object of derision" (30:9). Since adversity strikes at the level of his flesh, his pain becomes inescapable. But when grief-stricken Job is unable to find support, he becomes dually disenfranchised: he suffers both the isolation of his bodily affliction and the ambiguous status of his "role right" to grieve.

Although Job repeatedly asks God to account for his suffering, to open the ledger books and let him see firsthand how the figures have been tallied, Job's request is never honored and the reason for his trial never revealed to him. Though tested to an unparalleled extreme, he never gains privileged access to the meaning of his suffering. He never learns why the hedges were lifted, allowing adversity to penetrate the protective barrier. To the extent that God answers Job's plea that He be accountable, he does so by putting an end to the trial. However, this end to his suffering only comes when Job lets go of his fantasy: that he has a right to expect God to answer his questions and that he can induce God to lift him from his pain. At the same time, Job learns that God "canst do all things, And that no plan is unrealisable" with Him (42:2). In other words, Job trades in his fantasy of being taken under God's wing for one in which no plan is unattainable so long as men and women admit that human affairs always elude the control of human thought and wisdom.

While we clearly know that Job is tested, we can never know for certain to whom the lesson is directed. We might imagine that the lesson is for anyone who has either inflicted or endured suffering. It is an education in grief and a means for beginning to heal. A parable of learning, the *Book of Job* reminds us that the fantasy of belonging to a community in which all feel each other's pain—and for that matter each other's joy—can never be fully realized. Nevertheless it obliges us to imagine the possibility of a university that would respond not only to its students but also to its mission of compassion and understanding.

Reference Matter

Notes

MacCannell: Introduction

1. The blanked-out scene in the crypt is analogous to the blank of Egaeus's visit to their would-be wedding bed earlier in the story.

2. Etienne Bonnot, l'Abbé de Condillac, *Le traité des sensations*, ed. and comm. François Picavet (Paris: Librairie Delagrave, 1919). The *Traité* came six years after Hume's *Treatise*.

3. For Kant, *Schmerz* is the correlative of ethical acts. Kant conceives the ethical good beyond and against any good conceived as vitally desirable (Jacques Lacan, *Séminaire, livre VII: L'éthique de la psychanalyse, 1959–60* [Paris: Seuil, 1986], p. 129). Kant cannot imagine an overestimation of the object of desire—he cannot imagine dying for his object, or that he will accept death so that he can have the pleasure of cutting up the woman he sleeps with (ibid., p. 131).

4. Kant's view of the "symbolic" mediation between sensibility and *reason* as only a weak approximation (in par. 59 of the *Critique of Aesthetic Judgment*) is succinctly reviewed by Philip Barnard and Cheryl Lester in their Translators' Notes to Philippe Lacoue-Labarthe and Jean-Luc Nancy, *The Literary Absolute: The Theory of Literature in German Romanticism* (Albany: SUNY Press, 1988), pp. viii–ix.

5. If, after Kant—as Philippe Lacoue-Labarthe and Jean-Luc Nancy argue in their classic study, *L'absolut littéraire: Théorie de la littérature du romantisme allemand* (Paris, 1978)—the impasse he marked becomes the object of romantic revolt, the bent is away from the materialist comprehension of the embodied *idea* and toward attaining an unmediated presentation of the Absolute Idea, working its logic out beyond the categories of the mere understanding. Literature, and thereinafter "pure Philosophy's" concern with "the express distinction of philosophy and literature" (*logodaedalus*), becomes the site for setting up what Auerbach once called the "battle between sensible appearance and meaning" that came to define mimesis at the end of the Classical period.

6. This figure appears in the *Traité des sensations*, and has haunted all versions of the automaton.

7. This marking out, or theory of the sense perception as sustained by the signifier, was made clearer in the work of Destutt de Tracy, which I will discuss below.

8. Ernst Cassirer, *The Philosophy of the Enlightenment*, trans. F. C. A. Koelln and J. P. Pettegrove (Boston: Beacon Press, 1951), pp. 117–18.

9. See Jacques Lacan, "Kant avec Sade," in his *Écrits* (Paris; Seuil, 1966). See also the recent translation of "Kant with Sade" by James B. Swenson, Jr., *October* 51, Winter 1989, pp. 55–104 (Swenson's notes, pp. 76–104).

10. The deletions marked on the Kantian body already portend the formations of the unconscious as Freud discovered it in his own critique of metaphysics, *Beyond the Pleasure Principle* (trans. James Strachey [New York: Bantam, 1959]).

11. See Diderot's *conte* "Mystification."

12. Diderot writes in a letter to a friend, "There is always a little bit of testicle at the bottom of our most sublime ideals."

13. In some ways Rousseau, who called Condillac his one faithful friend, might be understood as considering his work to be the presentation of Condillac's ideas. His *Second Discourse*, for example, seems to me to follow the contours of Condillac's *Traité des sensations*, wherein the "statue's" progress in the (literal) garden of consciousness precisely parallels the development of the "ideas" of the savage in the state of nature.

14. English citations are from the Penguin edition of the text, *Love*, translated by Gilbert Sale and Suzanne Sale (Harmondsworth, Eng.: Penguin, 1957), p. 235: "This philosopher made the little mistake of calling his principle *self-interest* instead of giving it the prettier name of *pleasure*; but what can we think of the common-sense of a whole literary culture which allows itself to be misled by such a little slip of the pen?" For the French version, see *Stendhal, De l'Amour*, ed. Michel Crouzet (Paris: Garnier Flammarion, 1965), p. 264: "Ce philosophe commit la petite maladresse d'appeler ce principe *l'intérêt* au lieu de lui donner le joli nom de *plaisir*, mais que penser du bon sens de toute une littérature qui se laisse fourvoyer par une aussi petite faute."

15. Comte Antoine Louis Claude Destutt de Tracy, *Idéologie proprement dite* (Paris: J. Vrin, 1970). Originally written at the height of the Revolution (1796–1800), this work was first published in two stages, in 1801 and 1803. Destutt de Tracy was of a younger generation than the "philosophes"—a generation increasingly marked by splits into "right" and "left" wings (de Maistre, Constant, Cabanis, etc.). He wrote as part of his design to create from scratch a central school system for the new France.

16. Stendhal's definition of ideology as "crystallization" is entirely formed on this basis.

17. See Teresa Brennan, "The Age of Paranoia," *Paragraph*, 14, no. 1 (1990).

18. Jacques Lacan, *Seminar, livre III: Les psychoses, 1955–1956*, trans. Russell Grigg (New York: Norton, 1993), p. 39. Subsequent references to this work are cited in the text.

19. Alain Badiou argues Lacan's relation to philosophy this way: after Hegel and Spinoza, but especially in Nietzsche's wake, modern philosophy, hooked on the body, has become an anti-philosophy. Lacan's criticism of "philosophy," then,

could be understood as a crucial defense, precisely, *of* the philosophy that the modern spirit conjures. Alain Badiou, "Lacan et Platon: le mathème est-il une idée?" in *Lacan avec les philosophes* (Paris: Albin Michel, 1992).

20. Spivak uses the term "Semitized Hinduism." This takes Christianity back to a source that Christianity itself has not always felt it necessary to recognize except as one religious tradition among others it presumed to supplant. To link the Christian missionary-as-imperialist to the Semitizing of Hinduism in the period of colonization is somewhat mystifying in this context.

21. See Juliet Flower MacCannell, *The Regime of the Brother: After the Patriarchy* (London: Routledge, 1991), on Duras's strong reformulation of the "psychotic" faceting of feminine *jouissance* in *The Lover, The Seawall,* and *Lol V. Stein.*

Nancy: *Corpus*

NOTE: This essay was written to be presented at the 1990 meeting of the International Association for Philosophy and Literature held at the University of California, Irvine; the overall topic of that meeting was "the body." We are grateful to Juliet Flower MacCannell and Avital Ronell for extensive suggestions that helped shape the final translation.

1. *Entrée* is being used here both in the sense of a dictionary entry and in that of the openings, or orifices, of the body.—Trans.

2. Bernard of Clairvaux, *De diversis*, sermo 74, *Patrologia Latina* 193, c; 695.

3. See the formula Origen uses to designate Christ as "visible image of the invisible God." Christ, the "new Adam," whose "glorified body" is the singular property beyond death, has not always been thought of as a savior. His incarnation has also been thought of, especially in the high Middle Ages, as pure manifestation, as the radiance of God in his creation, or as the supplement that perfects creation.

4. Plato, *Phaedo*, 82e; *Gorgias*, 493a.

5. In Merleau-Ponty, the same obsession characterizes the thought of "the joint property between feeling and being felt" ("L'oeil et l'esprit," *Temps modernes*, no. 184–85 [1961], p. 187), or that of the "body [that] belongs to the order of things in the same way that the world is universal flesh" (*Le visible et l'invisible* [Paris, 1964], p. 181), or that of the flesh as "an *internally* shaped mass" (emphasis mine; ibid., p. 193). For the body in Hegel, see *The Phenomenology of Mind*, trans. J. B. Baillie (New York, 1967), pp. 337–72.

6. Merleau-Ponty, *Résumés de cours* (Paris, 1968), p. 177.

7. Roland Barthes, *Essais critiques* (Paris, 1982), p. 143.

8. How is this played back in the other areas of art? According to which identity and which difference? This would have to be investigated elsewhere.

9. St. Thomas Aquinas, *Summa Theologica*, Ia, qu. 91, 3.

10. Merleau-Ponty, *Le visible et l'invisible* (Paris, 1959), p. 192.

11. See n. 4 above and also Valéry: "There is no name to designate our sense of the substance of our presence, our actions and feelings, not only in their actuality, but also in an imminent, deferred, or purely potential state—something more re-

mote and yet less intimate than our secret thoughts." "Some Simple Reflections on the Body," trans. Ralph Mannheim, in *The Collected Works of Paul Valéry* (New York, 1964), 13: 36.

12. Derrida has analyzed the insidious return of the "spirit" in Heidegger after his setting aside Spirit in *Being and Time* (*De l'esprit* [Paris, 1988]). One could also investigate the absence, in *Being and Time*, of an analysis of the body, which Heidegger considers extraneous to his project (p. 108 of the German edition). Heidegger keeps certain references to the phenomenology of the "body proper" and to Scheler, but their status is not clear.

13. See my *L'insacrifiable*, forthcoming.

14. Marcel Henaff, *Sade, l'invention du corps libertin* (Paris, 1978), p. 322.

15. Elaine Scarry, *The Body in Pain: The Making and Unmaking of the World* (New York, 1985), pp. 35, 45.

16. The author is playing here on *ravaler ses mots*, "to retract one's words," but literally to "swallow" them.—Trans.

17. Gilles Deleuze and Félix Guattari, "How Do You Make Yourself a Body Without Organs?," in their *A Thousand Plateaus: Capitalism and Schizophrenia*, trans. Brian Massumi (Minneapolis, 1987), pp. 149–66.

18. The author uses the idiom *se réjouir*, "to look forward to something," in its literal sense "enjoy oneself again."—Trans.

19. Al Lingis, "L'ivresse des profondeurs," trans. N. and D. Janicaud, *Po&sie* 51 (1989).

Spivak: Response to Jean-Luc Nancy

1. Martin Heidegger, *Being and Time*, trans. John Macquarrie and Edward Robinson (New York: Harper, 1962), p. 25. Any remark about deconstruction and Heidegger must take into account the extraordinary reading of Heidegger in Jacques Derrida, *Of Spirit: Heidegger and the Question*, trans. Geoffrey Bennington and Rachel Bowlby (Chicago: University of Chicago Press, 1989). I have myself glossed at greater length the passage from Heidegger I have just quoted as a description of affirmative deconstruction, in Gayatri Chakravorty Spivak, "More on Power/Knowledge," in idem, *Outside in the Teaching Machine* (New York: Routledge, 1993).

2. Jean-Luc Nancy, "Corpus," trans. Claudette Sartiliot (with Avital Ronell and Juliet MacCannell), in idem, *The Birth to Presence*, trans. Brian Holmes et al. (Stanford: Stanford University Press, 1993). All citations of "Corpus" are taken from this translation, sometimes with modifications.

3. Jacques Derrida, *Glas*, trans. John P. Leavey, Jr., and Richard Rand (Lincoln: Nebraska Press, 1986) p. 214b. "Mise-en-oeuvre" comes from the following passage: "We are in an implacable political topography: one step further in view of greater profundity or radicalization, even going beyond the 'profound' and 'radical,' the principal, the *arkhe*, one step further toward a sort of original an-archy risks producing or reproducing the hierarchy. 'Thought' requires *both* the principle of reason *and* what is beyond the principle of reason, the *arkhe* and an-archy. Be-

tween the two, the difference of a breath or an accent"—what I have called a "tiny gap" in the text—"only the putting to work [*mise-en-œuvre*] of the 'thought' can decide. That decision is always risky, it always risks the worst. To claim to eliminate that risk by an institutional program is quite simply to erect a barricade against a future. The decision of thought cannot be an intra-institutional event, an academic moment," like a lecture or a book (Derrida, "The Principle of Reason: The University in the Eyes of Its Pupils," *Diacritics*, 13, no. 3 [1983], pp. 18–19). Although I reread this article for teaching only recently, long after the "original" response, I realize that my entire critique in this section resonates with Derrida's position.

4. Karl Marx, *Early Writings*, trans. Rodney Livingstone and Gregor Benton (New York: Vintage Books, 1975), p. 328; and idem, *Capital: A Critique of Political Economy*, vol. 3, trans. David Fernbach (New York: Vintage Books, 1981), pp. 958–59.

5. Jacques Derrida, "Declarations of Independence," *New Political Science*, 15 (1986), p. 11; translation modified.

6. Jean-Luc Nancy, *Corpus* (Paris: Metailie, 1992). Translations of passages are my own here and below.

7. Jacques Derrida, "Differance," in *Margins of Philosophy*, trans. Alan Bass (Chicago: University of Chicago Press, 1982), pp. 11–12.

8. The French "se" is active as a reflexive re-doubling of the self but gives passive meaning to active verbs. Thus it is a perennial worry to translators. When placed by itself, it is untranslatable. I have chosen the extremely awkward "transit" because for the body to redouble itself into a prediction would be for it to transit from *corpus*, and for the body to be acted upon is for it to become transitive. In the background is of course also *metaphora* as "transport."—Trans.

9. Derrida, *Of Spirit*, p. 57.

10. Jacques Derrida, "Shibboleth," trans. Joshua Wilner, in Derek Attridge, ed., *Acts of Literature* (New York: Routledge, 1992), pp. 373 and 393.

11. The following extract is from Gayatri Spivak, "Not Virgin Enough to Say that [S]he Occupies the Place of the Other," *Cardozo Law Review*, 13, no. 4 (1991), pp. 1343–44. The embedded extract is from B. K. Matilal and Gayatri Chakravorty Spivak, *Epic and Ethic in Indian Examples* (forthcoming).

12. Letter from Jean-Luc Nancy to Gayatri Spivak, Jan. 18, 1991, available at Cordozo Law Library, Yeshiva University.

13. See L. Dumont, *Homo Hierarchicus: An Essay on the Caste System*, trans. M. Sainsbury (Chicago: University of Chicago Press, 1970).

14. I have attempted to provide what is inevitably an impoverished and banal account of some ingredients of this "everyday" in Spivak, "Asked to Talk About Myself . . . ," *Third Text*, 19 (1992), pp. 9–18.

15. Romila Thaper, "Imagined Religious Communities? Ancient History and the Modern Search for a Hindu Identity," *Modern Asian Studies*, 23, no. 2 (1989), pp. 209–31.

16. Gayatri Spivak, " 'India,' Echo, and Two Postscripts," forthcoming in a volume edited by David Wills.

17. It is in this sense that Derrida writes, "I am psychoanalytically irresponsible," in Jacques Derrida, "Geopsychoanalysis: '. . . and the rest of the world,'" *American Imago*, 48, no. 2 (1991), p. 203. He is not and has not been where psychoanalysis attempts to be a performative ethics.

18. Gayatri Spivak, *Thinking Academic Freedom in Gendered Post-Coloniality* (Cape Town, South Africa: University of Cape Town Press, 1992), p. 27.

19. Derrida, "Shibboleth," p. 373.

20. Ibid., p. 384.

21. Paul Celan, "The Meridian," in *Paul Celan: Collected Prose*, trans. Rosemarie Waldrop (Manchester, Eng.: Carcanet, 1986), p. 54; translation modified. Partially cited in Derrida, "Shibboleth," p. 386.

22. Ibid., p. 52.

23. Gayatri Spivak, "Acting Bits / Identity Talk," *Critical Inquiry*, 18 (1992), pp. 776–79.

24. Derrida, *Glas*, pp. 232a–236a.

25. See William Pietz, "The Problem of the Fetish," *Res*, 9, no. 13 (1985), pp. 5–17; idem, "The Historical Semantics of Fetishism," *Res*, 16 (1987), pp. 23–45.

26. Jacques Derrida, *The Other Heading: Reflections on Today's Europe*, trans. Pascale-Anne Brault and Michel B. Naas (Bloomington: Indiana University Press, 1992), p. 76. I have discussed this passage at greater length in Spivak, *Outside in the Teaching Machine*.

27. Marx, *Capital*, vol. I, trans. Ben Fowkes (New York: Vintage Books, 1977), p. 131.

28. Elizabeth Grosz, *Sexual Subversions: Three French Feminists* (Sydney: Allen & Unwin, 1989).

29. The first-quoted phrase is to be found in Jacques Derrida, "This Strange Institution Called Literature," in Attridge, *Acts of Literature*, p. 34.

30. Jean-Luc Nancy, "*Menstruum universale* (Literary Dissolution)," *SubStance*, 21 (1978), pp. 21–35.

31. Ibid., p. 35.

32. Jacques Derrida, "White Mythology: Metaphor in the Text of Philosophy," in his *Margins of Philosophy*, p. 215.

33. This is a woman's reading of Derrida, "White Mythology," pp. 250–57.

34. Luce Irigaray, "Sexual Difference," in Toril Moi, ed., *French Feminist Thought: A Reader* (London: Blackwell, 1987), p. 124; translation modified.

Shapiro: *Nancy and the Corpus of Philosophy*

1. Jacques Derrida, "Ellipsis," in idem, *Writing and Difference*, trans. Alan Bass (Chicago: University of Chicago Press, 1978), p. 297.

2. See Jacques Derrida, "Violence and Metaphysics: An Essay on the Thought of Emmanuel Levinas," in his *Writing and Difference*, pp. 151–52.

3. Jean-Luc Nancy, "Sharing Voices," trans. Gayle L. Ormiston, in Gayle L. Ormiston and Alan Schrift, eds., *Transforming the Hermeneutic Context: Nietzsche to Nancy* (Albany: State University of New York Press, 1990), pp. 211–59.

4. See Jean-Luc Nancy, "Shattered Love," in idem, *The Inoperative Community*, ed. Peter Connor (Minneapolis: University of Minnesota Press, 1991), pp. 82–109.

5. Jean-Luc Nancy, "Vox Clamans in Deserto," trans. Nathalia King, in Norman F. Cantor and Nathalia King, eds., *Notebooks in Cultural Analysis*, vol. 3 (Durham, N.C.: Duke University Press, 1986), pp. 3–14.

6. See Friedrich Nietzsche, *The Gay Science*, no. 125, "The Madman."

7. Friedrich Nietzsche, *Thus Spoke Zarathustra*, trans. Walter Kaufmann (New York: Random House, 1966), p. 264.

8. Jean-Luc Nancy, "Wild Laughter in the Throat of Death," *MLN* Sept. 1987, pp. 719–36.

9. For the conception of laughter as verbal entropy, see *The Writings of Robert Smithson*, ed. Nancy Holt (New York: State University of New York Press, 1979), pp. 17–18.

10. See the entries for these words in the *Oxford English Dictionary*.

11. Cf. Michel Serres, *The Parasite*, trans. Lawrence R. Schehr (Baltimore: Johns Hopkins University Press, 1982), pp. 188–89; cf. also the chapter "Parasites and Their Noise," in my book *Alcyone: Nietzsche on Gifts, Noise and Women* (Albany: State University of New York Press, 1991).

12. Georg W. F. Hegel, *The Phenomenology of Spirit*, trans. A. V. Miller (New York: Oxford University Press, 1977), p. 210. I have substituted the English equivalent of Hegel's *Pissen* for Miller's "urination."

13. Friedrich Nietzsche, *Twilight of the Idols*, "How the True World Finally Became a Fable."

14. Derrida, *Writing and Difference*, p. 296.

15. Nancy, "Vox Clamans in Deserto," p. 8.

16. Nietzsche, *The Gay Science*, no. 125.

17. Jean-Luc Nancy, *L'oubli de la philosophie* (Paris: Galilée, 1986).

18. Nietzsche, *Thus Spoke Zarathustra*, p. 32.

19. Jean-Luc Nancy, "Dum Scribo," trans. Ian McLeod, *Oxford Literary Review*, 3, no. 2 (1978), p. 12.

20. See Nancy, "Dum Scribo," pp. 15–16.

21. Georg W. F. Hegel, *The Difference Between Fichte's and Schelling's System of Philosophy*, trans. H. S. Harris and Walter Cerf (Albany: State University of New York Press, 1977), p. 88.

22. Jean-Luc Nancy, "Elliptical Sense," trans. Peter Connor, *Research in Phenomenology* (1988), pp. 175–90; the words I cite are from pp. 188–90.

23. Nietzsche, *Thus Spoke Zarathustra*, p. 217.

Žižek: *How to Give Body to a Deadlock?*

1. Such utopian worlds are of course structured as a counterpoint to the aggressive, patriarchal Western civilization: the realm of matriarchy (*She*), of black rule (*King Solomon's Mines*), of harmonious contact with nature (*Tarzan*), of balanced wisdom (*Lost Horizon*). The message of these novels is, however, more am-

biguous than it may seem. For the heroes who entered the idyllic worlds, life in the domain of saturated desire soon becomes unbearable, and they strive to return to our corrupted civilization. The universe of pure fantasy is a universe without surplus enjoyment, i.e., a perfectly balanced universe where the object-cause of desire cannot be brought to effect.

2. This is the reason why this pass is always shown in the film in a way that points out its artificial character (one perceives immediately that it is a studio set, with its entire background—including the "Rancho Notorious" in the valley below—painted on a gigantic cloth). The same procedure was used by Hitchcock in his *Marnie,* among others.

3. A homological inversion in the domain of painting occurs in the work of Edward Munch; the despair of his "expressionistic" phase is followed by a quasi-magical appeasement when Munch found support and a stable point of reference in the rhythm of Nature, the life-giving power of the Sun, etc.

4. Cf. Jacques Lacan, *Séminaire, livre VII: L'éthique de la psychanalyse 1959–60* (Paris: Seuil, 1986), chap. 20.

5. Beside the "*real*-impossibility" and "the *symbolically* prohibited," there is a third, *imaginary,* version of incest, the economy of which is psychotic: incest is necessary and unavoidable since every libidinal object is incestuous. An exemplary case of it is the Catharic heresy, which proscribed *every* sexual relation, claiming intercourse with any libidinal object, not only with one's relatives, as incestuous. On these three modalities of incest (its impossibility, prohibition, necessity), see Peter Widmer, "Jenseits des Inzestverbots," *Riss,* 2, 4, and 6 (1986–87).

6. Here we encounter the function of the "subject supposed to believe": the existing order is legitimized by the scruple that a doubt about it would betray the naive belief of the other (of the foreign worker who believes in the USSR, who by means of this belief confers meaning and consistency upon his life). On the notion of the "subject supposed to believe," see Slavoj Žižek , *The Sublime Object of Ideology* (London: Verso, 1989), 185–86.

7. For another reading of this paradox, see my *Sublime Object of Ideology,* pp. 45–47.

8. See Sigmund Freud, *Interpretation of Dreams* (Harmondsworth, Eng.: Penguin, 1977), chap. 2.

9. *The Seminar of Jacques Lacan, Book II: The Ego in Freud's Theory and in the Technique of Psychoanalysis,* ed. Jacques-Alain Miller, trans. Sylvana Tomaselli (Cambridge, Eng.: Cambridge University Press, 1988), p. 159.

10. Ibid., p. 154.

11. Ibid., pp. 154–55.

12. Ibid., p. 168.

13. Ibid., p. 161. This reversal of trauma into bliss is equivalent to a kind of symbolic lobotomy: excision of the traumatic tumor, like the operation to which Frances Farmer was submitted in order to "feel good" in the American everyday ideology.

14. Hegel's philosophy is consequently radically antievolutionary. To ascertain this, one only has to recall the notional couple *in-itself / for-itself.* This couple is

usually taken as the supreme proof of Hegel's trust in evolutionary progress (the development from in-itself into for-self); yet it suffices to look closely at it in order to dispel this phantom of evolution. The in-itself in its opposition to for-itself means at one and the same time (a) what exists only potentially, as an inner possibility, contrary to the actuality wherein a possibility has externalized and realized itself, *and* (b) actuality itself in the sense of external, immediate, "raw" objectivity that is still opposed to subjective mediation, that is not yet internalized, not yet rendered conscious. In this sense, the "in-itself" is actuality insofar as it has not yet reached its Notion.

The simultaneous reading of these two aspects undermines the usual idea of dialectical progress as a process of gradual realization of the object's inner potentials, as its spontaneous self-development. Hegel is here quite outspoken and explicit: the inner potentials of the self-development of an object and the pressure exerted on it by an external force are *strictly correlative*, they form the two sides of the same conjunction. In other words, the potentiality of the object must also be present in its external actuality, under the form of the heteronomous coercion. For example (the example is from Hegel himself), to say that a pupil at the beginning of the process of education is somebody who potentially knows, somebody who, in the course of his development, will realize his creative potential, *is equivalent to saying* that this inner potential must be, from the very beginning, present in the external actuality as the authority of the master who exerts pressure upon his pupil. Today, one can add as a further example the sadly famous case of the working class *qua* revolutionary subject: to affirm that the working class is "in itself," potentially, a revolutionary subject, is equivalent to asserting that this potentiality must already be actualized in the party, which knows in advance of this revolutionary mission and therefore exerts pressure upon the working class, guiding it toward the realization of its potential. This way, the "leading role" of the party is legitimized, that is, its right to "educate" the working class in accordance with its potential, to "implant" in it its historical mission.

15. Jacques Lacan, *Écrits: A Selection*, trans. Alan Sheridan (London, Tavistock, 1977), p. 286.

16. Before one accuses Hegel of introducing the triad thesis-antithesis-synthesis as a formal principle of order into every kind of chaotic content, one should note that the terms are not Hegel's: Hegel *never* speaks of "thesis-antithesis-synthesis"; the terms were introduced by his pupils years after his death.

17. Within a "non-antagonistic" relation, the identity-with-itself of every moment is grounded in its complementary relationship to its Other (woman is woman through her relationship to man; together, the two of them constitute a harmonious whole, etc.), whereas in an "antagonistic" relation the Other truncates our identity, prevents us from achieving it, from "becoming fully what we are" (the relation between the sexes thus becomes "antagonistic" when woman starts to perceive her relationship to the opposite sex as something that prevents her from fully realizing her female subjective position, from fully "being herself"). For such a notion of antagonism, see Ernesto Laclau and Chantal Mouffe, *Hegemony and Socialist Strategy* (London: Verso, 1985).

238 *Notes to Pages 72–76*

18. Theodor W. Adorno, *Negative Dialectics* (New York: Continuum, 1973), p. 5.

19. The Lacanian name for this unbarred Other *qua* de-subjectivized symbolic machinery is "immixing [*immixion*]." See Jacques Lacan, "Of Structure as an Inmixing of an Otherness Prerequisite to Any Subject Whatever," in Richard Macksey and Eugenio Donato, eds., *The Structuralist Controversy* (Baltimore: Johns Hopkins Press, 1970).

20. The best indicator of this inherent impasse of the "pleasure principle" is the existence of the popular ideology in the U.S.A. called "nonism," i.e., the ideology of NON—the attitude of radical renunciation (of pollution, of fat and cholesterol in food, of stressful situations, etc.). In short, the final price for a pleasure-oriented life is that the subject is bombarded from all sides by prohibitions from the superego: don't eat fat and beef, avoid food with pesticides, don't smoke, don't pollute . . . "Nonism" is a new empirical confirmation of Lacan's paradoxical inversion of Dostoyevsky's famous proposition from the *Brothers Karamazov*, "If God doesn't exist, then everything is permitted": nothing at all is permitted, not even the innocent pleasures of eating, drinking, and smoking.

More precisely, the form taken by nonism in America is consumption-nonism: we may have anything, but in an aseptic, substanceless form—anything, including the most cruel fantasies, like that of the "Ratman," Freud's famous analysand of being tortured by a rat who penetrates the anus. A recent hushed-up scandal involving a movie star revealed that the staging of this fantasy is currently fashionable in Hollywood: A veterinarian cuts off the teeth and claws of a mouse; it is then put in a bag and its tail tied to a string. When the bag is deep in the anus, the excitement is provided by the animal's desperate motion till it suffocates; then it is pulled out by the tail. (The problem was the Hollywood star pulled the string too hard, so that it came off the tail, and stayed inside. The star thus had to seek medical help to remove the dead mouse.) Here we have the paradox of consumption-nonism: you can have everything, but in a form robbed of substance—cake without sugar and fat, beer without alcohol, coffee without caffeine, mouse without teeth and claws.

21. We all know the crucial step accomplished by the theory of relativity, the step from the thesis that matter "curves" space to the thesis that what we call "matter" is *nothing but* the curvature of space. Perhaps, this homology enables us to grasp the Lacanian proposition on the purely formal status of *objet a*: far from being the positive, material *cause* of the curvature, of the derailing of the path of desire, *objet a*—insofar as it is perceived as a positive entity (the Lady in courtly love, for example)—is nothing but a chimerical materialization of the curved structure of the space of desire itself. And since the only "substance" ("matter") acknowledged by psychoanalysis is enjoyment, we can also say that enjoyment is ultimately nothing but a certain purely formal curvature of the space of pleasure/displeasure, a curvature that makes us experience pleasure in displeasure itself.

22. As to the paradoxes of the notion of "beyond the pleasure principle," see the incisive developments of Joan Copjec in "The Sartorial Superego," *October*, 50 (1989).

23. On this prehistory, see Slavoj Žižek, *Le plus sublime des hystériques—Hegel passe* (Paris, Point Hors Ligne, 1988), chap. 11.

Sánchez-Eppler: *Por causa mecánica*

This study would not have been possible without the exchanges and the support provided by Doris Sommer, Eduardo González, Karen Sánchez-Eppler, and the students in the course "The Literature of Racial Difference in Latin America" (Spring 1990, Fall 1991) at Brandeis University.

1. Orlando Patterson, *Slavery and Social Death* (Cambridge, Mass.: Harvard University Press, 1982), summarizes this tenet of slaveholding ideology as follows: "If the slave no longer belonged to a community, if he had no social existence outside of his master, then what was he? The initial response in almost all slaveholding societies was to define the slave as a socially dead person" (p. 38).

2. Robert L. Paquette, *Sugar Is Made with Blood: The Conspiracy of La Escalera and the Conflict Between Empires over Slavery in Cuba* (Middletown, Conn.: Wesleyan University Press, 1988), pp. 84–85.

3. Manuel Moreno Fraginals, *El ingenio* (Havana, 1978), pp. 36–70; Paquette, *Sugar Is Made with Blood*, pp. 9, 30, 92.

4. Cirilo Villaverde, *Cecilia Valdés* (Mexico City, 1972).

5. "[Q]uiero por lo menos, que por sabios artífices se trace al instante, el plan que debe seguirse para *blanquear nuestros negros*, o sea, para identificar en América a los descendientes de Africa con los descendientes de Europa. Quiero que, al propio tiempo que con prudencia se piense en destruir la esclavitud, (para lo cual no hay poco hecho), se trate de lo que no se ha pensado, que es borrar su memoria. La Naturaleza misma nos indica el más fácil y más seguro rumbo que hay que seguir en esto. Ella nos muestra que el color negro cede al blanco, y que desaparece, si se repiten las mezclas de ambas razas; y entonces también observamos la inclinación decidida que los frutos de esas mezclas tienen a la gente blanca." Francisco Arango y Pareño, *Obras* 2 (Havana, 1952), p. 307; cited in translation by Verena Martínez-Alier, *Marriage, Class and Colour in Nineteenth Century Cuba* (Cambridge, Eng.: Cambridge Univ. Pres, 1974), p. 35.

6. With regard to the Gamboas, Doris Sommer states: "Father and son are seduced as much by the absolute power of their racial and sexual advantage as by their partner's sexual charms. This is no modern free market of feeling where unprotected desire could produce social growth, but a bastion of colonial custom where erotic protectionism nurtures desires in surplus of social needs." Doris Sommer, *National Romance, Foundational Fiction* (Berkeley: University of California Press, 1991), p. 128.

7. "Es querer decir que Magdalena, negra como yo, tuvo con un blanco a *señá* Chepilla, parda; que *señá* Chepilla, tuvo con otro blanco, a *señá* Charito Alarcón, parda clara, y que *señá* Charito tuvo con otro blanco a Cecilia Valdés, blanca" (Villaverde, *Cecilia Valdés*, p. 241).

8. For further analysis of how the black slaves are the ones who control the

information about the problems of Cuban miscegenation, and of how the whites and the *mulatos* refuse, at their peril, to recognize the validity of that knowledge, see Sommer, *National Romance*, pp. 129–30.

9. "Por entre aquel estrépito infernal, se oía distintamente el crugir de los haces de caña que otros esclavos desnudos de medio cuerpo arriba, metían de una vez y sin descanso, en las masas cilíndricas de hierro" (Villaverde, *Cecilia Valdés*, p. 190).

10. "Es, sin embargo, coincidencia rara, que a un tiempo se hayan alzado tantos negros y de aquellas fincas precisamente que han cambiado de poco acá su sistema de moler caña. ¿Será que estas estúpidas criaturas se han figurado que se les aumenta el trabajo porque en vez de moler con bueyes o mulas, se muele con máquina de vapor?" (ibid., p. 200; also quoted in Paquette, *Sugar Is Made with Blood*, p. 54).

11. "Si se hubiera pedido informe a las señoritas sobre lo que habían visto en la enfermería, habrían referido muy diferente historia de la relatada por el médico y Leonardo. Hubieran dicho que el Hércules africano tendido boca-arriba en la dura tarima, con ambos pies en el cepo, con los hoyos cónicos de los dientes de los perros aún abiertos en sus carnes cenizas, con los vestidos hechos trizas, . . . , Jesucristo de ébano en la cruz, como algunas de ellas observó, era espectáculo digno de commiseración y de respeto" (Villaverde, *Cecilia Valdés*, p. 210).

12. "Guiaba la procesión el cura de Quiebrahacha. . . . Marchaban a su lado dos caballeros conduciendo cada uno un haz de cañas, atados con cintas de seda blanco y azul, que sujetaban por la punta cuatro señoritas. Llegados delante del trapiche, murmuró el cura una breve oración en latín, roció los cilindors con agua bendita, valiéndose para ello del hisopo de plata, los caballeros colocaron enseguida las cañas en el tablero de alimentación y dio comienzo la primera molienda con máquina de vapor" (ibid., p. 219).

13. "He aquí lo que el vulgo llama tragarse la lengua y que nosotros llamamos asfixia por causa mecánica" (ibid., p. 220).

14. For an alternative fantasy on the coupling of the steam engine and the bodies of the slaves, see Reinaldo Arenas's *La loma del Angel*, translated as *Graveyard of the Angels*, trans. Alfred J. MacAdam (New York: Avon, 1987). This parody of *Cecilia Valdés* turns the just-installed steam engine of the Gamboas into a slave-eating machine that swallows the black bodies and ejects them explosively into the air, a process interpreted by the slaves as a return flight to Africa (chap. 24).

15. For a critique of this and other abolitionists' "solutions" to the problems of slavery by means of the literal enactment of "give me liberty or give me death" or by means of a return to Africa after emancipation—the Liberian option—see Karen Sánchez-Eppler "Bodily Bonds: The Intersecting Rhetorics of Feminism and Abolition," *Representations*, 24 (1988): 50.

16. "Seamos realistas: el Atlántico es hoy el Atlántico (con todas sus ciudades puertuarias) porque alguna vez fue producto de la cópula de Europa—ese insaciable toro solar—con las costas del Caribe; el Atlántico es hoy Atlántico—el ombligo del capitalismo—porque Europa, en su laboratorio mercantilista, concibió

el proyecto de inseminar la matriz caribeña con la sangre de Africa" (Antonio Benítez Rojo, *La isla que se repite: El Caribe y la perspectiva posmoderna* [Hanover, N.H., 1989], p. vi).

17.   Ass-swanking the Queen advances,
             and hot oscillations, which the drum coalesces
             into rivers of sugar and molasses,
             ooze from her huge rump.
             Dark grinding-mill for sensuous harvest,
             the hip-works, mass against mass,
             squeeze out rhythms bloodsweating/sweatbleeding,
             and the grinding climaxes in dance.

Ronell: *Finitude's Score*

1. *On the Genealogy of Morals*, trans. Walter Kaufmann and R. J. Hollingdale (New York: Vintage Books, 1989), p. 59. Follow these strains from *The Birth of Tragedy* onward, where the Dionysian figure presents itself as a space of telephonic reverberation: "The Dionysian musician is, without any images, himself pure primordial pain and its primordial re-echoing"; *Friedrich Nietzsche*, trans. Walter Kaufmann (New York: Vintage Books, 1967), p. 50. The negative trope of *ressentiment* (see below) covers the modes of operatic transmission. See Sarah Kofman's discussion "La musique, art privilégié," in her *Nietzsche et la métaphore* (Paris: Galilée, 1972).

2. One might mobilize the inscription coined by Peter Canning in which symptom and syntax are made to merge in *symtax*, for Nietzsche is indeed exploring the "symptax" of nihilism. See Peter Canning, *Sleepwalking* (Ph.D. diss., Harvard University, 1989).

3. Catherine Clément, *L'opéra ou la défaite des femmes* (Paris: Grasset, 1979); translated as *Opera, or the Undoing of Women*, trans. Betsy Wing (Minneapolis: University of Minnesota Press, 1988). Quotations below are from Wing's translation and are cited by page number in text.

4. Friedrich Kittler discusses Wagner's displacement of the orchestra to the pit in "Weltatem. Über Wagners Medientechnologie," in his *Diskursanalysen 1*, ed. F. A. Kittler, M. Schneider, and S. Weber (Opladen: Westdeutscher Verlag, 1987), pp. 94–107.

5. I am accompanying the score set by Jacques Derrida in "Des Tours de Babel," in *Difference in Translation*, ed. Joseph F. Graham (Ithaca: Cornell University Press, 1985).

6. The tense reopening of an aesthetics of closure is treated by David Carroll in his *Paraesthetics: Foucault, Lyotard, Derrida* (New York: Methuen, 1987).

7. Ibid., 191.

8. I have tried to follow the logic of Acquired Immune Deficiency Syndrome in the shared text of Mozart and Nietzsche in "Queens of the Night: Nietzsche's Antibodies," *Genre XVI* (1983), pp. 405–22.

9. Jean-François Lyotard, *Driftworks* (New York; Semiotext(e), 1984), p. 104. Of course, to the extent that they are both engaged in rebabelizing the Word, Moses and Luther are compatible figures. We might recall here Michel Foucault's assertion in *Les mots et les choses* that the modern age began with two great hysterics: Don Quixote and Luther. The first to introduce desire, Luther deposes the Father in the name of the Other.

10. Jean-Luc Nancy, "*Vox Clamans in Deserto*," trans. Nathalia King, in Norman F. Cantor and Nathelia King, eds., *Notebooks in Cultural Analysis* (Durham, N.C.: Duke University Press, 1986).

11. Francis Steegmuller, *Cocteau: A Biography* (Boston: Little, Brown, 1970), p. 112.

12. Other operas fascinated by the telephone include Gian-Carlo Menotti's *The Telephone*, subtitled *L'amour à trois*, in which interruption and scrambling are thematized, and Lee Hoiby's *Three Women: Composed for Miss Beardsley, 1988*, "Miss Alma Calls . . ."

13. Keith W. Daniel, *Francis Poulenc: His Artistic Development and Musical Style* (Ann Arbor, Mich.: Studies in Musicology, No. 52, UMI Research Press, 1982), p. 29.

14. Jean Cocteau, *The Human Voice*, trans. Carl Wildman (London: Vision, 1930).

15. On the links between background music and the death drive, see Laurence A. Rickels, *Aberrations of Mourning: Writing on German Crypts* (Detroit: Wayne State University Press, 1988).

16. Francis Poulenc, *Correspondance 1915–1963* (Paris: Seuil, 1967), p. 270.

17. Pierre Bernac, *Francis Poulenc: The Man and His Songs*, trans. Winifred Radford (New York: Norton, 1977), p. 184.

Schwenger: *Hiroshima in the Morning*

1. Jacques Lacan, "Of Structure as an Inmixing of Otherness Prerequisite to Any Subject Whatever," in Richard Macksey and Eugenio Donato, eds., *The Structuralist Controversy: The Languages of Criticism and the Sciences of Man* (Baltimore: Johns Hopkins University Press, 1970), p. 189.

2. Dean MacCannell, "Baltimore in the Morning . . . After: On the Forms of Post-Nuclear Leadership," *Diacritics*, 14 (Summer 1984), pp. 33–46.

3. Martha A. Bartter, "Nuclear War as Urban Renewal," *Science Fiction Studies*, 13, no. 2 (July 1986), pp. 148–58.

4. Robert Jay Lifton, *Death in Life: Survivors of Hiroshima* (New York: Random House, 1967), p. 33.

5. Michihiko Hachiya, *Hiroshima Diary*, ed. Warner Wells (Chapel Hill: University of North Carolina Press, 1955), p. 54.

6. Elaine Scarry, *The Body in Pain: The Making and Unmaking of the World* (New York: Oxford University Press, 1985), p. 80.

7. Jacques Lacan, *The Four Fundamental Concepts of Psycho-Analysis*, trans.

Alan Sheridan (New York: Norton, 1979), p. 203. Subsequent citations of this source will be given in text with the abbreviation *FFC*.

8. Fredric Jameson, *The Political Unconscious* (Ithaca: Cornell Unviersity Press, 1981), p. 35.

9. Thomas Pynchon, *Gravity's Rainbow* (New York: Viking, 1973).

10. Jacques Lacan, *Écrits: A Selection*, trans. Alan Sheridan (New York: Norton, 1977), p. 284.

Tomiche: *Writing the Body*

1. All references to the text will be to the French edition, Marguerite Duras, *L'amante anglaise* (Paris: Gallimard, 1967); all translations are my own. The other texts by Duras to which I refer are: *Moderato cantabile* (Paris: Minuit, 1958); *Les viaducs de la Seine-et-Oise* (Paris: Gallimard, 1959); *Hiroshima, mon amour* (Paris: Gallimard, 1960); *La maladie de la mort* (Paris: Minuit, 1982); and "Sublime, forcément sublime," *Libération*, July 17, 1985, pp. 4–6.

2. Interview with Marguerite Duras, reprinted in *Cahiers du cinema*, 312–13. Special issue on Marguerite Duras entitled *Les yeux verts* (June 1980), p. 76.

3. Duras, "Sublime," pp. 4–6. Duras's gesture of applying aesthetic categories (the sublime) to a murder was doubled and reinforced by the textual blurring between the "real" case and a Durassian fiction: throughout the article the accused mother was exclusively named Christine V., turning her into a Durassian character such as Lol V. Stein.

4. Jacques Lacan, "Hommage fait à Marguerite Duras du *Ravissement de Lol V. Stein*," *Cahiers Renaud-Barrault*, 52 (Nov. 1965), p. 9.

5. Lacan develops this concept of aggressivity as constitutive of subjectivity in terms of the "*imagos* of the fragmented body." This notion of the "imagos du corps morcelé" is at the heart of his articles on the mirror stage ("Le stade du miroir") and on aggressivity in psychoanalysis ("L'agressivité en psychanalyse"), both of which appear in *Ecrits* (Paris: Seuil, 1966). In the dialectical process of the constitution of the self, the "fragmented body" characterizes the imaginary mode of identification, which is then overcome by access to the symbolic order. Not only are these images part of the "normal" development of the subject, but they are constitutive of it, they cannot be dissociated from the "imago du corps propre" (the images of one's own body as a unified body), and they lead to the constitution of the forever alienated subjectivity.

6. Jacques Derrida, *Dissemination*, trans. Barbara Johnson (Chicago: University of Chicago Press, 1981), p. 301.

7. Jacques Derrida, "The *Sans* of the Pure Cut," in *The Truth in Painting*, trans. Geoff Bennington and Ian McLeod (Chicago: Unviersity of Chicago Press, 1987), p. 89.

8. Jacques Derrida, *Glas*, trans. John P. Leavey, Jr., and Richard Rand (Lincoln: University of Nebraska Press, 1986).

9. I am indebted to Juliet Flower MacCannell for reminding me of this point.

10. Maurice Blanchot, *L'entretien infini* (Paris: Gallimard, 1969), p. 269.

Librett: *Writing (as) the Perverse Body in "Lucinde"*

1. Jacques Lacan, *Encore: Le séminaire*, bk. 20 (1972–73), ed. Jacques-Alain Miller (Paris: Seuil, 1975), p. 31. Translation mine, J. L.

2. Friedrich Schlegel, *Philosophical Fragments*, trans. P. Firchow (Minneapolis: University of Minnesota Press, 1991), p. 29; *Kritische Friedrich-Schlegel-Ausgabe*, vol. 2, ed. E. Behler, J.-J. Anslett, and Hans Eichner (Paderborn: Schöningh, 1967), p. 179. References to fragments given parenthetically in text and notes below provide first the name of the collection in which the fragment originally appeared, then the number of the fragment, then the page references first to the English, then to the German edition. Occasionally I have altered Firchow's translations to bring out the connotations important to my reading.

3. Compare the reading of this fragment (along with others) in terms of the equation of system and fragment in Rodolphe Gasché's "Ideality in Fragmentation," which is the foreword to Schlegel, *Philosophical Fragments*, pp. vii–xxxii. Explaining Schlegel's concept of the fragment in terms of its background in Kant's philosophy, Gasché clarifies the difference between the romantic conception of the fragment—as fragmentary totality, or as *essentially* fragmentary—and two other conceptions: on the one hand, classical notions of the fragment, which see in the fragment the remains of a totality conceived as formerly or potentially existing beyond the fragment in a nonfragmentary form, and on the other hand, contemporary writing practices, which would neither see the fragment in terms of an essential "closure" (p. xxxi) nor revert to a classical conception of the fragment as part of a whole separate from it. "To call [contemporary writing] fragmentary would be to erase a fracture that resists all dialectics of part and whole" (p. xxxi). Still, one wonders whether Gasché is not being as it were too generous to contemporary thought or too ungenerous to Schlegel. Rhetorical questions: Can contemporary writing be said to resist *totally* all dialectics of part and whole? Is for example Derrida *simply* outside of metaphysics? And on the other hand, if Schlegel's concept of fragmentation simply acquiesces to the desire for the metaphorical totalization of synecdoche, then where is the basis of Hegel's dissatisfaction with Schlegel?

4. In the wake of Walter Benjamin's emphasis (e.g., with reference to "terminology," in his *Der Begriff der Kunstkritik in der deutschen Romantik*, in *Gesammelte Schriften*, vol. 1, pt. 1, ed. Rolf Tiedemann and Hermann Schweppenhäuser (Frankfurt/M.: Suhrkamp, 1974, pp. 47–51) on the importance of the motif of the "literal" in the work of the early German romantics, Philippe Lacoue-Labarthe and Jean-Luc Nancy have noted (in their *L'absolu littéraire: Théorie de la littérature du romantisme allemand* [Paris: Seuil, 1978], p. 77n) that Friedrich Schlegel began to develop a theory of writing analogous to that of Maurice Blanchot and Jacques Derrida, but failed to disentangle this thought from the guiding concerns of idealism to the extent to which these later thinkers seem to have done. I might be said to be testing the limits of this failure here.

5. Moreover, "association" is not identity, even if in Schlegel association may well be all that is left of identity, both in the logical and the psychological senses—senses that Schlegel in turn associates with one another in order to determine the

concept of wit (to the discussion of which I will return below): "Witz ist unbedingt geselliger Geist, oder fragmentarische Genialität" ("Wit is absolute associative [or social] feeling, or fragmentary genius" [*Critical Fragments*, 9; 2, 148]); "Witz ist logische Geselligkeit" ("Wit is logical sociability" *Critical Fragments*, 56: 7, 154]); "Manche witzige Einfälle sind wie das überraschende Wiedersehen zwei befreund-eter Gedanken nach einer langen Trennung" ("Many witty ideas are like the sudden meeting of two friendly thoughts after a long separation" [*Athenaeum Fragments*, 37; 23, 171]). Association is therefore as such precipitate in Schlegel's thought of *Witz*: it has the sudden quickness of a positioning, a *Setzung*. Since *Satz* can be translated not only as what is posited but also as what remains behind, or what precipitates out of a solution, the writing of wit is precipitate in this sense too, as the precipitateness of the chemical precipitate.

6. See Ernst Behler's essay "Friedrich Schlegels Theorie des Verstehens: Her-meneutik oder Dekonstruktion?" (in Ernst Behler and Jochen Hörisch, eds., *Die Aktualität der Frühromantik* (Paderborn: Schöningh, 1987), pp. 141–60), which describes in an extraordinarily precise and useful way the position of Schlegel within (or rather outside of) a hermeneutic tradition from Schleiermacher to Gad-amer. This tradition has found it necessary to marginalize (read: to ignore) his achievement. Behler argues persuasively for the legitimacy and importance of a re-consideration of Schlegel in light of the thought of deconstruction. His already ex-tremely helpful discussion (pp. 146–51) of Schlegel's peculiar take on the motif of "understanding the other better than he or she has understood himself or herself" gains, I think, somewhat greater focus when understood in terms of the considera-tions I am adumbrating here on Schlegel's thought of letter and spirit.

7. It is still coming our way in Paul de Man's essay "The Rhetoric of Tempo-rality," in his *Blindness and Insight: Essays in the Rhetoric of Contemporary Crit-icism*, 2nd ed. (Minneapolis: University of Minnesota Press, 1983), pp. 187–228. In this essay, first published in 1969, the temporal structures of irony (which de Man discusses in part with reference to Schlegel's text) and allegory, as the syn-chronization of the diachronic and as the diachronization of the synchronic re-spectively, are characterized as inextricably intertwined: "the two modes . . . are two faces of the same fundamental experience of time" (p. 226), which is an ex-perience of the demystification of the belief in the possibility of a demystified ex-perience of time's neither simultaneous nor successive (a)structure. Marike Finley (in "An Ironic Twist of a Semiotics of Narrative: Friedrich Schlegel's Roman," *Ca-nadian Review of Comparative Literature*, 11 [1984], pp. 559–95) has argued— in the wake of de Man, and by bringing to bear upon Schlegel's text with great acumen a formidable array of semiotic approaches—that a semiotic approach to irony is doomed to failure, in that irony is ultimately resistant to all metalanguage. This does not mean, however, that one can successfully resist the (ironic) tendency to metalinguistic formulations, as she acknowledges and perhaps also denies by suggesting that the semiotic model must be supplemented by a consideration of pragmatic discursive contexts. In "Rhetorik und Literatur: Anmerkungen zur poe-tologischen Begriffsbildung bei Friedrich Schlegel" (in Behler and Hörisch, *Aktu-alität der Frühromantik*, pp. 161–73), David Wellbery has commented upon de

Man's reading of Schlegel and extended it, focusing on Schlegel's Lessing essay, into an extraordinarily suggestive schematization of Schlegel's concept of text in its literal, spiritual, and labyrinthine dimensions. While fundamentally (and in almost all details) in agreement with Wellbery's essay, I would take issue, as the opening discussion of my own attempt makes obvious, with his characterization of the "geistigen Textes" in terms of "systematische Form, Totalität des Gehalts, und gesetzmäßige Entwicklung" (p. 168), since, for example, the annihilating effect of both systematicity and nonsystematicity upon spirituality makes the notion of "spirit" in Schlegel more complicated than this characterization allows.

8. See Immanuel Kant, *Kritik der Urteilskraft*, in his *Werkaugabe*, vol. 10, ed. Wilhelm Weischedel (Frankfurt/M.: Suhrkamp 1974), secs. 64–68, pp. 316–44.

9. The present essay is a piece of a longer reading in progress of Schlegel's novel in connection with *Florentin*, the novel by his wife, Dorothea. This reading will pursue the rhetorical and cultural-historical implications of the perverse scenario in which the two novels' lovers are involved, implications that are linked to the fact that Dorothea is a Jewess and the daughter of Moses Mendelssohn. That is, she is the daughter of "Moses," the daughter of the (displaced) author of the law *par excellence*, yet at the same time the daughter of the people whose presence in Germany constitutes, despite or because of its "juridical" identity, the subversion of the law of Protestant "faith" and the enduring "provocation" (willy nilly) of its Pauline dogma. The sense in which the publication of *Lucinde* violates both Dorothea Veit and those who are the enemies of her people extends the play of perversity within the novel into its politicohistorical context in important ways.

10. I may seem to be effacing the differences between deconstruction and psychoanalysis as the differences have been broached by the critical reading of Lacan undertaken by Jean-Luc Nancy and Philippe Lacoue-Labarthe in *Le titre de la lettre* (Paris: Galilée, 1973) and extended in Derrida's suggestion in *La carte postale: De Socrate à Freud et au-delà* (Paris: Flammarion, 1980) that the Lacanian letter is a letter in name only, i.e., a letter that is ultimately assimilated to a logocentric concept of writing in accordance with which the symbolic order would ultimately represent the law as a spiritualized logos taken to be prior to the writing of difference. But I am assuming that these differences are difficult to uphold (at least without further ado). Though I am unable to demonstrate this conclusively here, I would cite just a few reasons for it. For one, Barbara Johnson's essay "The Frame of Reference: Poe, Lacan, Derrida" (in her *The Critical Difference* [Baltimore: Johns Hopkins University Press, 1980], pp. 110–47) at the very least manages to make the reader uncertain whether Derrida is not projecting into Lacan what he thinks he finds there. In addition, the development of the "concept" of writing in Lacan's texts after *Ecrits*—perhaps under the force of the critical observations by Derrida, Nancy, and Lacoue-Labarthe—is particularly careful to evade or to pervert the law of logocentric conceptuality. Further, there can be no question of a *total* overcoming of metaphysics, for reasons by now well known, any more than there could be a question for romanticism of a total overcoming of enlightenment.

11. Freud discusses the possibility of the "Zusammenfassung" (comprehension, summation, synthesis) of the partial drives in the final section of the *Three*

Essays on Sexuality (Drei Abhandlungen zur Sexualtheorie [1905], in *Studienausgabe*, ed. A. Mitscherlich et al. [Frankfurt/M.: Fischer, 1982]). This section is entitled "Zusammenfassung"—a gesture that a perverse sensibility might be tempted to read as ironic.

12. In *Irony and Ethics in Narrative: From Schlegel to Lacan* (New Haven; Yale University Press, 1985), Gary J. Handwerk pursues the theme of an ethics of irony as an opening of the subject to the other from Schlegel to Lacan, but he establishes the correspondences at the level of the symbolic order (as a placing in question of the imaginary), whereas, drawing on the post-*Ecrits* Lacan, I am concerned with exploring the possibility of reading Schlegel in terms of the writing of the real (as a no-longer-theoretical placing in question of the signifying order).

13. In *Obscene: The History of an Indignation*, trans. Karen Gershon (London, Macgibbon and Kee, 1965), Ludwig Marcuse provides a partial account of the reception-history of the "scandal," if somewhat sloppily, and in a tone of indignation that makes of indignation an obscenity.

14. The word for "clumsy one" is "eines Ungeschickten," which means not only "clumsy" but also, literally, "unsent," and can be taken to imply here "undestined," as in one who has no destiny, no *Schickung* or *Geschick*, or one who, unlike Goethe's Wilhelm Meister, has no *Sendung*. Schlegel advertises this clumsiness and this lack of destiny in polemical contrast to the gracefulness of the "beautiful soul" (above all in Schiller and Goethe), conceived as the one who realizes the individuality of a destiny by fusing inclination and duty, i.e., natural and ethical necessities, into the higher necessity or destiny of pure existence. The subject of Schlegel's confessional narrative is clumsy and undestined in the sense that his destiny has been interrupted by the nonrelationality or undecidability of the relation-without-relation between "his" inclination, becoming, asystematicity or genesis, and "his" duty, being, systematicity, or structure: interrupted by the living-dying of their singular (non)community.

15. Friedrich Schlegel, *Lucinde*, in *Kritische Friedrich-Schlegel-Ausgabe*, vol. 5, p. 7. All references to *Lucinde* are to this edition; page references will be given parenthetically in text below. The translations are my own.

16. On the interplay between positing and reflexion in Fichte and the early German romantics, see Walter Benjamin, *Begriff der Kunstkritik*, pp. 18–40.

17. To begin to make the link between the hysterical and the perverse here, suffice it to cite two passages from Freud's *Drei Abhandlungen zur Sexualtheorie* (my translations): "neurosis is so to speak the negative of perversion" (p. 74), hence perversion is the supplement of neurosis, and as Freud quotes Möbius, "we are all a little bit hysterical" (p. 79). The ubiquity of a little bit of hysteria communicates here with the ubiquity of the little bit of polymorphous perversity that completes it.

18. For a recent discussion of Schiller's notion of grace important for the view taken here, see the last essays of Paul de Man, for example "Aesthetic Formalization: Kleist's *Über das Marionettentheater*," in his *The Rhetoric of Romanticism* (New York: Columbia University Press, 1984), pp. 263–90.

19. See Finlay, "Ironic Twist," p. 565–66, who briefly mentions the possibility

of reading the passage under discussion here in terms of Lacan but provides no detailed reading of the passage, and assimilates the letter to the signifier, in accordance with what Lacan seems to be suggesting in his middle phase.

20. "Romantic writing . . . alone is infinite, just as it alone is free; and it recognizes as its first law that the will of the poet can tolerate no law above itself" (*Athenaeum Fragments*, 116; 32, 183).

21. "Denke nur nicht so arg von mir und glaube, daß ich nicht allein für dich, sondern für die Mitwelt dichte. Glaube mir, es ist mir bloß um die Objektivität meiner Liebe zu tun. Diese Objektivität und jede Anlage zu ihr bestätigt und bildet ja eben die Magie der Schrift, und weil es mir versagt ist, meine Flamme in Gesänge auszuhauchen, muß ich den stillen Zügen das schöne Geheimnis vertrauen. Dabei denke ich aber ebensowenig an die ganze Mitwelt als an die Nachwelt. Und muß es ja eine Welt sein, an die ich denken soll, so sei es am liebsten die Vorwelt" (p. 25).

Sarris: *American Indian Lives and Others' Selves*

1. In this paper I have written from memory my conversations with Mabel McKay. "Aunt Violet" is Mrs. Violet Chappell. "Aunt Anita" is Anita Silva.

2. Arnold Krupat, *For Those Who Come After: A Study of Native American Autobiography* (Berkeley: University of California Press, 1985), p. 31.

3. David H. Brumble, *American Indian Autobiography* (Berkeley: University of California Press, 1988).

4. John G. Neihardt, ed., *Black Elk Speaks* (Lincoln: University of Nebraska Press, 1979 [1932]).

5. Sally McClusky, "Black Elk Speaks, and So Does John Neihardt," *Western American Literature*, 6 (1972), pp. 231–42; Michael Castro, *Interpreting the Indian: Twentieth-Century Poets and the Native American* (Albuquerque: University of New Mexico Press, 1983); Raymond DeMallie, *The Sixth Grandfather: Black Elk's Teachings Given to John G. Neihardt* (Lincoln: University of Nebraska Press, 1984).

6. Neihardt, quoted in DeMallie, *Grandfather*, p. 49. [Note also that the Indian is not portrayed as having a real body, something physical in a real world that is political and historical. Some editions of *Black Elk Speaks* provide photographs of Black Elk. Yet I would suggest the text frames any viewing of the photographs. Accordingly, Black Elk is seen as "the man" who is "spiritual," not *physical, political,* or *historical.*

7. Carlos Castaneda, *The Teachings of Don Juan: A Yaqui Way of Knowledge* (Berkeley: University of California Press, 1968).

8. Ruby Modesto and Guy Mount, *Not for Innocent Ears: Spiritual Traditions of a Cahuilla Medicine Woman* (Angelus Oaks, Calif.: Sweetlight Books, 1980).

9. Roy Pascal, *Design and Truth in Autobiography* (Cambridge, Mass.: Harvard University Press, 1960), pp. 182–83.

10. Louis P. Renza, "The Veto of the Imagination: A Theory of Autobiography," *New Literary History*, 9 (1977), p. 2.

11. Paul John Eakin, *Fiction in Autobiography: Studies in the Art of Self-Invention* (Princeton: Princeton University Press, 1974), pp. 213–14.

12. This pertains not only to the spiritual or cultural self that is presented but also to the "embodied" physical self in a world that is political and historical. What is portrayed concerning the American Indian in his or her physical world? To what extent do readers see bodies that may be rich or poor, oppressed or free?

13. Gretchen Bataille and Kathleen Sands, *American Indian Women: Telling Their Lives* (Lincoln: University of Nebraska Press, 1984), p. viii.

14. Again, *how* is an American Indian woman "embodied" in a given text?

15. Brumble, *Autobiography*, p. 111. Also see Alexander H. Leighton and Dorothea C. Leighton, eds., "The Life Story," in their *Gregorio, the Hand-Trembler: A Psychological Personality Study of a Navaho Indian*, Papers of the Peabody Museum of American Archaeology and Ethnography, vol. 40, no. 1 (Cambridge, Mass., 1949), pp. 45–81.

16. Marjorie Shostak, *Nisa: The Life and Words of a !Kung Woman* (Cambridge, Mass.: Harvard University Press, 1981).

17. James Clifford, "On Ethnographic Authority," *Representations* 1, no. 2 (1983), pp. 118–46.

18. Donald Bahr, J. Gregorio, D. I. Lopez, and A. Alvarez, *Piman Shamanism and Staying Sickness* (Tucson: University of Arizona Press, 1974).

Ekotto: *Body in Cameroonian Women's Writing*

1. Werewere Liking, *Orphée d'Afric* (Paris: Harmattan, 1986), p. 30 (translations of this and other quotations from Cameroonian novels are mine).

2. Lydie Dooh-Bunya, *La brise du jour* (Yaoundé, Cameroun: CLE, 1977), p. 102.

3. Calixthe Beyala, *C'est le soleil qui m'a brûlée* (Paris: Stock, 1987), p. 73.

4. Ibid., p. 173.

5. Julia Kristeva, *Powers of Horror: An Essay on Abjection* (New York: Columbia University Press, 1982), p. 4.

6. Ibid., p. 3.

7. This term comes from Jahnnes Fabian's *Time and the Other: How Anthropology Makes Its Object* (New York: Columbia University Press, 1983), p. 47.

8. Rey Chow, "Violence in the Other Country: China as Crisis, Spectacle and Woman," *Racial America*, 22, no. 4 (1990), p. 9.

Kamdar: *Corporal Politics*

1. See Jay Caplan, *Framed Narratives: Diderot's Genealogy of the Beholder* (Minneapolis: University of Minnesota Press, 1985); James Creech, *Diderot: Thresholds of Representation* (Columbus: Ohio State University Press, 1986); Elisabeth de Fontenay, *Diderot, ou le matérialisme enchanté* (Paris: Grasset, 1981); Pierre de Saint-Amand, *Diderot, le labyrinthe de la relation* (Paris: J. Vrin, 1984).

2. Rosalina de la Carrera, *Success in Circuit Lies: Diderot's Communicational Practice* (Stanford: Stanford University Press, 1991), pp. 19–20.

3. See Gayatri Chakravorty Spivak, "Can the Subaltern Speak?" in Cary Nelson and Lawrence Grossberg, eds., *Marxism and the Interpretation of Culture* (Urbana: University of Illinois Press, 1988), pp. 271–313.

4. See Mira Kamdar, "Subjectification and Mimesis: Colonizing History," *American Journal of Semiotics*, 7, no. 3 (1990), pp. 91–100.

5. Philippe Lacoue-Labarthe, "Diderot, le paradoxe et la mimésis," in his *L'imitation des modernes: Typographies II* (Paris: Galilée, 1985), pp. 15–36.

6. Denis Diderot, *Apologie de l'abbé Galiani*, in his *Oeuvres politiques* (Paris: Garnier Frères, 1963), p. 112.

7. Denis Diderot, *Le rêve de d'Alembert*, in his *Oeuvres philosophiques* (Paris: Garnier Frères, 1964), p. 346.

8. Francis Barker, *The Tremulous Private Body: Essays on Subjection* (London: Methuen, 1984), p. 55.

9. Denis Diderot, *Entretien entre d'Alembert et Diderot*, in his *Oeuvres philosophiques* (Paris: Garnier Frères, 1964), p. 260.

Olkowski: *Bodies in the Light*

1. Roland Barthes, "From Work to Text," in Josue V. Harari, ed., *Textual Strategies* (Ithaca: Cornell University Press, 1979), p. 77.

2. Jane Gallop, *Reading Lacan* (Ithaca: Cornell University Press, 1985), p. 61.

3. See, for example, Joan Copjec's statement in "The Orthopsychic Subject: Film Theory and the Reception of Lacan," *October*, 49 (Spring 1989): "The subject's own being breaks up between its unconscious being and its conscious semblance. . . . In sum, the conflictual nature of Lacan's culpable subject sets it worlds apart from the stable subject of film theory" (p. 71). Also see Mignon Nixon, "You Thrive on Mistaken Identity," *October* 49 (Spring 1989). Nixon finds a strategy that "blocks identification and destabilizes subjectivity, disrupts masculine viewing and exposes the construction of gender stereotypes" (p. 65), not in film, the moving image, but in the art of Barbara Kruger.

4. Judith E. Stein and Ann-Sargent Wooster, "Making Their Mark," in Nancy Grubb, ed., *Making Their Mark, Women Artists Move into the Mainstream: 1970– 1985* (New York: Abbeville Press, 1989).

5. Laura Mulvey, "Visual Pleasure and Narrative Cinema," in Gerald Mast and Marshall Cohen, eds., *Film Theory and Criticism* (New York: Oxford University Press, 1985).

6. Constance Penley, "The Avant-Garde and Its Imaginary," in her *The Future of an Illusion* (Minneapolis: University of Minnesota Press, 1989), p. 10.

7. See ibid., p. 12.

8. Jean-Louis Baudry, "The Apparatus," *Camera Obscura*, 1 (1976), p. 113.

9. Plato, *Symposium*, trans. Benjamin Jowett (Indianapolis: Bobbs-Merrill, 1956), p. 42.

10. Gilles Deleuze and Félix Guattari, *Anti-Oedipus: Capitalism and Schizo-*

phrenia, trans. Robert Hurley, Mark Seem, and Helen R. Lane (Minneapolis: University of Minnesota Press, 1983), p. 2.

11. Svetlana Alpers, *The Art of Describing: Dutch Art in the Seventeenth Century* (Chicago: University of Chicago Press, 1983), p. xix.

12. Friedrich Kittler, *Discourse Networks 1800/1900*, trans. Michael Metteer, with Chris Cullens (Stanford: Stanford University Press, 1991), p. 222, emphasis added.

13. Gertrude Koch, "Why Women Go to the Movies," *Jump Cut*, 27, p. 53.

14. Friedrich Kittler, "Dracula's Legacy," *Stanford Humanities Review*, 1, no. 1 (1989), p. 150.

15. Kittler, *Networks*, p. 284.

16. Elizabeth Grosz, *Jacques Lacan, a Feminist Introduction* (London: Routledge, 1990), p. 22. Grosz makes this statement in reference to feminist thinkers who, in their retrieval of psychoanalysis, unquestioningly accept the dominant patriarchal structures as inevitable and unchangeable, coded as natural. Nonetheless, I see it as directly relevant to the argument at hand. See ibid., pp. 22–23.

17. Ibid., p. 20.

18. Ardele Lister, *Split*, in *We Are Not Sugar and Spice and Everything Nice*, from the series What Does She Want?, available from Video Data Bank, School of the Art Institute of Chicago.

19. Alpers, *Art of Describing*, p. xix.

20. Gilles Deleuze, *Cinema 2, the Time-Image*, trans. Hugh Tomlinson and Robert Galleta (Minneapolis: University of Minnesota Press, 1989), p. 26.

21. Ibid., p. 26.

Brunette: *Electronic Bodies / Real Bodies*

1. This process is of course also operative in the other forms of the media, both electronic, such as radio, and nonelectronic, such as the written press. My emphasis in this essay is on a particular form of the process that is characteristic of television news.

2. Many theorists see television as quintessentially postmodern in that its normal mode of reception is disjointed and fragmented (primarily because of the use of the remote control to change channels quickly and because of television's status in most homes as the unremarkable and unremitting background of everyday life). Television's inherent disjointedness leads to some interesting contradictions with the prevailing ethos and "standards" that television news personnel seem to hold, which are invariably based on the older, more clearly logocentric print medium.

3. John Fiske, *Television Culture* (New York: Routledge, 1987), p. 308. It should be clear that such terms as "masculine" and "feminine" in this quotation and elsewhere in this essay are to be taken as descriptions of social constructions, not as empirical definitions.

4. Laura Mulvey's seminal 1975 article, "Visual Pleasure and Narrative Cinema" (*Screen*, 16, no. 3, pp. 6–18; reprinted in Karyn Kay and Gerald Peary, eds., *Women and the Cinema* [New York: Dutton, 1977], and elsewhere) first described

the gender dynamics of the cinematic gaze and, in so doing, spawned more than a decade of intense and important work in feminist film theory. In this essay, Mulvey claimed that the cinematic apparatus functioned principally to allow the male spectator to gaze voyeuristically upon the female characters in the film, a gaze that in turn led to castration anxiety, which then resulted in various psychic strategies of containment and fetishization that could only further diminish women. Despite the power of this claim, most feminist film theory since that time (including Mulvey's own recent work) has attempted to counter it by theorizing a place for the female spectator that defines her as something more than lack, more than a mere signifying necessity for the male's construction of meaning.

In a recent article, Craig Saper argues convincingly that all film theory has for years massively misunderstood and misrepresented Lacan's theory of the gaze. ("A Nervous Theory: The Troubling Gaze of Psychoanalysis in Media Studies," *Diacritics*, 21, no. 4 [Winter 1991], pp. 33–52.) But while the theory's parentage in Lacan may be suspect, it still seems useful as a kind of shorthand for what goes on psychologically between us and the characters when we watch a film. The psychoanalytic details of Lacan's version of the gaze do not seem to me to be crucial to the limited use to which I put the idea in this essay. (For a recent overview of film theory from the perspective of the gaze, see Joan Copjec, "The Orthopsychic Subject: Film Theory and the Reception of Lacan," *October*, 49 [Spring 1989], pp. 53–72.)

5. See Fiske, *Television Culture*, pp. 99–105, and Raymond Williams, *Television: Technology and Cultural Form* (London: Fontana, 1974). See also Henry Jenkins, *Textual Poachers: Television Fans and Participatory Culture* (New York: Routledge, 1992), for a convincing counterargument that television is not always received in a fragmented fashion or as part of background familial flow.

6. The functioning of the female anchor is of course even more complicated than that of the male. She must somehow be able to negotiate the gap between authoritativeness and beauty or glamour—does the handsome male anchor also have this problem?—not an easy task in a patriarchal society that has traditionally seen these qualities as opposed. In any case, this question deserves an essay of its own and cannot be adequately dealt with here.

7. A comparison with the old-fashioned newsreels that used to precede feature movies in theaters, before the advent of television, is instructive. Here, voice did all—remember the famous, stentorian voice invoked and parodied in Welles's *Citizen Kane*—and in the otherwise complete absence of the real body, the mastery effect was necessarily stronger and less compromised than it inevitably is on the network television news, where the news deliverers are seen as well as heard. But changes in media technology demand new strategies and negotiations.

8. But contradictions abound, as always. For example, as Fiske rightly points out, television news's obsession with speed and immediateness serves not only to parade but also to *disguise* the costs involved and the fact that only huge corporations can have access to such technology (*Television Culture*, p. 289).

9. Ibid., p. 289.

10. To invoke a personal anecdote, I have for years been automatically taping

the news each evening, then watching the show 30 minutes later so that I might fast-forward through, and thereby avoid, the commercials. I find that, despite the further alienation of the "natural effect" produced by the frequent fast-forwarding, once *in* a news story, my normal (that is, un-self-conscious) viewing mode is to watch it as something natural and not produced—and thus as eminently worthy of being believed—unless a particularly egregious interpretation is given of the events depicted.

11. Technology, in its essential reproducibility, is traditionally related to death, and the eyes of the anchor that follow us around the room do indeed suggest an automaton, an effect of technology from which the life has been removed.

12. For a discussion of the "postal principle," see Jacques Derrida, *The Post Card*, trans. Alan Bass (Chicago: University of Chicago Press, 1987), pp. 3–256; Peter Brunette and David Wills, *Screen/Play: Derrida and Film Theory* (Princeton: Princeton University Press, 1989), pp. 172–98; and Richard Dienst, "Postcards in TV Land," in Peter Brunette and David Wills, eds., *Deconstruction and the Visual Arts: Art, Media, Architecture* (Cambridge, Eng.: Cambridge University Press, 1994).

13. As Derrida points out in *The Post Card*, "the entire history of postal *tekhnē* tends to rivet the destination to identity. To arrive, to happen would be to a subject, to happen to 'me'" (p. 192). Subjectivity is also protected by the fact that the 50 different television sets always—when examined more closely—end up presenting themselves as difference (through reception, picture tube quality, improper tuning, etc.) rather than as perfect identity, reproduced 50 times.

14. Something of the same dynamic occurs throughout everyday life, for example, in the clash between the physician's medical discourse and the physician as human interlocutor, say, before or after the medical opinion has been dispensed.

15. Laudable efforts at affirmative action have paradoxically increased the depersonalizing effect—one thinks, ah, here is the black reporter, here the Hispanic female, here the Asian-American—abstracting them by making them typical or representative rather than (or as well as), strictly speaking, individually real.

16. The use of the first name can of course be overdone, the result being the opposite of what was desired. Thus in a recent "60 Minutes" segment (whose prosecutorial format alters all the intersubjective dynamics), convicted Wall Street con man Dennis Levine called Ed Bradley by his first name again and again, actually adding to the impression of Levine's ingratiating slickness that CBS was obviously happy to promote.

17. This aspect of the oftentimes laborious production of an individual personality for the newsman or newswoman seems to be related to stereotypes of the "reporter" derived from popular culture.

18. Fiske, *Television Culture*, p. 288. In this chapter of his book, Fiske uses an Australian news program for his principal analysis. Things are somewhat different on American network evening news shows, however, for here the fact that the anchors are all experienced journalists who decide and even write what they will say is heavily foregrounded. (Again, a product of the desire for the validation normally accorded to print media.) This point is emphasized in Fiske's use of the British/

Australian term "news reader," which of course has not been in use in the American context for many years.

19. This structural impossibility is similar to one Jacques Derrida elaborates in *Droit de regards* (Paris: Minuit, 1985), pp. 27–28. English translation: "Right of Inspection," trans. David Wills, *Art & Text*, 32 (Autumn 1989). There Derrida explores the impossibility of photographing two people looking into each other's eyes. See Brunette and Wills, *Screen/Play*, pp. 134–37, for discussion.

20. CBS has recently taken to regularly executing this address-switching maneuver in the studio itself, with extremely awkward results.

21. It is simultaneously both a real space and a representation of that real space. The news set, by contrast, represents no analogous space in the real world.

22. In late 1992, Louis Rukeyser, of *Wall Street Week*, began to effect this shift much more smoothly, mostly by looking down at his papers and thus suspending eye contact with the camera while the cut takes place.

Canning: *Transcendental Narcissism Meets Multiplicity*

1. Sigmund Freud, "Zur Einführung des Narzissmus," in his *"Das Ich und das Es" und andere metapsychologische Schriften* (Frankfurt/M.: Fischer, 1960), p. 33.

2. See Jacques Lacan, *Les quatre concepts fondamentaux de la psychanalyse* (Paris: Seuil, 1973), p. 180.

3. Freud, "Zur Einführung," p. 35.

4. Lacan calls this libidinal complex "hainamoration." On reciprocity, see Jacques Lacan, *Encore* (Paris: Seuil, 1975), p. 11.

5. Ibid., p. 12.

6. Sigmund Freud, *The Ego and the Id* (New York: Norton, 1960), pp. 26–39. The "id" is another name for primary erotic and aggressive power, which doubles back upon itself with the advent of consciousness.

7. Martin Heidegger, *Kant und das Problem der Metaphysik* (Frankfurt/M.: Klostermann, 1973).

8. Freud, "Zur Einführung," p. 40.

9. Heidegger, "On the Essence of Truth," in his *Basic Writings*, ed. David Farrell Krell (New York: Harper & Row, 1977), pp. 117–41.

10. Freud, "Zur Einführung," p. 35.

11. Sigmund Freud, *Beyond the Pleasure Principle*, trans. James Strachey (New York: Norton, 1961), p. 32 (translation modified).

12. Ibid., p. 36 (translation modified).

13. Ibid., pp. 36–37.

14. Sigmund Freud, *Civilization and Its Discontents*, trans. James Strachey (New York: Norton, 1961), p. 61 (translation modified).

15. See Jacques Lacan, "Kant avec Sade," in his *Ecrits* (Paris: Seuil, 1966), pp. 765–90, and Bernard Baas, "Le désir pur," *Ornicar?*, 43 (1987), pp. 56–91.

16. For an expansion of this argument, see Peter Canning, "Jesus Christ, Ho-

locaust: Fabulation of the Jews in Christian and Nazi History," *Copyright*, 1 (1987).

17. The Lacanian political thesis—theory of transcendental ex-pulsion—of Slavoj Žižek has made a major advance over the Bataille school of René Girard in exhibiting the structure and thus preparing diagnosis of the Christianomorphic "historical a priori" of European anti-Semitism, the historical conditioning and preparation of an eventual "sacrificial crisis."

18. It is true that the *objets a* are theorized and defined to be without image. But this is complicated by the fact that the ego, the conceptual basis of the *objet a*, is all image, i(a), concealing the lack of image wholeness that is the cause of its anxiety, its being-in-time-consciousness. The paradox is resolved by reference to the (idealizing) Other, I(A), which accords imaginary satisfaction (self-image), forming the ego by conferring its gaze and voice (*objets a*) upon the ego-in-formation, to complete Self-Image with non-imageable desirability and admiration.

19. Freud, "Zur Eiführung," p. 33.

20. See Lacan, *Encore* passim.

21. Suturing processes the subject in the dialectic of symbolic realization (social-institutional alienation). It is "the relation of the subject to the chain of its discourse. The subject figures there as the lacking element, under cover of a place-holder (under the aspect of a lieutenant). For missing from the chain, the subject is nonetheless not purely and simply absent. Suture, by extension, names the relation in general of lack to the structure of which it is a [constitutive] element, in as much as [something missing] implies the position of a placeholder" (J.-A. Miller, "La suture," *Cahiers pour l'Analyse* 1/2 [1966], p. 41).

22. "Self-ahead (of oneself)-already-being-in (the world) as being-by [and among] beings encountered (in the world)" (Martin Heidegger, *Sein und Zeit* [Tübingen: Max Niemeyer, 1986], pp. 231, 249; cf. 192 *et passim*).

23. Gilles Deleuze, *Kant's Critical Philosophy*, trans. Hugh Tomlinson and Barbara Habberjam (Minneapolis: University of Minnesota Press, 1984), p. ix.

24. Paul de Man, *Blindness and Insight* (Minneapolis: University of Minnesota Press, 1983), pp. 225–26. De Man elsewhere moves closer to the limit of the classical modernist subject: "absolute irony is a consciousness of madness, itself the end of all consciousness; it is a consciousness of a non-consciousness, a reflection of madness from the inside of madness itself. . . . [T]he ironist invents a form of himself that is 'mad' but that does not know its own madness; he then proceeds to reflect on his madness thus objectified" (ibid., p. 216). (Again, experimentally replace "mad" with "dead" or even, with a further twist, "conscious.") This is a concise diagram of something urging, implicating, and explicating itself in Kierkegaard and Dostoevsky and at least a phase of Nietzsche, in whom it breaks through. . . .

25. Heidegger, *Sein und Zeit*, p. 271.

26. Lacan, *Quatre concepts*, p. 181.

27. Marcel Proust, *A la recherche du temps perdu* (Paris: Pléiade, 1954), 3: 184.

28. Pierre Klossowski, *Le Baphomet* (Paris: Mercure de France, 1965); and idem, *Nietzsche et le cercle vicieux* (Paris: Mercure de France, 1969); cf. the "Pythagorean memoires" cited by Jean-Pierre Vernant, *Mythe et pensée chez les Grecs* (Paris: Maspero, 1965), 1: 96n: "When the soul gathers strength and remains concentrated in itself, it is its discourses and operations that become its links." These *logoi*, reasons, discourses, "ce sont des souffles [breaths], *anemoi*."

29. Gilles Deleuze and Félix Guattari, *A Thousand Plateaus*, trans. Brian Massumi (Minneapolis: University of Minnesota Press, 1987), p. 55.

30. See Rupert Sheldrake, *The Presence of the Past: Morphic Resonance and the Habits of Nature* (New York: Vintage, 1988).

31. Lacan, *Encore*, p. 27. But it is Deleuze who sustains and develops this *devenir* wherein the predicate transfuses the subject into the event.

32. Of course we have heard "there is no Other of the Other" (Lacan). But this must be understood in a logical and "existential" sense (there is no ground of the ground). The BwO is the Other *life*—the only one, but the one that was never recognized, while recognition was of death and misrecognition the denial of death (putting the transfinite outside and beyond "this" life). Now it is time to see that whatever is alive in me is simply alive and knows nothing of death, which *for me now* becomes (by that fact) a passage into other lives. Naturally this raises further questions—about escaping from "the wheel of incarnations"—but we must find the connection through disjunction before eluding determinate conjunctions.

33. Gilles Deleuze and Félix Guattari, *Anti-Oedipus: Capitalism and Schizophrenia*, trans. Robert Hurley, Mark Seem, and Helen R. Lane (Minneapolis: University of Minnesota Press, 1983), p. 331.

34. On affirmative disjunction, see Gilles Deleuze, *Logique du sens* (Paris: Minuit, 1969), pp. 198–211; on the polymorphic, multivocal expression of univocal being, see idem, *Expressionism in Philosophy: Spinoza*, trans. Martin Joughin (New York: Zone, 1990). At the limit is not Bakhtin suggesting such a break-up and "dialogic" proliferation of novelistic identity? Is it not then a mark of intense and multiple creation, as well as a "strategy" of resistance?

35. The question of Lacan's own affiliation with philosophy is deeply embroiled. But the restrictive or Kantian Lacan (also critic of Kant) may have mutated in the late 1960's, so that *Encore* (seminar of 1972–73) would be the sign of a Lacan that is transcending Kantian finitude ("phallic jouissance"). A Lacanian-Islamic philosophical critique of transcendental imagination is to be found in Christian Jambet, *La logique des Orientaux* (Paris: Seuil, 1983), pp. 52–93. The "imaginal" is the creational dimension of time.

36. Deleuze and Guattari, *Anti-Oedipus*, pp. 39, 289, 309, 324; quoting Lacan, *Ecrits*, p. 658.

37. See Jean-Luc Nancy, *L'expérience de la liberté* (Paris: Galilée, 1988).

38. On long-distance connection with our other selves, see Avital Ronell, *The Telephone Book* (Lincoln: University of Nebraska Press, 1989).

39. Nietzsche, *The Gay Science*, sec. 337.

40. Gilles Deleuze, *Logique du sens*, p. 346.

41. Lacan, *Quatres concepts*, p. 180.

42. Deleuze and Guattari, *A Thousand Plateaus*, p. 141.

43. Deleuze and Guattari, *Anti-Oedipus*, p. 88 (translation modified).

44. See Gilles Deleuze, *Différence et répétition* (Paris: PUF, 1968), pp. 121–23; see also Bruno Paradis, "Le Futur et l'épreuve de la pensée," and Jacob Rogozinski: "Défaillances (entre Nietzsche et Kant)," *Lendemains*, 53 (1989), pp. 26–29 and 55–62.

45. Ilya Prigogine and Isabelle Stengers, *La Nouvelle Alliance* (Paris: Gallimard, 1979).

46. See Deleuze and Guattari, *A Thousand Plateaus*, esp. chap. 3, "The Geology of Morals." This chapter constructs the concept of an abstract Machine existing enveloped in earth's "stratic assemblages," developed (or developing?) on a "plane of consistency" or immanent metamorphosis, anthropogaiacosmic creation ("becoming"). Of course, any synthesis or combination, the ones we assemble when we get up and put ourselves together in the morning, can mutate along a "line of escape" and transform everything, change direction and dimension, connecting (at points of egoic disjunction) on a plane of immanence (BwO) with other mutating assemblages. Losing proper Me-Here-Now spatio-temporal identitarian coordinates throws anyone into becoming, fast or slow. But what is a great Multiple City like New York if not a place where anybody could meet anything and change nature?

Zakarin: *God(')s Wink*

1. For an excellent working definition of *jouissance*, see Juliet MacCannell's essay in Elizabeth Wright, ed., with J. MacCannell, D. Chisolm, and M. Whitford, *Psychoanalysis and Feminism: A Critical Dictionary* (Oxford: Basil Blackwell, 1992).

2. The tale of the Student Body automatically eliminates the terror that individuality would arouse in academic institutions. In the long run, I wish to suggest that if the possibility of such difference were to be accounted for, universities could not conduct themselves as they do, making business decisions whose sole criterion is to keep their figures in line.

3. I here turn J. Hillis Miller's discussion of the parabolic character of parable in the direction of the question of studenthood. See J. Hillis Miller, "Parable and Performative in the Gospels and in Modern Literature," in his *Tropes, Parables and Performatives* (Durham: Duke University Press, 1991).

4. Here I am thinking of various texts on the Holocaust, most notable among them Maurice Blanchot's *The Writing of Disaster*, trans. Ann Smock (Lincoln: University of Nebraska Press, 1986), and Shoshana Felman's "In an Era of Testimony: Claude Lanzmann's *Shoah*," in *Yale French Studies*, 79 (Winter 1991), pp. 39–81.

5. Walter Benjamin, *Illuminations*, ed. Hannah Arendt, trans. Harry Zohn (New York: Schocken Books, 1969), p. 257.

6. See Friedrich Nietzsche, *Untimely Meditations on Schopenhauer as Educator*, trans. R. J. Hollingdale (Cambridge, Eng.: Cambridge University Press, 1989), p. 128.

7. See Jacques Derrida's most amazing essay, "The Principle of Reason: The University in the Eyes of Its Pupils," in *Diacritics*, 13, no. 3 (Fall 1983), p. 20. The essay, which meditates upon the possibilities of having institutions that would exhibit care for their students, was presented at Cornell University, a university known for the infamous "suicide bridge," from which students have leapt to their death. How would this chance be kept and from where in our academic reflections might the proceedings of an "instance of Studenthood" flash in our thinking?

8. See Walter Benjamin's essay "The Life of the Students," trans. Ken Frieden, in *A Jewish Journal at Yale*, 2, no. 1 (Fall 1984), pp. 46–55.

9. See Samuel Weber's discussion of the *desire not-to-know* and the result of nonknowing in "The Blindness of the Seeing Eye: Psychoanalysis, Hermeneutics, *Entstellung*," in his *Institution and Interpretation* (Minneapolis: University of Minnesota Press, 1987), pp. 73–84.

10. See Friedrich Nietzsche's *On the Future of Our Educational Institutions*, trans. J. M. Kennedy (New York: Russell & Russell, 1964), p. 16.

11. See Morris Jastrow, Jr., *The Book of Job* (Philadelphia: Lippincott, 1920), p. 124.

12. Werner Hamacher, "Interventions: Werner Hamacher," trans. Adam Bresnick, in *Qui Parle*, 1, no. 2 (Spring 1987), p. 41.

13. Rabbi Kushner, *When Bad Things Happen to Good People* (New York: Avon Books, 1975), p. 37.

14. For Bildad, punishment presupposes crime. Nevertheless, his suggestion that Job's children were sentenced to death by God for having committed some terrible crime is a particularly cruel one for him to make. As the Prologue tells us, Job himself worried that his sons might sin "in their hearts" and therefore habitually offered burnt sacrifices each morning to cover such hypothetical fault (Job 1:5).

Index

In this index, an "f" after a number indicates a separate reference on the next page, and an "ff" indicates separate references on the next two pages. A continuous discussion over two or more pages is indicated by a span of page numbers, e.g., "57–59." *Passim* is used for a cluster of references in close but not consecutive sequence.

Library of Congress Cataloging-in-Publication Data

Thinking bodies / edited by Juliet Flower MacCannell and Laura
  Zakarin.
    p.   cm. — (Irvine studies in the humanities)
    "Essays . . . presented at the 1990 meetings of the International
  Association for Philosophy and Literature held at the University of
  California, Irvine."—Introd.
    Includes bibliographical references and index.
    ISBN 0-8047-2306-0 (alk. paper):
    ISBN 0-8047-2304-4 (pbk. : alk. paper):
    1. Body, Human (Philosophy)—Congresses. 2. Literature—
  Philosophy—Congresses. I. MacCannell, Juliet Flower, 1943–
  II. Zakarin, Laura.   III. Series.
  B105.B64T55   1994
  128—dc20   93-34805
                                                         CIP
  ⊗ This book is printed on acid-free paper   REV.